THE FUNDAMEN
SPEECH COMMUNICATION
IN THE DIGITAL WORLD

Third Edition

Regina Williams Davis Deana Lacy McQuitty

Kendall Hunt
publishing company

www.kendallhunt.com
Send all inquiries to:
4050 Westmark Drive
Dubuque, IA   52004-1840

In memory of our beloved colleague and friend, Dr. Tracey Booth Snipes

CONTENTS

FOREWORD

"ttyl . . ." This lowercase acronym means "talk to you later . . .," which is most often used when texting on mobile phones. Who would have thought that texting would be the re-invention of shorthand coded in acronyms. Recognizing that most of my readers may not be familiar with "shorthand," I am certain that through context clues you have concluded that shorthand is, or was, an efficient way of coding communication. All of communication are messages that are coded, decoded, and have meaning; just as "lol," "lmao," "idk," and "btw" have become commonly communicated phrases for almost anyone who uses the texting function on their mobile phones. Yet, it has a nonverbal component as well (which will be discussed in Chapter 7 in this textbook). Texting, along with most other social media today, has blurred the lines of fundamentals of speech communication and general communication formalities and protocols.

This text has "ttyl" as part of its title because it is a simple example of the complex nature of communication today. When we are referring to the fundamentals of speech communication, it is not the typical speech course your grandmother took in college. It is so much more. Speech communication is multifaceted when it comes to sending and receiving messages. It still involves public speaking presentations, but it also involves the broad academic study of communication, message delivery, mediums for sending and receiving messages, meaning making, interpreting, culture, credibility, and confidence-building.

This textbook is adapted to learning objectives that are recommended by the National Communication Association (NCA) for college-level students who desire to become effective communicators. The learning objectives overlap and are applicable to all other social disciplines. How can one be social without communicating? In fact, how can one do anything without the use of some form of communication? Therefore, we believe that communication has developed a level of multidimensionality and a high level of sensitivity. This use of the term, "Hyper" in mathematical terms means multidimensional and hyperbole is the use of exaggeration as a rhetorical device or figure of speech. It may be used to evoke strong feelings or create a strong impression, but it should not be taken literally. Thus, we deemed labels for our units from the concept of hypersensitivity—hence, "hypercommunication." This textbook is organized by the following list of units:

Unit I: HyperCommunication
Essential Concepts and Guidelines
The reader will learn about becoming a responsible communicator, which will cover the basics of what communication is: listening, stating ideas clearly, and learning how to structure a message for

effectiveness with a clear format for organization. This format will include an introduction, main points, sub-points, useful transitions, and a conclusion that distinctly identifies your communication goals. You will learn about the health, wellness, anatomy and acquisition of vocal communication, and some of the pathologies of speech and language.

Unit II: HyperPerception
Perception, Culture, and Society

The reader will become aware of language that indicates bias on gender, age, ethnicity, sexual orientation, ethical communication, and communication behavior in the digital age. The reader will learn how and why to adapt messages to and for audiences, how to provide a narrow topic for an occasion, and the best medium to deliver messages in the digital age.

Unit III: HyperRelationship
Communication with Self, Relationships, and Groups

The reader may discover their intrapersonal communication, the importance of self-awareness, self-concept, perception, and the importance of the relationship between self, others, and with the greater society with questioning social media as a tool or a veil. The reader will practice interpersonal and group communication to learn to recognize when another does not understand your message and how to manage misunderstandings. Interpersonal communication will include recognizing when it is appropriate to speak, when to listen attentively to questions and comments from other communicators, friends, and family communication, and how to work on collaborative projects as a team.

Unit IV: HyperProfessionalComm
Persuasion, Argumentation, Business Communication, and Careers in Communication

The reader will learn ways to develop and enhance a message with the intent to persuade, using supportive arguments with relevant and adequate evidence. The reader will learn how to bargain and negotiate and demonstrate competence and comfort with persuading audiences. The reader will be introduced to techniques for handling "good news" and "bad news" messages in business communication. In addition, various careers that individuals can pursue with a degree in Communication and Communication Disorders are presented in Chapter 20.

Hopefully, you will enjoy reading this text, because of student contributions, engaging exercises, and personal stories. More importantly, this text should be thought of as a reference for improving and maintaining effective and responsible communication.

ACKNOWLEDGEMENTS

In a faculty meeting, it was suggested that because we teach the fundamentals of speech to about 1,500 students each year, why not create our own textbook. We are a unique faculty because half of us are experts in communication studies and the other half of us are speech language pathologists or audiologists. We believe that we bring a unique blend to the study of communication and communication disorders.

Although we know communication is **highly** influenced by the digital age, there are some solid pragmatic ideas regarding how we communicatively interact with each other that should clearly be stated. It is our hope that when you read the works of the magnificent faculty and friends listed below that contributed to the content of this textbook, you will learn that communication is truly a transaction of giving and receiving. Give words of kindness and integrity and you will receive the same.

"Give, and it will be given to you. A large quantity, pressed together, shaken down, and running over will be put into your lap, because you will be evaluated by the same standard with which you evaluate others." Luke 6:38, ISV, 2008

To the best Speech Faculty on this side of Heaven – Thank you!
Stephanie Sedberry Carrino
Johnetta E. Chavis
Dwight Davis
Ingram Land-Deans
Marissa R. Dick
Amanda M. Gunn
Hope Jackson
Claretha Lacy
Carolyn M. Mayo
Carl McQuitty
Zakeya Renay Mitchell
Daniel Richardson
Javon Robinson
Myra M. Shird
Kimberly Smith
Sheila M. Whitley

UNIT I

HyperCommunication

Essential Concepts and Guidelines

UNIT OBJECTIVES:

- *State ideas clearly*
- *Awareness of language bias*
- *Ethical communication*

. . . .

This unit covers the process of becoming a responsible communicator, which includes the basics of communication: listening, stating ideas clearly, and learning how to structure a message for effectiveness with a clear format for organization. This process includes an introduction, main points, sub-points, useful transitions, and a conclusion that distinctly identifies your communication goals. In addition, topics related to the health, wellness, anatomy and acquisition of vocal communication, and some of the pathologies of speech and language are presented in this unit.

. . . .

CHAPTER 1

Everything Is Communication!

by Regina Williams Davis

Introduction:

Communication is . . .

A collective definition for communication is a method of assigning meaning and transmitting thought-filled information to another with the goal of producing a mutual understanding. Everything is communication and we are doing it, in some way, at all times. It is cultural, practical, and emotional. There was a time when one could blame *lack of communication* as the primary reason for poor relationships—be it family, romantic, business, or otherwise. Such a statement can no longer be a true or an acceptable one. Why? Because EVERYTHING IS COMMUNICATION! Silence communicates a message. Please believe me when I say that there is no such thing as "lack of communication!" The objective is to understand that often the message is either not effectual or is perceived as ineffective.

The Responsible Communicator

It starts with a thought . . .

Usually, on the first day of class, I will ask my students what it means to be responsible. They will brainstorm words like, "accountable, dependable, in charge, conscientious, liable." These words start the critical thinking process. It is essential because we are learning to become responsible communicators. The "we" is necessary because I am still learning as well, although I am the instructor. We want to be clear and concise as we deliver our messages and be respectful and considerate of others.

In order to be clear and concise, it is important to be aware of the process of communication, often referred to as the "Transactional Model of Communication". The process of communication will begin with a thought that one (the sender) wants to share with another (the receiver).

Learning to state our ideas clearly begins with a thought. A thought is encoded into a message and is transmitted through a medium that may contain interference, noise, or detraction. The receiver will, in turn, decode the message to the best of their ability and attempt to construct meaning through thought. (See Figure 1.1, the transactional model of communication). This process is reversed and has enormous room for error and misinterpretations, yet it requires the intelligence of humans and biological, physiological, and psychological functions.

A thought is cognitive. It happens in your mind. Your experiences from birth and even before birth will affect your thought and the meaning you want to express. The responsible communicator must understand that our experiences are unique, thus causing each of us to have a personal field of meaning.

An individual's uniqueness is a double-edged sword. It is good to embrace your individuality, but it may make finding a shared field of meaning between you and others to be challenging. For example, my personal field of meaning includes the fact that I am 50-years-old. I am a woman. I am a college graduate. I am from Texas. I am from a two-parent home. I am a mother. I am a grandmother. I am short. All of these aspects affect my personal field of meaning and can either enhance or take away from finding that shared field of meaning.

Transactional Model of Communication

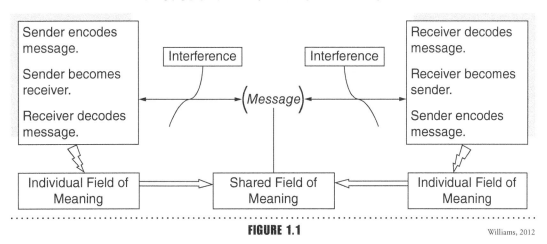

FIGURE 1.1

Williams, 2012

Considering your individual field of meaning, you must also consider others. Stating your thoughts and ideas clearly will require planning . . . thinking before speaking!! You will learn to *organize your thoughts . . .*

. . . .

Organizing Your Thoughts . . .

. . . .

by Regina Williams Davis

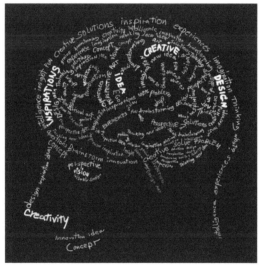

© MR.LIGHTMAN, 2012. Used under license from Shutterstock, Inc.

What do you want to communicate? My grandson is only three years old. His eyes tend to light up when a thought comes to his mind. He hesitates and then opens his mouth and I'll hear, "Nahnah, I to eat!" He is trying to say, "Nahnah! I want to eat" or "I am hungry." I can see him desperately trying to put the right words together to make me understand what he wants. Strangely, I understood his desires prior to his ability to use words. But now that he knows about two thousand words, he is attempting to organize his thoughts first.

The first step in organizing your thoughts is to get the attention of the person you are speaking to. This is important so that the person is prepared to listen. Think about how there is an alert sound or vibration when a "text" or "tweet" is coming through on your phone. The next step is to state what you intend to say in the most concise way possible. I know that a "tweet" must be about 140 characters or less. This forces the responsible communicator to focus on the essence of the message. Well, your message need not be necessarily always limited to a number of characters, but the thought placed on being clear and concise is great practice. When ending your message, a responsible communicator seeks confirmation that the receiver heard you and/or understood you.

The Interactive Bases of Communication: Foundation in the Cognitive Principles of Learning

by Deana Lacy McQuitty

The process of organizing our thoughts begins with the evolution of cognition. Cognition plays a critical role in our ability to understand and develop effective language, thus enhancing the communication process.

Jean Piaget became fascinated at a very young age with the study of origins and knowledge known as **epistemology**. The knowledge of biology and epistemology later became the foundation in his studies of cognition. According to Piaget, the driving force behind our developing cognition is **equilibrium**. When children encounter novel experiences or experiences that are unfamiliar, equilibrium is disturbed. There must be a balance that is regained in order for the child to understand and experience their environment. Piaget (1970), posited another principle essential to the nature of cognition and intelligence known as **organization**. As organisms evolve, their biological system (e.g., respiratory), which is discussed in Chapter 2, organizes and interacts more effectively. "As we begin to understand the world and everything in it, we also organize physical systems and cognitive responses to interact with the environment" (McLaughlin, 96). For example, remember the scenario with the 3-year-old young child who said "Nahnah, I to eat!" As the child begins to feel hungry, the message is then sent to his biological mechanism (brain). He begins to anticipate the desired act and in turn becomes excited and stimulated. By opening his mouth (nonverbal communication act) and eliciting a response, although not grammatically correct, his caregiver knows how to meet his wants and needs.

According to Piaget (1970), individuals organize behaviors into an identifiable pattern called **schema**. These organized patterns, or schemata/matrices, are not static but ever changing based on biological structures and experiences. As children are exposed to various experiences, these experiences help shape, assemble, and organize their cognitive structures. Children develop cognitive structures that in turn represent organized information about all of their experiences in a multi-modal concept which includes the use of sensations, movement, sounds, locations, people, objects, and speech, to name a few.

Just as the young child's schemes evolve with new experiences and exposure, so will their cognitive structures, their ability to organize and understand the changing world. The process of adjusting our understanding of an ever-changing environment is called adaptation. The ability of the child to adapt to the environment is a fascinating phenomenon. I often think about the young child that is able to, at a very young age, understand that if they drop the ball and it rolls under the sofa they will need to bend over and find it; a concept known as **object permanence**, which occurs around 9–10 months of age. The sophistication of their cognitive ability at such a young age further substantiates the amazing adaptation ability that occurs regarding cognitive structures. Two critical skills in the process of adaptation are known as **assimilation** and **accommodation**. Assimilation refers to the ability to adjust to new situations based on the available cognitive structures. Accommodation is a supplemental process in which the individual changes existing structures or develops newly learned skills to understand and process new experiences.

....

Thanks for Listening . . .

....

by Regina Williams Davis

"Sydney is someone I can really talk to. I know that she listens to what I have to say!" How can you assure that you are listening and that the speaker feels confident that you are listening as well? If it is your desire to listen to what another is saying, then it is probable that you want them to know that you are listening. This can be accomplished simply by employing an **active listening** technique. This particular technique is tailored for a small group—specifically, two to five persons that are engaged in conversation. Active listening is a series of activities performed to ensure a message is transmitted *successfully*.

Successfully is the key word because, it is my belief that, communication is complete only when the message has been decoded at its destination. If the message did not successfully reach its destination, then it was an unsuccessful communiqué. This unsuccessful communiqué is as futile as sending an e-mail to someone who lacks access to a computer. Therefore, active listening is a way of assuring the success of a transmitted message from the receiver's point of view.

When you are the listener, there is a series of activities you will perform to ensure that you are listening and that the speaker knows you are listening. The series of activities involved in active listening tend to be more effective when performed as follows:

a. Provide nonverbal clues that you are interested (i.e., eye contact).
b. Wait for a pause.
c. State to the speaker exactly verbatim some of the sentences you heard them say; but only the main points.
d. Look for the speaker to express agreement.
e. Give the speaker an opportunity to share more details.
f. Wait for a pause, and then paraphrase what you heard. Be sure to include some of the words from the speaker, but use more of your *own* words that convey the speakers' message.
g. Look for the speaker to express agreement either verbally or nonverbally (i.e., head nodding as an affirmation).

Example:
Jordan has an idea and begins to tell you about the idea.

1. Provide Jordan with nonverbal clues that you are interested in what she has to say. Some nonverbal clues are eye contact, nodding your head, or leaning in her direction.
2. Wait for Jordan to pause.

3. Restate some of her sentences that Jordan used to describe her idea. Be sure to use many of the same words she used to express herself.
4. Observe her response to you; watch for her to say, "Yes," or watch for her to nod her head in an affirmative manner. [If this does not occur, seek clarification from her until you agree on what she said.]
5. Give her an opportunity to add to her statement and wait for her to pause.
6. At this point, paraphrase her statements using some of her words, but use more of your own words to describe her idea.
7. Observe her response to you; watch for her to say, "Yes," or watch for her body language to provide affirmation that you understood her idea.

© StockLite, 2012. Used under license from Shutterstock, Inc.

Using the technique of active listening will decrease the noise or interference that takes place during the communication transaction and will improve your ability to understand what another is saying. Active listening also helps the speaker feel as if you, the listener, valued his/her comments, and that you took the speaker's comments seriously.

Unfortunately, active listening does not seem to be a natural process in our American culture. This is a technique that must be practiced and, intentionally and consciously, used when listening to another. I believe it is a skill worth practicing. I have heard many individuals who often describe strained relationships with their significant others because one of them did not take the time to listen to the other. I believe that managers and employees as well as parents and their teen-aged children will improve their relationships when they choose to actively listen to one another. As with most things, there is a caution to active listening if it is performed slightly incorrectly. Do not attempt to "fake listen" by nodding your head and parroting someone's words without attempting to process meaning for yourself. This is why paraphrasing and restating the speaker's comments in your own words is an essential part of active listening.

Why Do We Need Competent Communicators?

Effective communication is an extremely important and highly valued skill. In this digital age and its effect on message delivery, it is more important now than ever before to be sensitive to your audience. Later, we will learn more about analyzing your audience (Chapter 19). However, we live in a unique world where we will have an audience that we may never meet or even see. Making a public speech or being interviewed by news reporters suggests that there will *definitely* be an audience that you may never meet. The concern for the speaker is that you may never know who will hear your message. You may be intending to send a private message to an individual or a select group of people and, unknown to you, your message might "go viral."

A **viral video message** is one that is shared through email, websites, Instagram, and other means. In these communication environments there is a virtual curtain between the speaker and the audience (Figure 1.3). A competent communicator *must* be prepared for the unexpected audience. Therefore, it is necessary to be highly sensitive about the "who," "what," "where," "why," and "how." Who will hear my message? What will be perceived from my message? Where will this message be heard? Why would individuals want to listen and/or share my message with others? And how will my message be received?

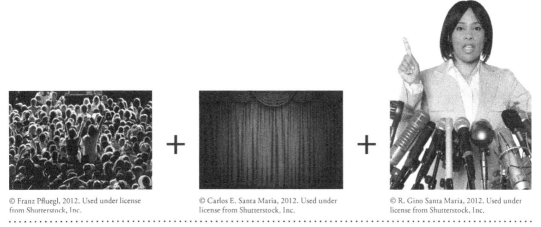

© Franz Pfluegl, 2012. Used under license from Shutterstock, Inc.

© Carlos E. Santa Maria, 2012. Used under license from Shutterstock, Inc.

© R. Gino Santa Maria, 2012. Used under license from Shutterstock, Inc.

FIGURE 1.3

In this digital age, the task of communication is more sensitive than ever before. The digital age ushered in the **social media** explosion. The sudden increase of communication mediums for dating, chatting, socializing, interviewing, campaigning, diagnosing, and who knows what else has taken the culture of how we express ourselves into uncharted territories. You may send a message to one person, but it may be read or heard by many—unintentionally. This makes it virtually impossible to ignore the ever-growing spider-web-like **transactional model of communication**.

Message delivery requires activity between at least two sending/receiving entities. The standard transactional model of communication is typically a description of the sender-receiver relationship among two individuals: (See Figure 1.1)

1. Sender Encodes a message;
2. As The Message is travelling to the receiver, it is often distorted by Interference (noise);
3. The Message is Decoded by The **Receiver**;
4. The Receiver provides Feedback to the **Sender** by Encoding a New Message;
5. The New Message is distorted by **Interference** (noise);
6. The Original Sender is now The Receiver of the **Feedback** (the New Message).

The standard transactional model of communication (which will be discussed later in this unit) is still correct, useful, and employable for face-to-face (one-on-one) communication or a single layer of a communication line. However, now that we *Skype* with our computers and may use *FaceTime* with our phones and notebooks, face-to-face communication has evolved and it is yet only one layer of the hypercommunication phenomenon.

This social media explosion has caused a cultural revolution resulting in unclear social guidelines. A "blind date" is not so "blind" anymore. The digital age is putting newspapers out of business that were a medium for personal ads. A personal ad is a notice traditionally in the newspaper, similar to a classified ad but personal in nature. With its rise in popularity, the Internet is the most common medium for people to meet and make connections—be it romantic, friendship, or casual (sometimes sexual) encounters from digitally mediated interviews. Interestingly, because newspaper prices were based on characters or lines of text, people used abbreviations, acronyms, and code words in personal ads, which seemed to have carried over to the Internet; abbreviations like SWF (single white female). Dating websites or any other self-promoting digital media might allow you to view or present a video introduction, with a preview of all likes and dislikes, after narrowing a search for "Mr./Mrs. Right." (Figure 1.4)

© Goodluz, 2012. Used under license from Shutterstock, Inc.

© Monkey Business Images, 2012. Used under license from Shutterstock, Inc.

© Yuri Arcurs, 2012. Used under license from Shutterstock, Inc.

© Monkey Business Images, 2012. Used under license from Shutterstock, Inc.

FIGURE 1.4

The internet gives us options for multi-layered, web-like communication connectivity instantaneously. Communication protocols, ethics, and privacy concerns that result from the technical ability to instantaneously express our thoughts without being in close proximity, promote a dichotomy of liberation and enslavement. For example: Alexander Graham Bell might be responsible for the development of the phrase, "I can't leave yet because I'm waiting for a phone call." The picture in my mind is someone chooses to remain in their home because leaving may cause them to miss a phone call that is very important to them. But today, with the mobile phone epidemic, individuals expect to be available to receive personal phone calls at absolutely any location. This provides liberation and freedom of movement. Yet, the culture of telephonic communication has changed so much that individuals seem addicted to having their mobile phones with them at ***all*** times (enslavement); so much that announcements at public gatherings requesting mobile phones to be turned off are commonly heard!

If face-to-face (one-on-one) communication is only one single layer of a communication line, what does the spider-web-like transactional mode of communication represent? Well, in the decade of the nineties, I would have considered email as a representation of the spider-web. (Figure 1.5)

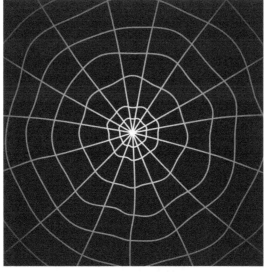

FIGURE 1.5

It made sense because of Internet access. One email could be sent to a mass number of people both simultaneously and instantaneously. But in this decade—2010–2020—the communication web has multiple layers of connectivity. (Figure 1.6)

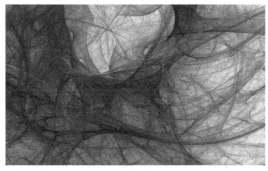

FIGURE 1.6

The information age is the pragmatic result of digital technology and it has transformed the fundamentals of speech communication into a less clear and concise set of rules and protocols. Nevertheless, the **competent communicator** will seek appropriate and effective communicative behavior. The primary characteristics of a competent communicator will be discussed in more detail later in this book: 1. personal motivation; 2. knowledge; and 3. skills (Sptizberg, 377). These are discussed in more detail later in this book. Briefly, personal motivation is the core reason for wanting to send your message. Knowledge is not only knowing the information you're presenting, but also knowing the potential impact your message may have on your audience. Skills are the intentional statements and actions to accomplish a specific objective. Therefore, the competent communicator now has to be aware that they may have messages that could "go viral" almost anytime.

Key Terms:

Accommodation

Active Listening

Assimilation

Cognitive

Competent Communicator

Decode

Encode

Epistemology

Equilibrium

Feedback

Individual Field of Meaning

Interference

Noise

Object Permanence

Organization

Process of Learning

Receiver

Schema

Sender

Shared Field of Meaning

Social Media

Transactional Model of Communication

Viral Video Messages

Application Activity: *"Picasso?"* Understanding the Transactional Model of Communication

Time: 25–30 Minutes

Objective:

- Students will identify and apply the basic concepts of the Transactional Model of Communication, the complexity of human communication, and the contextual issues of everyday interaction.

Materials:

a. One drawing, distributed by the instructor for each pair of students
b. One blindfold, distributed by the instructor for each pair of students
c. An 8 x 10 blank sheet of paper for each pair of students
d. A writing utensil
e. A flat surface

Directions:

1. Select a partner.
2. Arrange your desks/seats with your partner so you are sitting back-to-back.
3. Decide which of you will be the artist (drawing the picture wearing the blindfold) and which one of you will be viewing the picture to be drawn.
4. The instructor provides the drawing to the student who will be viewing the picture.
5. The instructor provides an 8 x 10 black sheet of paper to the student who is wearing the blindfold. This student should have access to a flat surface and a writing utensil.
6. After the instructor provides a signal to begin, the student with the drawing attempts to explain to the blindfolded student what to draw on the blank sheet—with the objective that the blindfolded student replicates the picture.
7. The blindfolded student is not to see the picture throughout the entire activity.
8. When signaled by the instructor, students may compare their pictures and discuss their communication challenges.

MINI QUIZ

1. True or False: According to the Transactional model of communication, both the sender and receiver encode messages.
2. Multiple Choice: "Understanding our experiences through mental processes such as perception, recall, and reasoning" is referred to as
   A. Listening
   B. Effective communication
   C. Cognition
   D. None of the above
3. Fill in the Blank: Using the techniques of _____ will decrease the noise or interference that takes place during the communication transaction.
4. Essay: Explain why it is imperative that we become competent communicators in the context of the social media explosion.

5. Who was Jean Piaget? What was the premise of his philosophy underlying the development of cognitive skills?

CHAPTER 2

The Clear Communicator

by Regina Williams Davis

Introduction:

Let's be crystal clear . . .

When my son was in the seventh grade, he was so excited to be acting in his school play, The Wizard of Oz. He had more lines than most of his peers and learned each of them with confidence. As a busy working mother, I would just briefly check-in with him to be sure he was ready for opening night, but I really did not take the time to listen to his lines. Finally, it was time for opening night. The entire family, including grandparents, was seated in the first two rows, ready to watch my son's acting debut. He looked great! The stage scenery, costuming, and make-up seemed advanced for a seventh-grade production. We knew we were in for a treat. Unfortunately, my wonderful son spoke, and . . . not one word was comprehendible! All of his words were mumbled and his voice did not project loud enough for the audience to hear past the first or second row. I was so upset with myself for not taking the time to work on his articulation and projection, especially being a speech professor.

A great way to practice articulation is to practice tongue twisters (See Figure 2.1). I have my students do these in teams of two and then share their mastery in front of the class. A **tongue twister** is a phrase that is designed to be difficult to articulate properly and can be used as a type of spoken game.

> Luke Luck likes lakes.
> Luke's duck likes lakes.
> Luke Luck licks lakes.
> Luck's duck licks lakes.
> Duck takes licks in lakes.
> Luke Luck likes.
> Luke Luck takes licks in
> lakes duck likes.
>
> from Dr. Seuss's *Fox in Socks, 1975*

FIGURE 2.1

We often teach a course in **voice** and **diction** to people who want to improve their speech and voices for communication arts, drama/theater majors, executives, lawyers, doctors, or entrepreneurs. We also work with individuals who have English as a second language and assist with accent modification.

Remember, communication does not occur until a message is received and understood. An unintelligible message is the same as mail returned marked undelivered.

Voice and Diction

by Johnetta Chavis

What's the name of the class you teach again? Voice and Diction? What is Voice and Diction? What is that class about? As we all know, there is always room for improvement with anything we do. Do you ever think about improving your voice and diction?

Many fail to realize that voice and diction are important components of communication. I like to think of voice and diction as the mechanics of vocal presentation. The mechanics of speaking include the following body parts: lungs, diaphragm, teeth, tongue, lips, lower jar, alveolar ridge, hard palate, soft palate, nasal, oral and pharyngeal cavities, and the larynx (voice box) that house the vocal folds. These body parts assist with the production of your vocal presentation. However, speaking is secondary to breathing because sustaining LIFE is the primary function of these body parts. Breathing is more important than talking!

The lungs, through the process of inspiration and exhalation, provide the air flow needed to make our vocal folds vibrate. Along with our lungs, the diaphragm allows our voice adequate breath support as well as projection. Articulation refers to the manner of producing a speech sound. The **articulators** include teeth, tongue, lips, lower jar, alveolar ridge, hard palate, and soft palate. Resonance refers to the amplification and shape of the vocal tract. The resonating components include the nasal and oral and pharyngeal cavities. Phonation occurs when air from the lungs flows through our vocal folds to produce vocal sounds.

The voice distinguishes us from another person. People can look alike and even favor another person, but there will always be a slight difference in the sound of their voices. When we try to disguise our voices, we change the pitch, rate, quality, volume, and duration to slightly change the way we sound. Vocal presentation includes the way in which we utilize all of these variables. On a daily basis, we use these vocal qualities to relate, transfer, and communicate messages to others.

The actual content of the information may not have as much significance as how you actually transfer the message. For example: Ari is super excited! She just won two tickets from the local radio station to meet her idol, Beyoncé. She decided to invite her friend, Kyra, who is also a huge fan. Ari calls Kyra and says, "I just won tickets to meet BEYONCÉ, would you like to go!!!?" Depending on how Ari transferred this message could vary Kyra's response. If Kyra's response was, "OMG that is AWESOME!!! Let's go shopping!!" This response would mean Ari used a high-pitched voice with a loud volume, inflectional pattern, and a fast rate. She sounds excited about the news and knows Kyra would be excited as well. Let's imagine what would happen to the message if Ari's rate was slow, with a low pitch, monotone volume, and her vocal quality was hoarse (as if she was sick). What do you think Kyra's response would be? How would her vocal qualities change the meaning of the message?

When a student has to present a speech, their successful manipulation of pitch, quality, volume, and rate will enhance the listeners' ability to be alert and attentive to the presentation. When our vocal presentation lacks a varied pith, intonation, appropriate volume, rate, and quality, the receiver of the message can misinterpret our intended message.

While presenting, speakers must also be aware of distractors. Distractors include vocalized pauses such as "uh," "um," "and um," "like," "you know", etc., lip smacking, nail tapping, hand punching/pounding, and the awkwardness of not making eye contact with the audience. These distractors may give the listeners the impression you have not practiced and are unfamiliar with the topic.

Your voice and diction can also be affected by stage fright. **Stage fright** is a psychological condition of speaking and can be distracting to the speaker. It is also referred to as performance anxiety, which is the anxiety, fear, or persistent phobia that may be aroused in an individual by the requirement to perform in front of an audience. The voice and diction course practices strategies to overcome stage fright and decrease distractions while speaking. The first strategy to overcome stage fright is to be prepared. Be sure to know your topic well and be comfortable in knowing what you do not know. It is okay to not know everything. A second strategy is to consciously take deep breaths minutes before your presentation in order to release tension and decrease stress levels. Finally, the most important strategy is to be aware of your own behavior and actions when you feel nervous. Self-awareness is the beginning of making conscious efforts to change.

It is also important that the speaker does not incorporate variations of Standard American English (SAE) such as slang. Although dialect is important regarding cultural sensitivity because it reflects the region in which they represent, we should learn to **"code-switch"** and use SAE during formal presentations and in professional settings.

The next time you add "improvements" to your list of things to do, be sure to list improving your speaking or presentation voice. Remember all changes take time and improving your voice and diction will take lots of practice. You will present the way that you practice!

The Speaking and Listening Human: A Case for Communication Wellness

by Carolyn M. Mayo and Deana Lacy McQuitty

Alexander Graham Bell was correct when he said ***"Communication is Power; Communicators-Powerful"***. When my colleagues and I in speech-language pathology and audiology (also called communication sciences and disorders) examine the evolution of communication in humans, we are indeed amazed at our ability as humans to engage in such an activity on a daily basis across our entire life span. Think about it. From the time we wake up in the morning until the time we fall asleep at night, we are talking, listening, writing, reading—in other words, communicating with ourselves, other humans, and with our environment to express our ideas and to receive information. Some of the information is old but needs to be reconfirmed or reinforced in our collective thoughts and perspective on how we fit into our culture, our society at large, and the world. As discussed in Chapter 1, the explosion of communication technology in our society has been a growing phenomenon. Along with this explosion has come a multitude of new vocabulary and products that define and describe our latest forms of communicating.

When we are healthy, we communicate effectively, efficiently, and dynamically with absolutely no idea how intricate and complex human communication is. In other words, we tend to take our ability to communicate for granted, not knowing that this ability involves systems of the body that were designed for other biological needs in human beings. Speech is a secondary or overlaid function that has been superimposed or placed on top of biological functions that are important for your basic survival.

Let's look at one biological system for now—your breathing mechanism.

The Lungs and Respiration

Our lungs are two large sponge-like structures encased within our rib cage. The primary purpose of the lungs and their associated structures is respiration—the act of taking fresh air in and expelling used air out of the body. Although the top priority of the lungs is to serve respiration, humans have adapted them for communication.

To put it simply, breathing in and out allows us to take in air from our atmosphere that is filled with rich oxygen. It comes into your body through our nose where it is filtered, warmed, and moistened before entering your lungs. The air molecules continue to travel deep into our lungs, eventually reaching the tiniest portion of our lung tissue—the alveoli (pronounced /AL VEE OH

LEE/)—where the air enters the blood stream. Rich oxygen is then released into our blood stream while simultaneously collecting the carbon dioxide and carrying it back up through the lungs, through our throat, and out of our nose; thereby releasing the carbon dioxide into the atmosphere which our trees and other plant life love to absorb so they can survive. Figure 2.1 provides an illustration of the breathing (respiratory) mechanism.

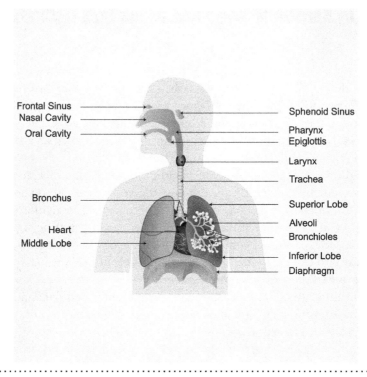

FIGURE 2.1   © stockshoppe, 2012. Used under license from Shutterstock, Inc.

Now, let's look at this same system from a speech production perspective. The breathing mechanism is what I call the "Power Supply for Speech." Speech requires us to draw in a supply of air to use for an outgoing flow of air. The mechanism of breathing for speech is essentially the same as for respiration. Biologically, the throat area of your body is responsible for making certain that the food you are swallowing and the air you are breathing goes down the correct pipe. In other words, air should go into the lungs through the larynx (pronounced /LAIR-RINKS/), while the food is supposed to go into the esophagus (pronounced /EE-SAF-A-GUS/), which is connected deeper in your throat behind the larynx. The esophagus permits food to travel to the stomach for digestion. The larynx, also commonly called the "voice box", is the body structure used to produce your voice to speak, sing, yell, or cry. Thus, this structure is the vocal source for speech.

Interesting, did you know that we restrict the outward flow of air at different points along the way? The vocal folds, tongue, and lips, especially, impede the airstream as they generate speech sounds. The respiratory muscles, also very important, extend the duration of the expiratory cycle for speech. Additionally, our speech volume such as speaking softly and loudly is also controlled by our respiratory muscles. Have you ever known someone who sounds breathy when they convey a message? Have you ever encountered someone who talks so soft you can barely understand what they are saying? Likewise, have you ever run out of breath when climbing stairs, walking fast, or running away from something? What happens to your speech and voice? If you are like me, you tend to sound breathy, your speech is choppy, and you eventually wait until you catch your breath before you resume talking. Well, that occurs because your power supply for talking is not functioning properly!

Our ability to control our respiratory mechanism depends largely on how we sound to others and if we are effective in conveying our messages. Therefore, breathing and the respiratory system are very important to our communication effectiveness. Breathing to speak is as important for you as a communicator as your need to plug into an electrical socket so your iron, blow dryer, or any other electrical device works!

A diagram showing you these biological structures that contribute to your overlaid ability to talk is seen in Figure 2.2.

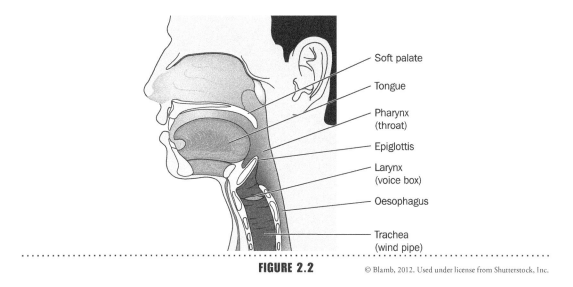

Soft palate

Tongue

Pharynx (throat)

Epiglottis

Larynx (voice box)

Oesophagus

Trachea (wind pipe)

FIGURE 2.2   © Blamb, 2012. Used under license from Shutterstock, Inc.

Communication Wellness: Reflecting on the Power Supply for Breathing and Speech

Communication wellness is an important concept to consider when identifying factors that are important in our ability to be a clear and concise communicator. As described previously, that individual who just completed a 5K run or that person that just finished climbing a flight of stairs will not, immediately after these events, be able to provide a clear communication exchange. I recently had a student enter my office after taking the stairs to reach the 3rd floor of the building. As soon as she came into my office she began to initiate communication and describe the purpose of her visit. However, I encountered a problem. I could not understand anything she was saying. Immediately, I had to redirect the student and instruct her to slow down, take several breaths, and sit down. She explained she had just taken the stairs instead of the elevator and she was out of breath, as she sipped her water and gasped for air. It was very apparent that until she was able to control her breathing mechanism and allow the "power supply for speech" to stabilize, she was not going to be an effective communicator.

....

Delivery Methods

....

by Regina Williams Davis

A clear communicator knows the best method to deliver their public message, face-to-face. There are four major delivery methods for public, face-to-face, information-giving communicators: 1. a memorized speech; 2. a scripted speech; 3. an impromptu speech; and 4. an extemporaneous speech.

Memorized speeches tend to be theatrical when presented. For talented actors, this may work well. However, for the rest of us, it can come across slightly insincere. This will affect how your message is received and perceived by your audience. It will not matter if it is an audience of one or many. Consider the scenario below:

> Sean and Sarah had a fight. Sean got some advice from a friend about what to say verbatim to fix things. Although these words were not what Sean would use, he thought Sarah would appreciate and forgive him based on his friend's comments. Well, Sean went to Sarah with his memorized speech. He stumbled over a few words and when Sarah asked him what he meant by some of his statements, Sean did not know what to say. It was awkward for both of them. Sarah really felt that Sean was completely disingenuous with his conversation.

Scripted speeches are appropriate for technical presentations and when it is important not to miss a specific procedural or intricate detail. These are often heard at professional conferences and seminars. Frequently, people are so afraid of their potential nervousness when speaking publicly that they will script every word of their speech. When they deliver this speech, they will read each word. This may annoy your audience because it will not feel as though you are speaking to them. An effective presentation should resemble a conversation with your audience. Reading decreases eye contact, which may cause you to miss the audiences' feedback. Another problem occurs when you make an attempt to look out to the audience and causing you to lose your place on the script. This causes mistakes and affects the delivery of your message, thus adding more pressure and nervousness that is reflected in your presentation.

An **impromptu speech** is delivered without any notes or preparation. Occasions for impromptu public speaking may come from a job interview or being questioned by an investigator or a journalist. The impromptu speech is an unprepared response, but well thought through. This happens in dialogue, but should not happen when given notice to provide a public presentation. There are ways to practice impromptu speaking in order to express your thoughts clearly and concisely, but impromptu public speaking should not occur unless there is no other choice or if you are in a less formal dialogic exchange.

The best and most effective delivery method is **extemporaneous speaking**. An extemporaneous presentation is a prepared presentation in terms of research, an outline, or bullet points. It has a distinct organization and communication goals. To use the extemporaneous method for your public presentation most efficiently, you must first know the two or three points you intend to make (Figure 2.3):

Body:
A. Point 1
B. Point 2
C. Point 3

FIGURE 2.3

Next, you can develop each point with two or three sub-points that will bring substance and augment your presentation. These sub-points are data and facts that provide supporting evidence with the purpose of enhancing each main point. Conciseness and brevity are still important so that none of the main points seem over emphasized. Nevertheless, your sub-points may be substantiated by the use of a statistic, an illustration, a personal story, an expert testimony, a visual aid, or all of the aforementioned examples as outlined in Figure 2.4.

Body:
A. Point 1
1. Sub-point A
2. Sub-point B
B. Point 2
1. Sub-point A
2. Sub-point B
C. Point 3
1. Sub-point A
2. Sub-point B

FIGURE 2.4

After you have the "body" of your speech with the sub-points, then you may prepare your introduction and conclusion. The introduction should contain an "attention-getter," a "credibility" statement, and a "preview" of what will be discussed.

The "attention-getter" will be your opening statement that will direct your audience's focus on you and what you are prepared to say. Attention-gaining devices may be as simple as a rhetorical question, a joke, or a startling statistic.

The "credibility" statement is one of the most important aspects of your speaking presentation. It is imperative that your audience is made aware of why they should take their valued time to listen and trust anything that you have to say. What makes you an expert or knowledgeable of the topic of what you are speaking? Where did you get your information? This information needs to be stated explicitly in the introduction section of your presentation.

Your "conclusion" will have only two parts: a summary and a memorable statement. The summary will consist of an extremely brief review of your main points. Please try to end with a profoundly memorable statement. See Figure 2.5.

I. Introduction

    a. Attention-getter

    b. Credibility

    c. Preview

II. Body

    a. Point A

        i. Sub-point

        ii. Sub-point

    b. Point B

        i. Sub-point

        ii. Sub-point

    c. Point C

        i. Sub-point

        ii. Sub-point

III. Conclusion

        i. Summarize

        ii. Memorable Statement

FIGURE 2.5

Finally, you may add to your draft outline for your speaking presentation "transition" statements. Transition statements are words that bridge previous parts of your presentation to the next part. Transitions are like directional signs or signals for your audience to know where you are in your presentation and what to expect next. See Figure 2.6.

I. Introduction

    a. Attention-getter: *"Have you ever wanted to feel and be healthier than you are but hate hearing that all you need is diet and exercise? Well, you are going to hear it again."*

    b. Credibility: *"I read an article in the March issue of Prevention Magazine, interviewed my certified personal trainer, and surveyed ten women who recently lost twenty pounds, which they intended to lose within the past year."*

    c. Preview or Thesis Statement: *"I will share with you three major activities that will improve your health: exercise, healthy eating, and mind control."*

II. Body
Transition Statement: *"My first point is . . ."*

    a. Point A

        i. Sub-point

        ii. Sub-point

Transition Statement: *"My next major point is . . ."*

    b. Point B

        i. Sub-point

        ii. Sub-point

Transition Statement: *"My final and most significant point is . . ."*

    c. Point C

        i. Sub-point

        ii. Sub-point

III. Conclusion

        i. Summarize

        ii. Memorable Statement

FIGURE 2.6

Key Terms:

Alveolar Ridge	Inhalation
Alveoli	Larynx
Articulators	Phonation
Articulation	Respiratory System
Code-Switch	Resonance
Communication Wellness	Soft Palate
Diaphragm	Stage Fright
Diction	Tongue Twister
Esophagus	Vocal Folds
Exhalation	Voice
Hard Palate	

Key Concepts:

Speech Delivery Methods:

Scripted	Extemporaneous
Impromptu	Memorized

Application Activity: *Informative Speech*

Time: 3–5 Minutes

Objective:

- The purpose of the Informative Speech is to give your audience information in an organized manner. Be sure to know your audience well enough to present your material in ways that may be engaging and meaningful to them. Be mindful that an informative speech is not to persuade but simply to give facts. If you begin to share your opinion, you have transitioned your speech into a persuasive presentation; thus, your personal opinions are not allowed in an informative speech!

Directions:

PART ONE:

Prepare an extemporaneous self-introductory speech. Share information about yourself. Please be certain you are not persuading your audience. Enlighten the audience of some aspect of your life. Some ideas might be to share your background, influences, interests, or a challenge you had to overcome. Consider informing the audience of your heritage, regional influences, artistic abilities, and athletic or scholastic achievements. Be sure to develop a clear:

I. **Introduction**
   a. Attention-getter
   b. Credibility statement
   c. Preview of the main points contained in the body
   d. Transition statement to the "Body"

II. **Body**
   a. Two or three main points; elaborate them using examples, explanations, or narrations
   b. Transition sentences or phrases between each point and a main transition statement to the "Conclusion"

III. **Conclusion**
   a. Signal that you're ending your speech
   b. Memorable statement

PART TWO:

Prepare a video of your speech using ACCLAIM. Reviewing your video will allow you to see and hear how you present your information. Are you presenting your information with confidence? Confidence will be evidenced with eye-contact, clear articulation of words, and minimal fillers. (Fillers are "uh, uhm, leaning, pacing, fidgeting).

PART THREE:

Two or three of your peers will review your video and complete a peer review. Consider their feedback and prepare a typed 1-page reflection paper. Please include in your paper the following:
   a. What were your strengths and weaknesses, considering: organization, content, and delivery?
   b. What will you do to improve your presentation?

Peer Evaluation—The Informative Speech

Directions: With four (4) being the highest and best score, please select the number to rate each component of the Informative Speech.

INTRODUCTION
Attention-Getter (Opening story, rhetorical question, quotations, etc.)

0	1	2	3	4

Credibility

0	1	2	3	4

Preview

0	1	2	3	4

Central Message

0	1	2	3	4

Transition Sentence

0	1	2	3	4

BODY
2–3 Appropriately Organized Points

0	1	2	3	4

Sufficiently developed with support for each point

0	1	2	3	4

Transition sentence

0	1	2	3	4

CONCLUSION
Signal of Wrapping-up/Transition Phrase

0	1	2	3	4

Summarize

0	1	2	3	4

Memorable Statement (Final, strong, connected . . .)

0	1	2	3	4

Vignettes are portrayals of a brief evocative description, account, or episode that will illustrate an important lesson.

VIGNETTE A: MUMBLING WORDS

Have you ever discovered you were in a conversation with someone and struggled to understand what they were saying? Sometimes they seem to be mumbling. Sometimes their way of describing a situation is so convoluted that the story they're telling is too hard to follow. Some people are so longwinded that their main point is completely lost. You may find yourself drifting and zoning out, dismissing the conversation, and leaving the other individual feeling devalued. How can this be avoided? More importantly, suppose you're the longwinded, convoluted, mumbling communicator? How might you improve to become clear and concise in future dialogues? Create a vignette that will demonstrate this lesson.

MINI QUIZ

1. True or False: The primary function of the larynx is speech.
2. Multiple Choice: Which of the following anatomical parts is responsible for directing air into the lungs?
   A. Esophagus
   B. Larynx
   C. Diaphragm
   D. Alveolar Ridge
3. Fill in the Blank: A memorized speech and an extemporaneous speech are types of

   _____ methods.

4. Essay: Explain why it is important to prepare a formal outline for an extemporaneous speech.

5. Discuss the four major types of speech delivery methods. Explain how they are different.

UNIT II
HyperPerception
Perception, Culture, and Society

UNIT OBJECTIVES:

- *Understanding perceptions of others*
- *Awareness of language bias and word of caution*
- *Nonverbal communication and culture*
- *Ethical communication*

. . . .

You will become aware of language that indicates bias on gender, age, ethnicity, sexual orientation, ethical communication, and communication behavior in the digital age. You will read how and why to adapt your messages to and for your audiences, how to provide a narrow topic for the occasion, and the best medium to deliver your message in the digital age.

. . . .

CHAPTER 3

Perception as Making Sense of the World

As the world evolves, so does communication. There are words and phrases that were used historically that may be inappropriate today. Being unaware of our responsibility as communicators will convolute our message and can ruin relationships, marriages, friendships, employment, and other significant concerns we have in our lives.

Perception as Making Sense of the World

by Myra M. Shird

Perception is the complex process of **selecting, organizing,** and **interpreting** information about people, events, activities, and situations. We rely on all of our senses to gather information about our surrounding environment. From the information we gain, we try to make sense of the world around us. Our perceptions, however, are deeply rooted in our personal experiences. **Perception is ultimately about how we select, organize, and interpret information so that we can understand our surroundings.**

Selection as Meeting Our Needs

We choose to focus on information that *meets our physiological and psychological needs.* Have you ever been really hungry and food was the only thing you seemed to smell? Probably, there were no more food smells in the air at that moment than there were at any other time. You were simply hungry. Therefore, you selected to focus on something that addressed that need.

We choose to focus on information that *interests* us. We are more likely to pay attention to presentations that offer us a benefit or a value. Likewise, we are much more likely to listen to someone we like, to someone who is like us, or to someone whose interests are similar to ours.

Finally, we choose to focus on *that which we expect to see.* Seeing what we expect to see instead of what is actually taking place is a cognitive error. Individuals tend to see what they expect to see. I was driving a red BMW. The policeman stopped me because there was a search for a black BMW. The only explanation for the policeman's behavior is that he saw what he expected to see. He made a cognitive error. Do you think it is easy to make this kind of mistake? Quickly, look at the phrases in the triangles below:

You probably read "Snake in the grass," "Once in a lifetime," and "Bird in the hand." Now, go back and reread. Did you have an accurate perception of what was in the triangles, or did you perceive what you expected to see? We easily miss the repeated words, because we don't expect to see them. Seeing what we expect to see rather than seeing what is really there hinders us from seeing change. It hinders our growth as social human beings. These cognitive errors occur without us ever realizing they are taking place. This is the type of cognitive error that costs innocent people their lives and their freedoms. Check yourself one more time. Read the following.

How did you do?

Perception as a Means of Categorizing

We organize information based on our personal categorizing system. We categorize based on our personal experiences and based on the material and nonmaterial components of our culture. Cognitive psychology suggests that we organize information into *schema* or patterns that are coherent and meaningful. A variety of schemata helps us to organize our impressions: **prototypes, mental yardsticks,** and **stereotypes**.

An Example of *"Fine!"*: Prototype

One of my students, Angela, was crazy about another student, "Z." Angela constantly told her girlfriend, Regina, "Ooh, girl, he is so fine." For Angela, "Z" was the epitome of "fine." He was her prototype or best example of the concept "fine," the best example of male attractiveness. We organize our perceptions by defining a prototype or a best example. The **prototype** is the benchmark for how we categorize a person, object, activity, or situation.

How They Measure Up: Mental Yardstick

Angela and Regina do a lot of "boy watching." The young women usually categorize a male's attractiveness by measuring him against their prototype, their own best example of attractiveness, "Z." The young women have done what most humans do: they have created their own mental yardsticks for determining attractiveness. Our mental yardsticks provide a bipolar continuum for measuring how close new information measures up to the prototype. Prototypes provide the best example of a concept or phenomena. The mental yardstick allows us to measure new information, using the prototype as the primary basis of comparison.

No Acknowledgment of Uniqueness: Stereotypes

In our society stereotypes tend to flourish. When people say things like, "White rappers are just acting Black," or "female basketball players are lesbians," they are stereotyping. **Stereotyping** is the categorizing of people, situations, and objects without acknowledging unique individual characteristics. Stereotypes stem from our broad generalizations about phenomena. Communication professors William Seiler and Melissa Beall (2002) find that:

> "Stereotyping is pervasive because of the human psychological need to categorize and classify information. Through stereotyping we pigeonhole people. This tendency may hamper our communication, because it may cause us to overlook individual characteristics . . . stereotypes often oversimplify, over-generalize, or exaggerate traits . . . , and . . . are based on . . . , distortions, and false premises."

Finally, stereotypes repeat and reinforce beliefs until they come to be taken as the truth. Stereotypes ultimately perpetuate inaccuracies about people, and thus impede communication. How we organize our perceptions is inextricably linked to our past experiences. Past experiences may cloud or distort perceptions. It is a social responsibility to make sure that what we see and/or hear represents reality. If we do not, lives could be lost or negatively altered forever. Generally, stereotypes are negative when they hinder the social, psychological, physical, spiritual, and/or financial welfare of any individual or group.

Definition of a Redneck

by Stephanie Sedberry Carrino

What is a "redneck"? It depends on whom you ask. Like many other words, different people define it differently. If you are Black, chances are that you define the term as a White person who is racist. If you are White, it is entirely possible that the term refers to the stereotype of "poor white country folk"—uneducated individuals who live in a rural setting and live in trailers, smoke, drive pick-up trucks, and have lots of dogs and stuff in their yards. Many white people DO NOT use the term redneck to describe someone who is racist and do not know that the word is interpreted by some people as racist. Really?!

My daughter, Emily, was in a reading class in the third grade that had been divided into reading groups. The kids were asked to name their own groups and come up with a "cheer" for their group. There were the "Boxing Honey-buns," the "Crunchy Candies," and the "Rednecks." Really?! The "cheer" for this group was rubbing their necks whining "I'm so sunburned!" In this group, there were three White children and one Black child. When Emily told me about the reading groups, I almost choked. Although I am White, I spend a great deal of time in a predominately Black environment, so I know that "redneck" is often translated as racist by African-Americans. The next day, I spoke with her teacher, a white woman, who was appalled when I explained to her that to many Black Americans, redneck means racist. She had no idea. The next day, Emily told me that the reading groups had been reassigned, and that they had to come up with new names and cheers. The "Redneck" group was gone. That day, Emily's teacher learned an important lesson about how words can be interpreted differently by different people. I hope you have too!

There's a Redneck in My Backyard, HELP! A Case Study Perspective

by Sheila M. Whitley, Ph.D.

When you hear the term *redneck,* maybe many different stereotyped images pop into your head. Maybe you have a definite image and behavior in mind, because your stereotyped image has held true for every *redneck* you ever met. When I hear *redneck,* one stereotyped image pops into my head—southern white male. Let me clarify, I don't think all southern white men are *rednecks* and not all *rednecks* are the same. My stereotype may differ from your stereotype. Humor me as I label and poke fun at my stereotyped image of a *redneck.* I place *rednecks* on a continuum. On one side of the continuum is the friendly *redneck.* He is country-talking, gregarious, blue-jean wearing, never met anyone he couldn't get along with, will help anyone, and in general—just a nice guy.

The other side of the *redneck* continuum is the extreme opposite of our friendly *redneck.* He is the guy you don't want living next door. He out-cusses a sailor, guzzles beer, favors collecting unemployment money over a job, owns aggressive dogs, scurries off in his mufflerless car, is always itching for a good fight (especially in a bar), is overly proud of his race and sees all other races as inferior, has had at least one clash with the law before he could legally acquire intoxicating beverages, and in general is someone his friends won't turn their backs on out of fear or lack of trust. Almost forgot, he picks a woman with the same qualities.

Some guys on both ends of the continuum proudly proclaim their *redneck* status; while others distress if you call them a *redneck.* I know many self-acknowledged and in denial *rednecks.* I adore and appreciate the friendly *redneck.* They are good guys to have as friends and neighbors. But on the other side of the continuum, well . . . I rather only hear stories and be thankful it didn't happen to me. Sit back, 'cause I'm about to tell you a story that happened to me, and you can be thankful it wasn't you. I need to give you a bit of background so you can fully understand my befuddlement. The names have been changed to protect the guilty.

I was about 6 years old when Mr. and Mrs. Smith moved into the house on the left side of our home. Karen, their only child, was married and about to have her first baby. Her husband was away in the military, so she moved in with her parents so they could help with the new baby. Around Thanksgiving, Karen had a baby boy. For satirical emphasis, I'll call him Bubbbbba. His real name doesn't fit the stereotype and he's guilty. Bubbbbba was a cute baby and another neighborhood playmate. I don't remember how long Karen lived with her parents after the baby was born. Eventually, she joined her husband in another town. Bubbbbba visited his grandparents often and some of the visits were for extended periods of time. All the neighbors grieved when Bubbbbba was about three or four years old, and his grandfather was beaten to death in a convenience store robbery. It was about this time that Karen started her marrying and then divorcing spree. Mrs. Smith was financially stable and she paid the bill every time Karen got into a predicament. Karen was engrossed with her life and didn't devote time to raising Bubbbbba. The end result was Bubbbbba lived off and on with his grandmother. Looking back, I wonder if this shuffling back and forth was the birth of what would become his adult value system.

I know Bubbbbba loved his grandfather. It is possible that his grandfather was the only positive male role model in his life. Years after his grandfather's death, Bubbbbba told me he thought his grandfather was the only person who really loved him. Wow! I didn't know what to say then and I still don't know what to say. I think he was wrong. I believe his mother and grandmother loved him. He obviously didn't receive love the way he perceived it should be given. I can only speculate how Bubbbbba's life would have been different if his grandfather lived.

To sum up my relationship with Bubbbbba, we grew up together and had an amicable relationship. I'm told he looked up to me as an older sister. His grandmother affirmed to my mother many times that I was a good influence on Bubbbbba. I didn't see Bubbbbba much after he reached junior high school. I was away in college and he wasn't spending as much time with his grandmother. His high school years completed his transformation to a new value system. He converted into the type of *redneck* you don't want living beside you. Bubbbbba didn't try in high school and frequently got into trouble. His grandmother kept us updated on his ins- and outs-of-trouble during this time, mainly traffic violations. My father is a barber, so what wasn't told, he heard through the proverbial barber shop grapevine—gossip.

Throughout high school, Bubbbbba's grandmother bought him several cars. He wrecked, destroyed, or maimed every car. Mrs. Smith bailed him out of trouble every time he drove or walked into it. She lamented many times to my mother about how much it worried her the way Bubbbbba was living his life. I think she believed buying him things and bailing him out of trouble would wake him up. Conversely, it fueled his lifestyle and reinforced an absence of love. He knew her money was available to fix his mess with no parental discipline attached. So he messed and messed and messed. I saw Bubbbbba for the first time in many years at his grandmother's funeral. He was about twenty-three years old. Noticeably, he wasn't the same person as my childhood friend. We had a pleasant visit and relived some of the good ol' days. It was obvious to both of us that we didn't have any common interests or the necessary foundation for a friendship. Our value systems were too different. Even so, I continued hoping his childhood heart would resurrect. My mother had no doubts. She heard way too much from his grandmother and knew the type of person he had become. He was someone you didn't want in your neighborhood.

For the first time in two decades, Mrs. Smith's house was vacant. Hopefully, Karen would sell the house. The neighborhood's worst possible nightmare would be for Karen to allow Bubbbbba to move into the house. The neighbors prepared for the worse. I was living at home and would be affected by Karen's decision. I really didn't think Karen would let Bubbbbba move in because surely she knew the problems he would cause the neighbors. Not to mention, he would probably destroy the house. Karen wasn't like her mother; she wanted all the money for herself. I was sure she would sell the house for the money—if for no other reason. We all woke up to a nightmare. Bubbbbba moved into the house with several of his friends and his seven-month pregnant soon-to-be wife. Initially, it was difficult to see the intensity of his hostility because it was masked in lightheartedness. It wasn't long before Bubbbbba and I discovered we had nothing in common and no relationship. He no longer respected me as a friend, looked up to me as an older sister, or even talked to me.

I won't even talk about how he approached my parents and the rest of the neighbors. Bubbbbba and his live-in friends worked occasionally, but by far, spent most of their time messing around the house. They competed in front yard cussing episodes in the early morning, mid-morning, noon, night, and late night; drove noisy cars; kept an aggressive pit bull and chow inside the fenced-in backyard; hosted beer guzzling parties that encouraged their propensity for outdoor bladder relief and ended with empty beer cans all over the yard; and performed many other openly defiant behaviors aimed at upsetting the neighborhood old fogies. One peaceful Sunday afternoon sticks out in my mind and confirmed where Bubbbbba's belief system ended up. I just returned from Baton Rouge and was trying to take a nap since my early morning flight robbed me of a good night's rest. My bedroom was about fifteen feet from Bubbbbba's driveway and the side entrance into his basement. The driveway ran the length of his house and continued beyond the driveway-width chain-linked-fence gate, which wrapped around to the back of the house into the basement garage.

I was awakened from my nap by the jocularity of Bubbbbba and three or four of his friends in the driveway trying to fix his stentorian, but at the moment, broken car. I tried to ignore all the commotion and go back to sleep. Yeah, right! What was I thinking?

Suddenly, the mood changed. I heard an anguished, "No! . . . NO! . . . BUBBBBBA!" OK, that didn't sound promising. Could be a problem? Probably not! Drama was commonplace when they were messing around outside. I'm a bit upset. It's beginning to look a lot like I'm not going to get my nap. I'm sooooo sleepy. Why today Bubbbbba? You planned it this way, didn't you? Oh my, what's that? Surprise, surprise! The engine started. VAROOM, VAROOMMMMM, VA ROOMMMMM ROOM. Great! He got the strident engine started. The verdict's in. I lost my nap attempt. Can't sleep with that cacophony! I knew the usual routine. Race the engine in an attempt to break the sound barrier or annoy the peace and quiet out of the neighbors. Success, Bubbbbba! You drove my peace and quiet into the next county. No nap for this very tired gal.

A flash later . . . CRASH, KABOOM! . . . "OH . . . !" Sorry. I didn't quite catch that last part. Hummmmmm? I wondered what that was all about. Was that a whoops? Sort of sounded like damage. I knew I wasn't dreaming because I couldn't nap with all that racket! A split second later, my curiosity mounted beyond restraint. I sprang out of bed—interrupting my insomnia—with an inquiring mind. I was about to take the big risk and look out the window to see what they destroyed. Took a deep breath . . . Held it! Exhaled! Braced for the worse. Prayed! "Please, don't let it be our house." Looked out the window. Opened my eyes! Sighed with relief—"NOT our house." Sort of chuckled—"HIS house!!!!!" Based on visual scrutiny and what I heard, I surmised the chain of events. No one was behind the wheel of the car. The boys were all in or near the driveway close to my bedroom window. The hood was up. Bubbbbba and maybe one of his dudes worked on the engine while the rest joked around and made a lot of needless noise.

Stunner! Bubbbbba got the car started. Based on all the joking, I'm guessing his ability to start the engine took his buddies by surprise. After all, Bubbbbba wasn't a mechanic. Now for the whoops. . . . If you aren't a mechanic, it is in your best interest not to be under the hood trying to fix the engine. Even more so, it really isn't in your best interest to be under the hood with the engine running. You could blow up the engine, electrocute yourself, or accidentally put the car into gear. What? You think you know where I'm going with this?

For the second time that Sunday afternoon, Bubbbba had success. He didn't blow up the engine or electrocute himself. That's right, he got the car in gear and it took off down the driveway. I'm guessing this evoked the: "No! . . . NO! . . . BUBBBBBA!!" The car traveled about ten feet and ran through the double gates, busting them off the fence post hinges. It traveled another ten feet and rested after hitting the corner of the freestanding garage. Needless to say, there was a lot—and I mean a superfluity—of cussing. I could only shake my head in bewilderment over his accidental mechanical achievement. Shoot. This was more entertaining than television. Even my dreams aren't this whacked. Could my afternoon get any more entertaining? Could he appease for terminating my nap? Yea, he could and did! Bubbbbba decided to fix the gates. After all, he needed to keep his pernicious pit bull and chow incarcerated. Resourcefully, he got the necessary supplies to reattach the twisted gates. With twine in hand, he was ready to repair. Luckily, his friends were there for him and willing to help. You know, drink beer and laugh at him . . . I mean . . . laugh with him.

Each gate was half the width of the driveway. The two gates met in the mid-point of the driveway. One gate had a rod that anchored into the driveway. The other gate latched to the anchored gate to ensure the gates closed securely. Anyway, that was the design prior to the "whoops." Bubbbbba diligently worked to secure the mutilated gates back in place—original design in mind. He took his sturdy twine and wove the twine around each gate, reattaching it to its respective fence post. His comrades offered copious encouragement with each weave—laughter. Wonderful. Beautiful. Most excellent. Finished. Bubbbbba had a puff of pride. At last, the gates were shabbily tied to the fence posts. You ask, "What about the gate with the anchoring rod so the gates close securely?" Twine was used to hold the two gates closed. "Securely?" you ask. Get real. Of course, not! Bubbbbba's friends agreed with me. With mockery in their voices, they pronounced their judgment on Bubbbbba's workmanship. Bubbbbba retorted, "I ain't no nigger! I'm a white man and don't do no nigger job!" Ergo, Bubbbbba proved beyond a shadow of a doubt where he resided on my *redneck* continuum.

In addition to exhibiting all the other extreme end criteria (cussing, drinking, loud cars, vicious dogs, no job, police difficulty, and so forth), he announced to the world his racist stance. In doing so, he implied other races can't match his mastery—inferior to his white supremacy. In reality, race has nothing to do with quality of work. Quality of work is determined by knowledge, ability, skill, and talent. In this case, Bubbbbba was not qualified to fix the gate. Hence, I had to contemplate Bubbbbba's promulgation. I wondered why the "pride of the race" couldn't process that he didn't have the skill or knowledge to fix the fence. My first thought was, "You goof. You ran the car through the fence and into the side of the garage. The fence shouldn't be broken, and you park the car . . . in the garage." Perhaps, the best solution would have been to call the fence repair man. Needless to say, the gates fell off the "hinges" every time they tried to open the gates. Twine just doesn't work as well as steel bolts and an anchoring rod. Bubbbba's broken-down repair job kept the dogs inside the fence. We were thankful his dogs weren't smart enough to figure out they could push down the gates. He never fixed the garage. Bubbbbba, his wife (Bubbbbbett), their son (Bubba, Jr.), and friends lived next door to us for many more months. During his remaining time, Bubbbbba continued to do an array of things that reinforced his position on the extreme end of the *redneck* continuum.

Just as he was born with his mother living in that house, his oldest son was born with him living in that house. I only saw his son from a distance. Neither one of us made any attempts to rebuild our previous relationship. In telling this true story, I've used my *redneck* stereotype satirically. We all have stereotypes and use them daily. Is this fair? How often do you label a person and then judge him by that label? Was Bubbbbba a *redneck*? His attitudes and behaviors fit nicely into my extreme end *redneck* continuum. Our strife had nothing to do with a label. It was all about our opposing value systems.

I can only wonder why our lives took such drastically different paths. I know my family structure and situation was more stable. More importantly, my belief system prohibits me from viewing anyone as inferior or superior. Undoubtedly, our perceptions of a person greatly influences the way we interact with that person. I know attitude and behavior determines the type of relationship I cultivate with anyone. My perceptions and the time I spent with Bubbbbba as a baby and young boy were harmonious. Our opposing adult attitudes and behaviors shattered our childhood relationship. In spite of the challenges in Bubbbbba's life, he had the opportunity to take a different path. His grandmother was an elementary school teacher. She graduated from college when women were told and expected to stay home and have babies. She would have gratefully paid for him to go to college. What happened, and why did he choose the path of slothfulness instead of opportunity?

In retrospect, I regret I didn't encourage him more when we were growing up. He was six years younger which translated into light years away from my peer group. When I was with my friends, we didn't want him around us all the time—especially when boys entered the picture. It was difficult for twelve-year-old girls to woo the boys with a six-year-old boy hanging around. When I wasn't with my friends, I spent a lot of one-on-one time with him. Let me tell you the end of the story. Bubbbbba moved out of his grandmother's house about a year after moving in. His sister, Chick, moved in after he vacated. She is six years younger than Bubbbbba and I barely knew her. She was a better neighbor and cared—at least superficially—how the neighbors reacted to her shenanigans. Just like two peas in a pod, Chick had the same belief system. Consequently, she had conflicts with the neighbors. She lived in the house less than a year and moved out. Karen sold Mrs. Smith's house soon after Chick skedaddled. Once again, my parents have a real neighbor. The new neighbors put up a new gate and tore down the detached garage. After Bubbbbba moved, we didn't hear much about him until a neighbor heard his obituary on a local radio station. We found out Bubbbbba committed suicide in his mother's house in Charlotte. He died somewhere around his 30th birthday, the father of three boys, and divorced. His mother buried him in our hometown beside his grandfather and grandmother. I never told my parents, but I visited his grave shortly after he died. I think my parents did too.

After seeing Bubbbbba's lifestyle and attitude when he moved in next door, I'm not surprised he died young. I really thought he would die in a bar room fight or car wreck. He had two serious car accidents—alcohol related—a few years before he moved in next door. I never thought about suicide, because he had a gregarious personality and appeared to have a positive self-image. Shortly after Bubbbbba moved in next door, my father had his only serious conversation with him. My father asked him if he learned anything from his two near-death experiences. He responded, "Yeah, I'll do the driving next time we are all drunk." My father told him he was headed for a short life if he didn't get it together. He blew off my father's prophetic warning. I hadn't really thought about the potential reasons Bubbbbba became the person he was until now. I thought writing this essay would be easy, but it wasn't. I've told and laughed about the Sunday afternoon escapade many times. Bubbbbba was a friend. I remember him fondly as a child and cherish those days. I still think about him around Thanksgiving. As an adult, he became pure misery in our lives for a short period of time. I didn't like or respect him at all. His metamorphosis from friend to nemesis is why writing the complete story wasn't easy. As a matter of fact, it was down right painful.

There is no happy ending for this story. A wasted friendship. A wasted life. After this experience, I hope I never say, "There's a *redneck*—on the unenviable end of the continuum—in my backyard, HELP!"

Key Terms:

Perception   Mental Yardsticks
Prototype   Stereotyping

Application Activity: *Perception Lesson*

Can I Talk to You for a Moment?: Cultural Conversations
Soncerey L. Montgomery, Ph.D. Winston-Salem State University

Objectives:

- To demonstrate how our interpersonal relationships and cross-cultural interactions are influenced by social perceptions and cultural understandings (or misunderstandings).
- To increase awareness of individual perceptions and group generalizations through candid dialogue.

Directions:

Ask for about 12-15 student volunteers. (Numbers may vary depending on the size of the class.) Student volunteers should line up in the front of the room with their backs facing the audience. The instructor will then tape a different card on the back of each student volunteer. Each card should have the name of a different culture on it; as such, the student becomes a cultural representative for that particular group. The cultural representative should not be able to see which culture he/she will be a part of. Sample cultures include: *homeless person, Arab-American, welfare recipient, convicted felon, homosexual, Asian-American, person in a wheelchair, janitor, Muslim, elderly person, drug user, Baptist preacher, domestic abuse survivor, etc.* Once all cards are taped on the backs of the cultural representatives, the remaining audience members should join this group in the front of the room. (At this point, the audience members have seen which culture each cultural representative is a member of.) Audience members should mingle with and engage in conversation with the cultural representatives in a manner that they would typically interact with members of that particular culture. Based on the conversations and interaction (or lack thereof) cultural representatives will try to figure out which culture they represent. Please note: during the cultural conversations, audience members should not explicitly tell the cultural representatives which culture they represent. The representatives should determine their group affiliation based on others conversations, behaviors, and interactions with them. Once each cultural representative has figured out which culture he or she represents, everyone sits down and reassembles as a class. Then, serious discussion about this activity begins.

MINI QUIZ

1. True or False: Perception is a simple process based on our interpretation of the world.
2. Multiple Choice: Categorizing people, situations, and objects without acknowledging unique individual characteristics is referred to as:
   A. Prototypes
   B. Mental yardsticks
   C. Stereotyping
   D. A and B
3. Fill in the Blank: Our most ideal representation of phenomena is referred to as

   _____.

4. Discussion: Refer to the essay "There's a Redneck in My Backyard, HELP! A Case Study Perspective" and discuss in small groups how the author's perception of her friend changed from when they were children to when they became adults. Based on life experiences, was her perception accurate or inaccurate, regarding what she thought the term "redneck" meant? Why or why not?

CHAPTER 4

Accurate Stereotypes: Do They Exist?

by Myra M. Shird

We usually develop stereotypes based on our personal experiences or the experiences of those close to us. Stereotypes are linked to our frame of reference. It is sometimes difficult for people to release the baggage of the past and progress towards the future. However, past experiences may prevent us from seeing change and force us to see only what we expect to see.

Some stereotypes help us to make decisions more efficiently. Say you are at your local bank making a deposit on a warm summer afternoon and in walks a person wearing a ski mask. Do you think "**BANKROBBER**" and instinctively run? Your assessment may be a fair generalization. Some generalizations provide understanding and expectations for how people, situations, and objects should be. Generalizations sometimes provide a basis for us to compare our expectations with reality. In this society, generalizations or stereotypes frequently inform our behaviors, such as your decision to run. Let's take the bank scenario further. Say you get home that evening and kick back to watch the news. The news anchor reads, "Suspected bank robber tackled by customers. Find out more when the 6:00 o'clock news comes your way." You sit there on the very edge of your seat, waiting to hear about the ski mask assailant from your bank. You say to yourself, "I knew it. I knew that was a robber." Finally, the news comes on. The anchor reads:

> Today, a suspected bank robber was wrestled to the floor by a mob of customers and bank employees. The suspected robber entered the local ABC Bank wearing a ski mask. Two male customers jumped the suspected robber from behind and tussled him to the ground. As the three struggled, one of the customers discovered that the suspected robber was armed. One customer yelled to the others in the bank, "He's armed. We need help." The customers attacked the suspected robber, beating and kicking him until he was unconscious. Once the police and paramedics arrived, the suspected robber was identified as an off-duty police officer who had stopped at the bank after being released from the hospital. It appears the officer was wearing the ski mask for protection.

During an attempted arrest, a suspect doused the officer in the face with a lye-based chemical causing major burns to his face and neck. Doctors bandaged the officer and suggested the ski mask was protection from the ultraviolet rays.

You sit back in your chair. You are floored because here is an example of perception gone wrong. Yet, this scenario could have taken a completely different turn. The officer could have truly been a bank robber. Are stereotypes ever accurate? Not all stereotypes are completely inaccurate. At some time or some place, enough people have experienced a phenomenon in a similar way so that a generalization might be drawn. Hence, there may be a morsel of truth in some stereotypes. And some perceptions are accurate.

I'm a Product of My Environment

We usually assign cause to people's behaviors. I have often heard people justify behavior by claiming, "He's a product of his environment." This claim is a way of attributing cause to behaviors based on an individual's surroundings. **Attribution** is the process of understanding the reasons for our own as well as other's behaviors. We attempt to understand behaviors by attributing cause to either the individual's situation (environment) or the individual's disposition (personality traits). We must remember that the attributions that we make are not always correct. We make an **attribution error** when we overestimate dispositional causes and underestimate situational causes of others' actions. Research shows that humans are more likely to perceive others as acting the way they do because they are "that kind of person" rather than attributing their behavior to environmental causes (Gilbert and Malone 1995; Overwalle 1997).

The attributions that we make may influence our relationships with others as well as our relationship with ourselves. Research also concludes that we make attributions that serve our personal interests (Hamachek 1992; Sypher 1984). We claim that good things are caused by the power that we have exerted and disclaim responsibility for what we do poorly. This **self-serving bias** distorts our perceptions of our worth in relation to others in the world. We develop an unrealistic image of ourselves and our abilities when we perceive ourselves as invincible and omnipotent—the alpha and omega of any situation.

Factors That Influence Perception

So far, we have discussed the perception process in terms of selection, organizing, and interpreting. Now let's examine factors that impact our perception process. **Physiological, cognitive, cultural,** and **gender** factors influence perception. In addition, perception is greatly influenced by the **media**.

Perceptual Differences Based on Physiology

In the fall of 2002, people living in the D.C., Maryland, and Virginia suburbs were afraid to come outside of their homes to perform simple tasks like pumping gas. They feared they may be the next victims of the beltway sniper. A witness expert commented that it would be extremely difficult to develop a composite drawing of the sniper because witnesses' accounts vary so widely. The expert said that an old person may describe seeing a young person, and a young person may describe seeing an old person. The witnesses' descriptions are relative to their respective ages. An eighty-year-old may perceive a forty-year-old as young; whereas a twenty-year-old may perceive a forty-year-old as old. Physical factors such as age, weight, height, health, and body shape account for perceptual differences. Think back. As a child, was there someone who you thought was really tall? And now that you are older and taller, do you think of that person as being the same size giant? As age does in this case, other physiological factors may impact perception on multiple levels.

Perceptual Differences Based on State of Mind (Cognitive Function)

Think about when you are happy or sad. Do you perceive situations the same way? State of mind greatly influences perception. Quite frequently, people who suffer from depression are pessimistic about life. Their perceptions are distorted because of their negative state of mind. On the contrary, when we are up and everything is going our way, we perceive possibilities. These are examples of how cognitive functions influence perception. Remember a time when you broke up with a boyfriend or girlfriend? Right after a long-term relationship ends, we are usually fairly vulnerable. We are skeptical of intimate relationships. We sometimes perceive other individuals as being less trustworthy. These perceptions are based on the state of mind caused by the breakup.

Perceptual Differences Based on Culture

Culture is a way of life; it encompasses values, beliefs, and understandings shared by a group of people. The way people live in the "hood" and the way people live in the "burbs" are quite different. The way people live in the country and the way people live in the city are just as different. The way of life and understanding the assumptions about what is good, right, and worthwhile may vary from group to group. In Afghanistan, it is not right for a woman to go out unveiled. Women are not valued as equal to men. In the United States, although disparities in pay and certain other areas still exist between men and women, they are generally treated as equal. At least that is what is legislated.

Some cultures are very communal. The family is very important to the identity of individuals from these cultures. For example, certain African cultures that strongly value family relationships also greatly value and respect their elders. On the other hand, in the United States, elders are frequently perceived as expendable. Co-cultures are social communities within a macro or dominant culture. **Co-cultures** have a system of values and beliefs that may coincide or conflict with those of the dominant culture. People can belong to multiple co-cultures. Members of co-cultures have unique understandings of the world. Our perceptions are influenced by the personal knowledge that comes from our experiences as members of a particular social community.

Our perceptions are influenced by our cultural capital. **Cultural capital** is defined as the personal knowledge and experience that is directly related to membership in a particular social community (Shird 2001).

Perceptual Differences Based on Gender

by Myra M. Shird and Regina Williams Davis

Women tend to act as caregivers. They tend to perceive need. Although the maternal instinct may explain part of this proclivity, socialization can explain the other part. In this society, women have been raised to be caring—to take care of the house and the family. Women are the nurturers in this culture. Men, on the other hand, are less likely to stay at home and care for the ailing child. In this culture, fewer men tend to choose careers in such fields as nursing, classroom teachers, and even speech-language pathology.

Women and men have different socially-defined roles. We follow different scripts for how we are to behave. Our cultural capital is different because of our personal knowledge and experience as a male or female. Some people tend to defy the norms of the dominant culture. A man, for example, who chooses to wear a dress, makeup, and high-heel shoes may be perceived as weird, and at the least, different. Simply because a man wears a dress does not make him weird. Gender roles are socially constructed and greatly influence our understanding of the world.

An activity I like to do in my communication classes is a role reversal. I ask the men to meet me down the hall while I leave directions for the women. After the last male exits the room, I ask the women to create a dramatic representation of two men who were friends returning to campus after an entire summer away from each other. They happen to see each other for the first time since they were back in school in front of the campus bookstore where they greet each other. The women are asked to prepare to act the scene as they might imagine the meet and greet would progress. Then they are asked to prepare to act a second scenario. The setting for the second scenario is at a club downtown. They have to create a skit showing how a man asks them or another woman to dance with them and how they try to get their phone number. I tell them they have ten minutes to develop the two skits. Then I meet the male students down the hall and give them the same assignment, but the men must act their scenes out in the manner they would believe women might great their friend, ask a guy to dance, or try to get a guy's phone number.

As you might imagine, the skits are hilarious. To see the women act like the men and the men act like the women is extremely entertaining. However, the interesting phenomenon is how women and men coexist, yet we perceive and maintain a zillion stereotypes about the opposite sex. The point I like to make is how easy it is to take our limited experiences with a few individuals and extrapolate those experiences to the entire gender or segment of people.

....

Measuring Objectivity

....

by Dwight Davis

My wife is an ardent fan of NC State football. Strangely enough, a comment she made while watching a Wolfpack game on television one day led me to a revelation concerning the concepts of objectivity and subjectivity. Most of us think of objectivity as a state of mind without bias, and most of us believe we are quite capable of achieving this thought process. I, too, believed that I was an objective thinker. After all, as a longtime journalist I was trained to be objective. I believed this until a close third-down call went against the Wolfpack on this Saturday afternoon. As State drove down the field, the Wolfpack needed a crucial first down to pull out a victory in the waning minutes. The game hinged on a third-and-short yardage situation. This pivotal play required a measurement by the referees. It would determine if State's forward progress had met the required distance, which is ten yards for a first down. As the chains were stretched on the field to measure the yardage, the referee eyed the situation closely. He then held up two fingers inches apart, indicating my wife's beloved 'Pack had narrowly missed gaining the required yardage for a first down. My wife, June, was incredulous. She bellowed, "How can they (the referees) place the ball all over the field and then determine they (the Wolfpack) are short (of making a first down) by inches?"

Having covered many football games as a sportswriter, I began to posit an authority's argument. I told my wife that some degree of subjectivity on the part of the referees is a necessary and accepted part of the game. The measurements, though (such as the one made in the State game), are considered an objective standard. But, June countered, "How can the measurements be objective when the same referees have determined where the ball should have been placed the whole game?"

Ah! While definitely not an objective observer of NC State in any sense of the word, June caused me to realize that objectivity has to be obtained through subjectivity. Therefore, the concept of total objectivity cannot exist. Let's go back to the game for a moment. According to the rules, the ball should be spotted at the point where a ball carrier's knee has touched the ground. In many instances, however, it is impossible to determine exactly where a knee has touched, even with the use of slow-motion replays of television cameras. But we leave it to the game officials to determine these spots and assume they use their best judgment in determining as closely as possible where the ball should be placed. Over the course of any particular game, we can assume placements of the ball could vary by several feet, inches, or yards if compared to the exact spots where the ball should have actually been placed. Often officials or coaches request measurements to determine if indeed a team has moved the ball the required ten yards and should be awarded a first down. A chain attached to two poles measuring ten yards in length is brought on to the field to determine the exact distance a team has moved the ball.

After a measurement, a game official may hold his hands or fingers inches apart, indicating that a team is just shy of attaining the required ten yards to be awarded a first down, when in actuality the team may have exceeded the required distance by several inches, feet, or even by several yards, depending upon the point of the game at which the measurement has taken place—or the team may have fallen short by such margins. From the accepted subjective notion of maintaining fair play, an accepted objective notion is perceived when a measurement has been made, because when something is measured, this is perceived to be an act of objectivity.

But, this begs the question: How can objectivity be maintained if subjectivity is part of the equation? The example of spotting a football on the gridiron and subsequent measurements of yards is symbolic of the manner in which the skewed notions of objectivity are perceived. Subjectivity is defined as "existence in mind only; absorption in one's own mental states or processes; tendency to view things through the medium of one's own individuality" (*The World Book Dictionary*, 2085). Objectivity is defined as "intentness on objects external to the mind; external reality" (1432). It could be said, then, that subjectivity is inherent, and objectivity is an attempt to separate ourselves from subjectivity. The latter is not possible. An objective notion becomes a subjective attempt to separate one's self from preconceived ideologies, which makes the concept of objectivity a slippery one at best. Defining the concept of objectivity is a multi-dimensional dialectic dilemma within itself because the definition of the term may vary from one individual to another. Hence, defining the term and subsequently applying or attempting to apply the concept reaches to the roots of subjectivity.

Restivo (1994) argues that objectivity is "burdened by a history of interminable and inconclusive discussions and contradictory usages. It has been described as a value and an ideology that embodies and expresses detachment and alienation from self and society" (177). Philosophers of science, according to Restivo, formulated and systematically developed the social theory of objectivity, conforming to the canons of the sociology of science. Objectivity in this regard remains problematic. Even in the sterile, unfettered confines of a laboratory, void of "outside" influences, a subjective tenor remains, which is that of the scientist(s) performing the tests.

If objectivity cannot be fully realized within the concepts of science, it stands to reason objectivity cannot be fully accomplished in the realm of social communication. In this cluttered and complex realm, unbiased thought process—alienation from expressive paradigms in order to interpret the external world with impartiality—becomes layered with subjective issues from which we cannot escape. In order to become more effective communicators, it is important that we make attempts at objectivity, but realize we will always come up short of the goal.

Key Terms:

Attribution   Cultural Capital
Attribution Error   Self-serving Bias
Co-culture

Key Concepts:

Factors Affecting Perception:

1. Physiology
2. State of Mind (Cognitive Function)
3. Culture
4. Gender

Application Activity: *Gender Perception and Stereotypes*

We learn culture complicates the complex phenomenon of communication. It is our way of life. We all belong to many cultural groups. However, we may function more in an individualistic culture than in a collectivistic culture; or we may function more in a collectivistic culture than individualistic (p. 76, Shird). It is important to know that individualism and collectivism flow on a continuum and it's function in communication is dynamic.

Objectives:

- To acknowledge percept on is based on culture.
- To distinguish individualism from collectivism.

Directions:

1. Ask women to brainstorm a list in response to the following statements:
   - All men are . . .
   - Men think women are . . .
2. Ask men to brainstorm a list in response to the following statements:
   - All women are . . .
   - Women think men are . . .
3. Both groups will prepare to present a short skit to the class based on the following scenarios by switching gender roles (women depict men, and men depict women):
   - Two friends (of the same gender) meeting each other back at school for the first time this year.
   - A person flirting with a member of the opposite sex at a party (both actors are of the same gender).
4. After the skits, answer the following questions:
   - Do you believe the skits accurately depict your gender
   - What were the stereotypes you observed?
5. Explain the connection between this exercise and the concepts we discussed about perception and stereotyping.

MINI QUIZ

1. True or False: Media has little to no impact on our assigning of stereotypes.
2. Multiple Choice: The process of understanding the reasons for our own, as well as others', behaviors is referred to as
   A. Stereotyping
   B. Attribution
   C. Self-serving bias
   D. Attribution error
3. Fill in the Blank: Referring to an individual as "a redneck" is an example of

   _____.
4. Essay: Discuss how perception differs based on physiological, state of mind, culture, and gender variables.

CHAPTER 5

Perception and Social Media Influences

A Brief History of Social Media and Why We Are So Obsessed With It

by Kim Smith

What is social media? What is the extent of social media usage among young people? Why is social media used? These questions are explored in this section.

What is Social Media?

Kaplan and Haenlein (2010) defined social media as Web-based and mobile technologies that turn communication into interactive dialogue and allow for the creation and exchange of user-generated content. While Dominick (2011) argued that the first social media was the telephone, "because it connected friends and family and kept people in touch" (72), the first Web-based social media was founded in 1997 as sixdegrees.com (Boyd and Ellison 2007), followed by Friendster (2002), LinkedIn and MySpace (2003), Flickr (2004), and YouTube (2005). Facebook and Twitter began in 2006.

Today, millions of users—many of them young people—have integrated these popular and lesser-known examples of social media into their daily lives (Boyd and Ellison 2007).

Scholars refer to the evolution of the web in three web phases. **Phase 1** began in the 1990s and was dubbed Web 1.0, the so-called "read only" web. Web 1.0 is rooted in the basic static website that provides a one-way communication model where content is broadcast to many. There is little feedback (Mansfield 2012). **Phase 2** (Web 2.0), introduced in 2003, marked the beginning of the social media (i.e., the interactive web). It is characterized by YouTube, Facebook, and other programs that allow content providers to engage with an online audience, a two-way communication model often in "real time" (Cormode and Krishnamurthy 2008). **Phase 3** (Web 3.0) is the current phase and is described as the mobile web where mobile devices are used to connect to social media. Mansfield (2012) argued that integration of Web 1.0, Web 2.0, and Web 3.0 is critical to the successful use of social media by nonprofits. From a corporate perspective, businesses wanting a strong social media presence have to think beyond social media and develop an online social strategy that helps fulfill the online social needs of people using social media (Silverthorne 2009).

What is the Extent of Social Media Usage Among Young People?

Young people between ages 8–18 spend 7.5 hours a day using some type of electronic device as they access the Internet and text message (Lewin 2010), 66% of 8–18 year olds owned a mobile phone in 2009, compared to 39% in 2004, and 85% of 11–18 year olds owned a mobile phone in 2009, up from 56% in 2004. This generation of high school students grew up using the Internet and easily adopted social media. They have great confidence in their ability to perform computer-related tasks, what Bandura (1997) would describe as self efficacy.

Why Are Social Media So Popular?

In studying how people interact in online communities, Cutrona and Suhr (1992) discovered five social support functions of computer-mediated communication that help explain why people use the Internet, mobile devices, and social media. You can think of social support functions as needs that social media fulfill among people.

1. People seek informational support from a variety of sources, including their own research and information obtained from and about family and friends.
2. People seek emotional support through online interaction from family members and friends. They want to know that things will be OK when they have a bad day.
3. People seek esteem support (i.e., praise and admiration for a job well done).
4. People seek tangible aid online. They use social media to ask friends and family for help, such as moving furniture.

5. People also seek social network support among people who share common goals and experiences.

Informational support ("Stay in the know") can include using the Internet and social media for research to finding out from other social media users the location of the next party. In one aspect of social support that points to informational support, 71% of 18–29 year olds said keeping up with current friends and family was the main reason they use social media; 51% said they used it to find friends and family with whom they have lost contact. Based on the idea of "staying in the know," 11% of Latinos, 10% of African-Americans, and 3% of Whites said the main reason they used Twitter was to keep up with the trials and tribulations of their favorite public figures, athletes, and/or celebrities. Thirty-one percent of Blacks, 26% of Latinos, and 16% of Whites said that keeping up with public figures was a minor reason for using Twitter (Smith 2011).

Emotional support is demonstrated in how people use Facebook. Facebook users in 2011 had significantly more online confidants—people with whom they discuss personal matters—than Facebook users in 2008 (Hampton, Sessions, Raine, and Purcell 2011). Facebook users who accessed the site several times a day averaged 9% more in close, online social ties than people who used other types of social media.

I noted the power of emotional support when a cousin of one of my students died following a motorcycle accident. After the student posted the news on her Facebook page, along with a picture of the mangled bike, hundreds of friends responded with kind words. A virtual prayer service broke out on her Facebook page. It lasted for at least an hour.

Esteem support can be found in a study which noted that positive comments about an adolescent's online profile page enhanced self esteem, while negative comments decreased self esteem and well being. As positive comments increased, the more the adolescents visited their own site. As negative comments increased, the fewer times they visited (Valkenburg, Peter, and Schouten 2006).

Social network support can be seen on R&B singer Whitney Houston's Facebook page following her death in February 2012, where people shared a tragic yet common online experience. As of March 4, 2012, more than 3 million people had clicked on her "like" link and 21,571 had posted comments about the singer's death and what Houston had meant to them (Houston 2012).

Another part of the puzzle related to why people use social media is because some probably can't help it. A theory dubbed "media system dependency" (Ball-Rokeach 1985) proposes that the more people use a particular type of media such as the Internet, Facebook, and Twitter, the more they become dependent upon it. It becomes like a drug and some people experience withdrawal-like symptoms if they try to kick the media habit. To test this theory, students in one of my classes agreed to limit their use of media for three days. They kept a diary of their experiences. The rules were: no use of the Internet unless it was class related. Avoid using your cell/smart phones and no texting. No Facebook, Twitter, radio, TV, movies, or books/magazines unless it was class related.

In nearly all cases, students reported that this experiment was one of the hardest things they had ever done in their lives. Some reported being frustrated and angry over not being able to respond to Tweets or to post and read messages on Facebook pages. Most admitted they had a media system dependency problem. Some also said that from the experience they began to realize how much time they wasted doing nothing on social media. Some reported they were more relaxed, slept more, and got more homework done in a shorter amount of time. Most noteworthy, perhaps, was how some were able to reestablish face-to-face communication with friends, loved ones, and significant others. "We actually talked without the distractions of TV, radio, the Internet, and smartphones," said one student.

Not Having a Cell Phone is a Disability!

by Zakeya Renay Mitchell

© Lena Berntsen, 2012. Used under license from Shutterstock, Inc.

I lost cell phone privileges at the end of my junior year in 2010. Because there were multiple factors as to why I could not replace it right away, I simply went without one. One may think, in the age of technology, that it would be wise to figure out a different solution to my problem.

Thinking that I had nothing to worry about with respect to being socially missed, I took my time handling the situation. In the beginning, it seemed as though the only people that were missing the opportunity to contact me were the friends I spoke to religiously. Being inaccessible to my peers was not detrimental to me or my ability to successfully function, so I ignored all the comments such as: "Renay, you need a phone!" or "What if you get in trouble?" or "What if there is an emergency and we cannot contact you?" Now as real as those possibilities are, their probabilities are not nearly as high as my friends wanted me to perceive them to be.

After six months of being "mobile-less," I started to feel the irritation of not having a cell phone. It stemmed more from by disability than my friends inability to communicate with me. I was reduced to leaving messages with people in the Dean's office, and my counselors and professors had to call one of my friends' cell phones and have them deliver the message. Initially, not having a phone was supposed to be a liberating experience where I did not have to be bound to the use of technology. Using technology suggests that you are addicted to it. And if you are not, you are inaccessible and inconveniencing others.

Perception and Social Media Influences on Political Communication with the Masses

by Regina Williams Davis

Up until the last election, I would think of no other entity with as much influence on perception as the mass media in terms of defining what the public is to perceive as a crisis, as a scandal, as newsworthy, as trendy, as hot, and what to perceive as not. The news media might still translate what our congressional leaders define as national issues, but in the age of YouTube, the masses define it for the media. Now that anyone, anywhere, with an iPad, notebook computer, or smartphone, can post a video on YouTube; and the Internet can count the number of views one's video posting may accumulate, the masses determine what they like. They have a voice with the number of views and postings of "likes" and "dislikes." YouTube is a social media phenomenon that has taken the voice of the masses to an unbelievable level of strength.

Once the masses have influenced the social media, then the news outlets will pick up on it and make it news for "what's trending" online. So . . . Who's influencing whom?

Communication is the essence of a political campaign. Getting the politician's message to the masses and encouraging donors to give to the campaign is crucial. Barack Obama successfully used social media to influence the masses that, in turn, influenced the other media outlets. He embraced the new forms of communication by taking his campaign (with the help of Facebook founder, Mark Zuckerberg) to the digital age and making YouTube and social networking the central platform.

. . . .

Social Media Reflection

. . . .

by Brianna Bazile

As we look at the history of communication, we can say we have come a long way. From writing letters to being able to see each other face-to-face through video chat on our phones, technology has progressively become more and more advanced, especially in today's generation. Now, it has become easier to contact and interact with people through social media as it becomes popular. From pictures, to videos, and maybe even personal thoughts, social media has made it accessible and easier for people to share amongst friends and the Internet. As stated in the text, this generation of high school students grew up using the Internet and easily adopted social media (Smith 66). I, myself, can relate to this chapter as I grew up using the Internet at a young age. It first started off with computer games and other computer related tasks until eventually the first iPod came out. This became a gateway to our handheld Apple world to where they later started creating iPhones. iPhones then changed the computer world as they became smartphones and could access the Internet. With the Internet in the palm of our hands, we were able to do anything. It all suddenly became easier and convenient to access information by just a few keystrokes away. Facebook, Twitter, Instagram, and Snapchat also became popular within the younger generation as it kept friends and colleagues close-knit and in the loop. As a military kid, I can speak from experience that social media became my best friend. As it became hard for me to move every 3-4 years, I hated losing touch with my friends. Before social media took its course, keeping in contact was difficult. All we had were emails that we occasionally replied to and foreign telephone numbers that we could no longer call because we moved back to the United States. However, as time progressed and more people started creating social media accounts, I was able to reconnect with all my friends that I grew up with around the world. From Okinawa, Japan to Fresno, California, I was able to catch up and stay close with all my friends who I originally thought I lost touch with. Without social media, I wouldn't be able to see and check on my friends from all over the world. I wouldn't be able to see how much they've changed or the major milestones they may have accomplished. Amazingly, I was able to discover one of my peers, whom I met in South Carolina, from my 1st and 2nd grade class and is now running track for our school on scholarship. I was able to reconnect with him on Instagram after 10 years without any source of contact. After meeting him again in person, he instantly remembered me and became good friends. Not only is it odd that after over 10 years of separation of each other that we would attend the same school but that we were able to remember each other as if we had never left. Without social media, I wouldn't be able to reconnect with all the friends I've made. I wouldn't be able to see them graduate and attend college, wish them happy birthdays, or simply just converse with them. Social media has become our source of communication and more or less an outlet source for our generation. I personally think social media is a great way to stay connected in today's world, especially as it grows more advanced in technology. However, social media can become a problem if we rely on it too much for everything. As it was stated in the text, young people between the ages 8-18 spend 7.5 hours a day using some type of electronic device as they access the Internet (Smith 66). It is important that we don't allow social media and the Internet to consume or lives for it could lead to us forgetting what it was like to have human interaction.

....

Improving Perception Competencies

....

by Myra M. Shird

To maintain a socially just society, we must understand the impact our perceptions have on ourselves and on others in the world. There are several different ways to improve your perception competency.

Distinguish Facts from Inferences

We frequently mistake inferences for facts. For instance, you may perceive that Bill Clinton was a better president than George W. Bush. This is not a fact because "better" is a subjective term and at least in this case cannot be proven. A **fact** is a statement that can be demonstrated as true or false, regardless of our own personal beliefs. An **inference** involves personal preferences and opinions.

Look at the list of statements below and check to see if you can identify which ones are facts and which ones are inferences.

FACT OR INFERENCE

1. Fact _____	Inference _____	Beyoncé is the best singer in the world.
2. Fact _____	Inference _____	Men are strong.
3. Fact _____	Inference _____	Reported cases of HIV/AIDS within the co-culture of African-American women have risen over the last few years.
4. Fact _____	Inference _____	Children that do not perform well in high school will not perform well in college.
5. Fact _____	Inference _____	Christina Aguilera has won at least one Grammy.
6. Fact _____	Inference _____	In 1986, Run-D.M.C. became the first rap act to be featured on the cover of *Rolling Stone* magazine.
7. Fact _____	Inference _____	Children that misbehave deserve to be spanked.
8. Fact _____	Inference _____	Kareem Abdul-Jabbar is the best basketball player of all time.
9. Fact _____	Inference _____	Vanilla Ice paved the way for Eminem.
10. Fact _____	Inference _____	Sydney has been in five car accidents.
11. Fact _____	Inference _____	Sydney does not drive well.
12. Fact _____	Inference _____	Seniors are ready to graduate from college.

Answers:
Numbers 1, 2, 4, 7, 8, 9, 11, and 12 are inferences. Numbers 3, 5, 6, and 10 are facts.

It's easy to confuse inferences with facts. After my divorce, I went to a therapist so that I could deal with my feelings. I began explaining to the therapist, "John always . . ." She stopped me in mid-sentence to explain that no one ever always does anything. They may do it sometimes, most of the time, and sometimes they may even do it pretty much close to all of the time. Yet, it is virtually impossible for a person to always be in the act of doing one thing. Humans are much more complex.

From that experience, I learned to use more tentative language: "Tina sometimes arrives late." instead of "Tina is a late person." The latter description is evaluative. It sounds like a character judgment. By saying, "Tina is a late person," I am labeling Tina. Labels are notorious for hindering the progress of certain social communities. We are less likely to perceive change, and our perceptions may be distorted when we label an individual or a group based on our personal preferences. Eliminating evaluative language helps us to distinguish facts from inferences. Distinguishing facts from inferences increases our perception competency, which ultimately increases our interpersonal communication competency.

Key Terms:

Informational Support

Emotional Support

Esteem Support

Social Network Support

Fact

Inference

The Portrayal of African American Males in the Media

by Jordan N. Silverthorne

As technology has advanced over the years, the brainpower used for such innovations has not elevated what is displayed amongst said technological devices. The many television shows and movies continuously show and ridicule significant issues within society, as well as exhibit false assumptions of different ethnicities and cultures. Although certain media displays are created for the purpose of comedy and satire, some of the long running jokes and imitated behaviors are no longer amusing, but embarrassing and inaccurate. As an African American female, I am beyond annoyed with the mockery I have witnessed by engaging in technology in my leisure time and in the research I have found. The media presents stereotypes for African American men to being uneducated, bad fathers, and "thugs", and there are direct effects of these misrepresentations.

As if slavery was not enough humiliation, African Americans can turn on the TV and find discomfort from being something they cannot change. Apparently, it is a known fact that "all Black people love fried chicken, Kool-Aid, and watermelon. They are always so loud and obnoxious. These uneducated people do not know how to speak or write proper English." Such comments hold no truth. Skin pigmentation has nothing to do with what people enjoy because every individual is unique and has their own identity.

The existence of Historically Black Colleges and Universities (HBCUs) are enough proof that African Americans are choosing to further their education. "More black men are going to college than ever before" (Hagler, 2015). It is not as likely for students to drop out of high school. With the rate of high school completion rising, the enrollment rate for college has been increasing. The amount to African American males that are obtaining bachelor's degrees has more than tripled since 1976 from 6.3 percent to 20.4 percent (Hagler, 2015).

Bill Cosby introduced an educated and wealthy African American family to American society. Phylicia Rashad was a successful attorney and Bill Cosby was an obstetrician; they were an upper middle-class family with five children living in Brooklyn Heights. Former education was popularized by this outstanding comedy series. Along with The Cosby Show, the six season TV series, A Different World, gained a large, faithful audience from their take on struggling black college students at an HBCU. Seasons 1 through 4 of A Different Word were ranked in the top 5 for Thursday night TV show slots most likely due to the fact that it exposed America to a new educational experience (Harris, 1991). The idea of success physically, spiritually, and financially has become an ultimate goal for the African American community. No longer will skin color be a determining factor in the prosperity desired. This potential advancement in life, although not always achieved for personal reasons, but possibly in an effort to prove oneself to others, has helped African Americans identify a need and love for discipline and scholarship.

The black community has had some struggle through life fatherless. This notion is reoccurring in the entertainment business; it makes for good TV. African American fathers have taken an active role in their children's lives even though there are a significant amount of households that are led by females alone (Hagler, 2015). Black fathers that live with their children are closer with their children and more involved in their lives.

For example, in looking at two different Tyler Perry movies, *Meet the Browns* and *Daddy's Little Girls* both movies display an abundance of hardships within the Black community, as well as fulfilling a character with something they did not have at the beginning of the movie. In *Meet the Browns*, Angela Bassett plays the single mother of two kids, one in which plays basketball exceptionally. Angela Bassett is not single by choice, rather the father of her son, Michael, wants nothing to do with his son or her until Michael is signed to a professional basketball team. Michael's father appears at the press conference eager to share that he is the father of the extraordinary athlete, only to hear his son express to everyone how his father was not in his life. Without his father, Michael struggled to eat each day, keep his grades up, and stay out of trouble, and yet he beat the odds.

On the other hand, in *Daddy's Little Girls*, a father with three girls wants nothing more than to love and support his children while his ex-wife leads an unacceptable, deteriorating life with a drug dealer. He had to fight with everything he had to get full custody of his kids. The father figures in these movies are contrasting characters. Although these movies have happy endings, the African American families and their struggles are portrayed in an extreme manner. Such situations can occur, but are not likely. It is hard to distinguish as audience member, especially when life has afforded you other opportunities, that the people playing these roles are real, but their characters are not.

Black hoodies, du-rags, and saggy jeans often illustrate the image a "thug." In actuality, a thug is defined as a violent criminal. Video games often show Black characters as more aggressive and more violent than white characters (Riley, 2014). Nowhere does it state that a thug is defined by the way they dress or their race/ethnicity. In the media, an African American who has lost his way is portrayed as a thug. If the black teenager is not a good kid, he is considered a thug in the media. One sometimes assumes that if an African American child stops going to school, gets bad grades, or is inappropriately aggressive, that the child is a thug and has taken on the behaviors of a criminal. Under these same circumstances with a child of a different race, thug would not be the first assumption; an illness or another problem would be the first thought. Black kids can be suffering from other factors, like depression or a mental illness and still be considered "good kids."

Barriers are developed from the many harsh portrayals the media links with black men. Media distortions promote ill-feelings and agendas toward African American men. Often times, the debate on whether violence in video games impacts the thoughts and behaviors of children who play them. Children and young adults mimic what they see and hear. The name-calling and degrading characters on screen express negative associations with people of African descent. Racism and stereotypes will continue to parade the country from poor representations of any and all races, ethnicities, and cultures of people.

References

Hagler, J. (2015, March 19). The Media Narrative of Black Men in America Is All Wrong. Retrieved November 13, 2016, from http://www.newsweek.com/black-men-today-dont fit-old-stereotype-314877

Harris, M. (1991, April 12). The evolution of 'A Different World' Retrieved November 13, 2016, from http://www.ew.com/article/1991/04/12/evolution-different-world

Riley, R. (2014, December 10). 5 Offensive Stereotypes Reinforced by Video Games That Need to End - Page 4 of 5 - Blerds. Retrieved November 13, 2016, from http://blerds.atlantablackstar. com/2014/12/10/5-offensive-stereotypes-reinforced-byvideo-games-that-need-to-end/4/

Application Activity: *Virtual Ways We Communicate*

Software or communication technology also tells us how friendly, or maybe even intimate we are with another. It tells us to what degree a relationship might be considered casual. Please compile a list or a table of **virtual ways we communicate** and provide an example of the perception of the relationship might be when specific communication software is used. See example below:

Technology	Perceived Relationship
Skype	Old Friend From High School

MINI QUIZ

1. True or False: Young people between ages 8–18 spend 7.5 hours daily using some type of electronic device.

2. Multiple Choice: This form of support can be exemplified by people posting on social network pages of recently deceased celebrities to show support.
   A. Informational support
   B. Emotional support
   C. Esteem support
   D. Social network support

3. Fill in the Blank: A statement that can be demonstrated as true or false, regardless of our own personal beliefs is termed a _____.

4. Essay: Explain how inferences can be misinterpreted and may be erroneously accepted as facts.

CHAPTER 6

Intercultural Communication

by Stephanie Sedberry Carrino

Introduction
by Soncerey L. Montgomery, Ph.D.

Rationale:

Culture and communication cannot be separated because each influences and informs the other. Culture is reflected in communication practices, at the same time, communication practices shape cultural life (Wood, 2006, p. 96). Furthermore, due to the increase of cross-cultural encounters in today's shrinking world, it is impossible to avoid contact with individuals from other cultures. Undeniably, when dealing with members from different cultures or social communities, stereotypes may come into play. Sometimes we are aware of our stereotypical thinking, sometimes we are not. We engage in stereotyping and uncritical thinking when we fail to recognize differences between individual members of social groups (Wood, 2006, p. 95). Whether intentional or unintentional, conscious or unconscious, we need to be aware of the attitudes and perceptions *toward* differences as well as our responses to differences. Our attitudes and perceptions inform our interactions; our responses impact our relationships. As such, it is important for students to recognize differences and commonalities among different cultures or social communities with whom we communicate. It is also critical that we become more aware of factors that influence our conversations and perceptions of different groups which includes the media, material and nonmaterial components, historical and geographical forces, communication patterns, shifting cultural identities, just to name a few.

Globalization and Intercultural Communication: Interwoven Themes

by Andrea Patterson

Lisa, an American student at a university in North Carolina, was extremely frustrated. She could not install the software for her printer on her new laptop. After several failed attempts, she called the 1-800 product number for the printer.

The technical support person was extremely helpful and spent half an hour walking her through each step of the installation process. Lisa was relieved and grateful. She had her section of the group Power Point due for her intercultural communication class. The project focused on popular culture. Lisa's section highlighted the influence of Bollywood and India on popular culture. Lisa wanted to print her slides to preview and edit before submitting to her group.

Without realizing it, Lisa experienced the interwoven relationship of intercultural communication and globalization in a digital world. Her laptop was manufactured by a Japanese company, her printer was manufactured by an American company assembled in China. The technical support person was sitting in a cubicle in Bangalore, India. Her research focused on another part of the globe—India. What factors shaped the interaction described above? The scenario demonstrates the impact of globalization in today's world society. With advances in technology from communications (the cell phone, the internet) to global transportation technology and open global markets, intercultural communication and interaction have become a common occurrence.

This chapter begins with an introduction of the critical role history plays in the context of intercultural communication and globalization. To understanding the complexity of globalization, we will examine the aspects of social/cultural, economic, and political globalization. Following this section, we will analyze the role of power and the popular resistance to globalization. Our study will conclude with a discussion of the imperative to balance the explosion of technology in the context of globalization with intercultural sensitivity.

The Role of History in Intercultural Communication and Globalization

In the previous chapter, Carrino (2012) refers to globalization as the "increased connectedness of people from different cultural backgrounds. These connections can be economic, through goods and natural resources, or informational". In fact, people have traveled around the globe exchanging cultural goods, practices, and ideas, and have consequently been involved in intercultural communication for centuries. For nearly 3,000 years, Europeans have traversed sand and seas to buy from, and trade with, the Far East for silk and satin. It is important to note that Islamic and Mongol empires had far reaches. European domination and conquests, beginning in the 16th century, changed global migration patterns and have a profound impact on our world today. Authors Held, McGrew, Goldblatt, and Perraton (1999) note in the book *Global Transformation: Politics, Economics, and Culture* that during the European colonial period, people migrated not only from Spain, Europe, Portugal, and England, but also France, Belgium, and Holland to Asia, Africa, and Oceania with the goal of economic gain, territorial conquest, and religious conversion. Settlers from these countries formed colonies in these conquered countries. As we know from our study of history, between the 1600s and the 1850s, nine to 12 million Africans were forcibly moved, mainly to the Americas during the transatlantic slave trade. In the 19th century, Indians were forced to live under British colonial rule and some were subjected to relocate to colonies in Africa and Oceania (Young, 2001). This process of colonization, based upon the stripping and exploitation of natural and human resources, established Europe as a central world power and the colonies as the borders.

Further into the 19th century, after the British and Spanish colonies had gained independence in the Americas, a massive migration erupted with the working class and poor people from economically and war-distressed countries of Europe to the United States of America and other countries including Brazil, Chile, Argentina, and others (Young, 2001). The migration of indentured laborers from Asia—mainly Japan, China, and Philippines to the United States, Canada, and other former European colonies, made the number of migrants explode to more than 40 million people before World War II (Sorrells, 2013).

The Second World War ushered in the unparalleled restriction of national borders and the development and enactment of immigration legislation and border controls in the United States of America in recent history. The unprecedented ethnically-motivated violence, mass murder, and genocide of WWII led to the exodus of Jews from Europe to the United States, Latin America, and Israel. In response to the devastation of human lives, political structures, economies, and natural resources across Europe, Japan, and Russia, first organizations of economic and world political governing bodies were created, including the World Bank (WB), the International Monetary Fund (IMF), and the United Nations (UN; Sorrells, 2013).

Consequently, since the 1960s, with the rise of economic power in the United States and the rebuilding of Europe as an economic power, there is a migratory pattern shift. The migration of immigrants from Europe to the United States at the beginning of the 20th century is mirrored today by the influx of immigrants from Asia and Latin America to the United States.

In addition to this stream of people was the flow of people from Africa and Asia to the oil-rich countries of the Middle East, as well as regional migration patterns within Latin America, Africa, and East Asia (Young, 2001). During the latter part of the 20th century, the increase of people looking for asylum and refugees fleeing for a variety of reasons including war, famine, and natural disasters has risen substantially (Held et al., 1999).

Sorrells and Nakagawa (2008) argue that the current wave of globalization, deeply rooted in European colonization and Western imperialism, have thrust people from different countries and cultures together in physical and virtual spaces. All the facets of globalization including social/cultural, political, and economical depict the interwoven connection of people, culture, market, and the connection to power that is rooted in history and is evident in today's world. The intent of this chapter is not to highlight history and globalization. However, it is important to note that history plays a profound role in intercultural communication within the context of globalization.

In recent years, significant developments in governance, economics, politics, and educational institutions have combined with changes in communication technology and transportation to have exponentially increased the interaction and relations of humans from different religious, ethnic, social, national, and international cultures around the world (Sorrells, 2008).

Many people around the world, however, regard globalization with suspicion, apprehension, and trepidation. They worry about its impact on humanity. Some people view it as a threat to jobs, livelihood, and culture. It increasingly leads to inequality between countries—wealth for a few, and mounting poverty for many. Globalization is complicated and means many things to different people.

Globalization

Frank Lechner (2005) describes globalization as the "world-wide diffusion of practices, expansions of relations across continents, organization of social life on a global scale, and growth of a shared global consciousness". In India, China, or Vietnam, globalization may be viewed as economic prosperity and opportunity, while in Afghanistan or Iraq, globalization may be viewed as occupation and "democratic" terrorism and imperialism. Globalization may be seen on one hand as "the increase in worldwide networks of interdependence" (Nye, 2009, para. 3), whereas Thomas Palley, from the Economics for Democratic and Open Societies, defines globalization as the general concept incorporating the diffusion of ideas and cultures (as cited in Perkovich, 2006).

Although globalization is often viewed as the world economy and markets, it has, in fact, several dimensions—each impacting our lives. And while the term globalization became common in the 1990s, the various factors that constitute globalization have been in existence for thousands of years. Regardless of how one may view globalization, the one element that is ubiquitous involves communication. Author Kirk St. Amant believes that "in every instance, however, globalization involves one central factor—communication. Effective communication provides individuals with the information they need to participate in today's global society as consumers, workers, and citizens" (St. Amant & Olaniran, 2013, p. 2). In the following section, we will examine the social/cultural, political, and economic dimensions of globalization.

Social/Cultural Globalization

The first type of globalization is social/cultural globalization, which includes the dissemination, infusion or exchange of ideas, images, artifacts, customs, cultures, and interaction of people. The dimensions of social/cultural globalization impact people's ways of thinking, believing, and behaving and communicating. As people travel across the world, whether for work, military service, tourism, family, economic survival, or opportunity, they take their culture with them. People make efforts to recreate a sense of the familiar or home. In addition, people returning home from their travels take artifacts or reminders of the places they have visited. While the complicated notion of culture cannot be reduced to an item packed in a suitcase, the mementos we take or leave are important in representing our cultures, the languages we speak, the beliefs we hold, and the practices we carry out (Sorrells, 2008).

One specific example of social/cultural globalization is migration. During the 19th century, more than 80 million people crossed continents, oceans, and borders to new homes. In America, at the start of the 21st century, more than 11.5% of the population, or 32 million people residing in the United States, were born in another country (Nye, 2009). Consequently, the lives of people from various cultural backgrounds—ethnic/racial, religious, class, national and regional cultures—are increasingly intertwined and interconnected.

Political Globalization

The second type of globalization we will discuss is political. There is a growing trend toward political globalization. Following the toppling of the Berlin Wall in 1989 and the collapse of the former Soviet Union in 1990, there has been a growing assumption that capitalism and democracy together will bring about global prosperity and peace. Many observers suggest there has been a global trend toward democracy since World War II, and this move of "democratization" has been highly contested in different parts of the world (Fukuyama, 1992; Leys, 2001; Nsouli, 2008; Nye, 2009; Palley, 2006). Some observers and skeptics of globalization conclude that the political agendas associated with "democratization" are closely related to the free-trade agreements of the World Trade Organization (WTO), the World Bank, and the International Monetary Fund (IMF).

The impact of political globalization is also felt by women in the Kingdom of Saudi Arabia. According to CNN commentator Mohammed Jamjoom (2013), Saudi Arabian women face many restrictions—including driving. An interior minister spokesperson in Saudi Arabia issued a warning that women caught driving or participating in driving demonstrations during the Women's Driving Campaign slated for October 26, 2013 would be punished. The spokesperson went on to state that punishment for defiance of the ban on women driving would not only occur on October 26, but anytime before or after. According to Jamjoom (2013), there is no specific law which bans women from driving; however, "religious edicts there are often interpreted to mean women are not allowed to operate a vehicle" (para. 20). Saudi religious leaders warn that driving could negatively impact women's ovaries.

Despite repeated arrests, Saudi Arabian women have been practicing civil disobediance in relation to driving out of symbolic protest and practicality. News reports state that there have been several staged protests, and women have posted videos of themselves driving on YouTube. Women have also used social media to help organize demonstrations. An electronic petition was launched in September 2013 stating opposition to the stance of prohibiting women drivers. The movement has gained more than 16,000 signatures (Jamjoon, 2013). The Arab Spring, the political revolts in

Tunisia, Iran, Egypt, Syria, and other Arabic nations are indicative of how technology has helped initiate social changes through the use of social media including YouTube, Twitter, and Facebook.

Economic Globalization

Think about the coffee you drink that was harvested in Brazil, the chocolate you eat, grown in the Ivory Coast, the suit pants you wear, designed in Italy and assembled in China, and the tennis shoes you wear produced in Indonesia—all of these items are indicators of economic globalization. These examples point to the intercultural economic dimensions of globalization

Many economists, business people, and journalists view economic globalization and the world economy as one (Nye, 2002). Thomas Friedman views economic globalization as the international system that replaced the one established by the Cold War. It is perceived as the integration of capital, technology, and information across national borders, and in a manner that is creating a single global market—or in essence, a global village (Friedman, 2007).

But for some observers and skeptics, the ideology of globalization is deceptive and destructive. It represents imperialism, global capitalism, and inequity of power. It also appears shrouded in economic greed, corporate gain, capitalistic consumerism, and Western imperialism. The World Bank, in a report released in September of 2009, states that poorer countries face a $11.6 billion shortfall in key areas such as education, health, social protection, and infrastructure. The private capital flows to the poorest countries are projected to plummet. This represents a decrease from $21 billion in 2008 and $30 billion in 2007 (World Bank, 2009).

However, Kenya has infused technology into mobile banking and transformed its global economy with this innovation. The Economist Newspaper Limited ("Why does Kenya," 2013) reported that Kenya leads the world with Mobile banking. Kenya uses a mobile money operating system M-PESA which allows over 17 millions Kenyans to use their mobile phones as a banking system. With the stroke of a few keys, Kenyans are able to pay for services from taxicab fares to transferring cash with their phones.

Although economists, scholars, world leaders, businesspeople, and others distinguish between the variations in globalization, critical theorist Peter McLaren contends that they are all interconnected. The dimensions of globalization—economic, social, political, and environmental—have shaped conditions in our world society. Essential to our understanding of globalization is also the role of power in intercultural communication.

Power in the Context of Intercultural Communication and Globalization

The term power can be viewed as something that is imposed on or held over someone that other people do not have. In this sense, power can be seen as coercion, control, or manipulation through language, thought, or action. In some cases, people are rendered helpless, defenseless, and unable to respond or escape—physically or mentally.

In his writings, philosopher Michel Foucault (1977, 1984) challenges us to critically examine the relationship between power and the way it is understood, how it develops, its intricacy, how it functions, and how it is formed. Foucault notes that power is not something that is only hierarchical in nature, uniform or top down only in its approach; it is something that is pervasive, insidious, that grows, and manifests itself within society. Power not only rests on the elements of repression and ideology, but goes further. Power can also be understood in terms of discipline and the function of rules, norms, and regulations, reified through policies and procedures. It is through this normalization of power that it becomes a process, it is enforced, and the language becomes codified (Swartz, Campbell, & Pestana, 2009).

An example is Barber's (1992) concept of *McWorld*, which he describes as the capitalistic spell that mesmerizes consumers for fast food like McDonald's to MTV, fast computers, fast music, and glamorous makeup and clothes. George Ritzer (2000, 2004) discusses the concept of "McDonaldization." He refers to it as the development of a formal prototype originated from a few principles that can be duplicated anywhere around the globe. This view also extends to mainstream America where "McMansions" are becoming more prevalent in the suburbs—a sign of progress and affluence. The McDonalds mentality has become embedded in American culture. The McDonaldization mentality has been compared to the policies, procedures, operations, and marketing of the Disney theme parks, whose practices are being adopted across America as well as around the globe. Disney's amusement parks consist of fantasy worlds that transport the visitor to a different global location, and even to outer space.

The bigger-than-life theme is also evident in oversized malls such as the Mall of America in Bloomington, Minnesota. The casinos and hotels of Las Vegas, also often built around a theme, transport the visitor into another world. Hotel visitors can travel around the globe: Caesar's Palace becomes Italy; New York, New York becomes a cosmopolitan city; Circus Circus becomes the ultimate children's three-ring circus event. Visitors are constantly surrounded by merchandise, food courts, casinos, and amusement.

While intercultural encounters can be entertaining, delightful, and even memorable, they can also be contentious, challenging, and filled with protest. In the next section, I discuss the global protest and resistance to globalization.

Protest, Resistance, and Defiance

The debates over globalization are passionate and fierce. The resistance to globalization and its adverse effects are erupting around the globe. Protestors are angry about the inequities between rich and impoverished countries, the policies of the Group of Eight (G-8), International Monetary Fund (IMF), and the World Bank, the lack of intervention from the United Nations, and the increasing militarization and domination of foreign countries in the name of "democracy" and "freedom." In recent decades, anti-globalization protests have disrupted meetings around the world, including those of the IMF, World Bank, and World Trade Organization (WTO), among others. Demonstrations were held during the annual meetings of the IMF and the World Bank in 1988 in West Berlin, then a part of the German Democratic Republic. Many view these protests as a foreshadowing of the anti-globalization movement.

Since then, protesters against globalization have marched faithfully during WTO, IMF, and World Bank meetings. The first mass anti-capitalist, anti-globalization protest took place on June 18, 1999, when thousands of militant protesters took to the streets in more than 40 cities around the world, including London, England and Eugene, Oregon, in a mass movement known as The Global Carnival against Capital. This event also came to be known as J-18.

The second major anti-globalization protest, known as the Battle of Seattle or N30, occurred some five months later on November 30, 1999, in Seattle, Washington. With an estimated 50,000 to 100,000 protesters in attendance, the massive gathering turned violent; more than 600 people were arrested, and opening ceremonies of the WTO meeting were cancelled. The protest, however, continued throughout the four-day meeting.

On September 26, 9,000 protesters in Prague voiced their fury and frustration over economic globalization. *The Seattle Times* ("Prague protests," 2000) reported at least 69 people were injured and 44 hospitalized. News reports called Prague a "smoky battle zone" (para. 4), filled with the chants of demonstrators yelling "London, Seattle, continue the battle" (para. 3) as they converged on Prague's Wenceslas Square, where peace protesters had gathered more than ten years earlier to speak out against communism.

Since 2001, additional protests held in Quebec, Canada, Davis, Switzerland, and other places have become symbols of the festering and growing feelings of frustration and resentment about the unfair gap between rich and poor and the power inequities that exemplify globalization (Sorrells, 2008).

Meetings, rallies, and protests are being held around the world to develop programs, strategies, and oppositional forces to combat the various forms of globalization. The patchwork quilt of forces has formed a loosely-woven blanket of resistance. Activists have been energized across the globe.

The energy of activism was evident in Porto Alegre, Brazil, during the 2003 World Social Forum (WSF) where as many as 40,000 activists gathered to discuss the conference's two main themes: global justice and life after capitalism. More than 15,000 attendees packed a local soccer stadium to hear the keynote address of Scholar Noam Chomsky. Harsh criticism of the United States dominated the conference.

In his speech "Confronting the Empire," Chomsky (2003) said, "the most powerful state in history has proclaimed, loud and clear, that it intends to rule the world by force, the dimension in which it reigns supreme" (p. 1). During the course of the speech, Chomsky told the audience that many of them already knew how to combat the empire—through their "own lives and work. The way to 'confront the empire' is to create a different world, one that is not based on violence and subjugation, hate and fear. That is why we are here, and the WSF offers hopes that these are not idle dreams" (p. 2).

The local TV station reported that the fans cheered like "it was a rock concert" during Chomsky's speech. Organizers said the heavy turnout during the conferences proved the anti-corporate globalization movement had regained some of the energy lost after September 11. On the final day of the conference, thousands of protestors marched and danced through the city carnival style, waving red flags and banners. This demonstration and the World Economic Forum in New York occurred simultaneously.

In our study of globalization in relation to intercultural communication, it is important to think about how people, businesses, products, and global movements are shaped, influenced, and in some instances controlled by relationships of power.

Who is controlling these policies, positions, and relationships of power? How have these relationships been formed and maintained? How does the media impact and influence power? Who are the media giants that control the flow of information, news, and popular culture? How is this power disseminated in the context of globalization? Through innovations in communication technology, transportation technology, and economic technology, people around the world with different cultures, identities, ideologies, and beliefs are becoming more connected in the workplace, home, and community. Obviously, intercultural encounters are becoming a more everyday experience. One of the elements that connects globalization is technology.

Technology and Globalization

As Carrino (2012) mentioned in the previous chapter, one of the most significant impacts on globalization is technology. Technology, including the internet, computers, and mobile phones all impact globalization and consequently, intercultural communication. The current wave of globalization have thrust people from different countries and cultures together into shared physical and virtual homes, workplaces, schools, and communities in unprecedented ways. High school students in Senegal can SKYPE with a group of students learning French at an American high school.

A businessman from Brazil may participate in a virtual conference call in Spain. An activist in Egypt may organize a protest on Facebook. People also no longer have to rely on traditional media outlets such as television, newspaper, or radio. Social media including Twitter, Tumblr, YouTube, Flickr, and Facebook have also opened up many avenues for communication

Unfortunately, not all people benefit from globalization. The inequities in our society are evident in how communication technology is allocated in our world. Sorrells (2008) reports that while technological advances enable about 15% of the earth's inhabitants to connect to the world via the internet on wireless laptops at home or in our favorite coffee spots, more than 50% of the earth's population lives below the poverty line. These people start their day without the basic necessities of decent food, clean water, and safe shelter. These inequities point out that there is also a digital divide in relation to globalization.

Technology and Intercultural Sensitivity

It is also imperative that communicators in a digital age balance this explosion of technology in the context of globalization with intercultural sensitivity. On December 13, 2013, CNN reported an American public relations executive sent a tweet shortly before boarding a 12-hour flight to South Africa. Justine Sacco's tweet read: "Going to Africa. Hope I don't get AIDS. Just kidding. I'm white!" However, by the time Sacco landed in South Africa, Sacco's tweet was the biggest internet story of the week. Sacco received countless negative tweets condemning her comments. The public relations executive did release an apology a few days later. Subsequently, 53 characters caused her to lose her job. CNN commentator Brandon Griggs observed, "Think before you tweet. It only takes a few seconds to compose a dumb tweet. The damage can last much longer" (Griggs, 2013, "Think before you tweet," para. 4)

This example highlights how ethnocentrism, the belief that your culture is superior to another culture, can be instantly communicated in a digital age. In essence, whether you realize it or not, with only a few key strokes and characters you have created attitudinal and behavioral barriers to intercultural communication in the context of globalization via social media.

Understanding culture is imperative to success in the modern world of globalization. Therefore, successful interaction in the context of globalization, especially with online media, demands that communicators understand and respect the "other" culture (Kalafatoğlu, 2013). In a digital age, social media blunders can have an immediate and profound impact. Developing communication competence in the context of globalization requires one to not only develop intercultural competence skills, but also to learn how to use these skills responsibly and successfully in connection with technology.

Conclusion

In this chapter, we explored the social/cultural, economic, and political influences of globalization. We defined globalization as an increased connectedness of people from different cultural backgrounds. These connections can be social/cultural, economic, and political. While in reality it is unrealistic to divide globalization into facets, we recognize it is an extremely complex concept that is interrelated and interwoven, with the elements of history and power playing significant roles. We also looked at a few of the debates and resistance to globalization. Our discussion concluded with how technology is a driving force in intercultural communication in the context of globalization. We stressed that developing intercultural communication competence in the context of globalization requires one to understand and respect other cultures and learn how to use these skills in a complex, challenging, and rapidly-changing digital age.

Intercultural Communication

by Stephanie Sedberry Carrino

I would *never* talk to my mother like she does.

Married people shouldn't act like that!

Why do "they" live like that? Talk like that? Dress like that?

How can he *eat* that? Nasty!

Why is he looking at me that way?

What is Intercultural Communication?

Have you ever heard someone ask a question like one listed above? If so, you have probably witnessed a breakdown in intercultural understanding. ***Intercultural Communication*** occurs when people from different cultural groups communicate to try to co-create meaning or negotiate a shared understanding. The purpose of this communication might be to gather information, influence the other, establish a personal relationship, or just acknowledge the presence of another human being, and can occur in many settings. To be an effective, successful communicator, you'll need to add intercultural communication competence to your list of skills.

Like all communication, intercultural communication is complex and multi-faceted and can be best understood by examining the principles, or foundational elements. Intercultural communication is:

- **Transactional**: Communicators send and receive messages simultaneously, through numerous channels and by using both language and non-verbal symbols.
- **A Process**: Communication is ongoing, meaning that we are communicating even if we do not intend to communicate. As long as there is another person around who attaches meaning to what we say or do, then communication occurs.
- **Systemic**: All communication is part of a larger system in that what happens between people is affected by what has happened in the past. One aspect of your life affects others aspects and impacts your communication with others.
- **Dynamic**: Communication is not static, meaning that it is ever changing. Even the exact same phrase, stated in the same way to the same person, can mean something different every time.
- **Contextual**: All communication occurs within a context—a place and time—that influences the way we interpret what is communicated.

- **Symbolic**: All messages are symbolic, meaning that both the words we choose and the non-verbal signals are symbols we use to represent our ideas to others. We *encode* our thoughts and feelings into verbal and non-verbal messages and hope the other person *decodes* them in the way we intended.

Globalization, Immigration, and Technology

In past generations, intercultural communication was not as common as it is today. For many reasons, populations are shifting, resulting in the greater likelihood that we will encounter others who are culturally different. In fact, it may well be impossible to live in the United States today without having to connect with others from a variety of cultural backgrounds. *Globalization* refers to the increased connectedness of people from different cultural backgrounds. This connection can be economic, through goods and natural resources, or informational. Certainly, increased international and intercultural business and trade has had a significant impact on globalization.

The greatest force in expanding globalization is, of course, technology. The many ever-expanding digital technologies, including the Internet, have enabled many global citizens to connect with others despite physical distance. Satellites broadcast TV stations from all over the world giving us access to the perspectives of other cultural groups. Much of our experience with others is now mediated through technology rather than based on face-to-face personal experience.

Immigration and travel have allowed people more freedom to move from place to place, often locating diverse people right next door. Many colleges and universities, including North Carolina Agricultural and Technical State University, encourage students to study abroad for a semester or a year and welcome students from all over the world.

What are Cultural Groups?

I have used the term *cultural group* to refer to any group of people who share a set of values, beliefs, attitudes, practices, traditions, and norms. In other words, any group of people who share "a way of life." Your cultural groups teach you what is right and wrong, good and bad, and how people are supposed to communicate with others. Cultural groups share *fields of meaning*, and these shared meanings give us our identities.

This broad definition allows a cultural group to refer to more than just people of different nationalities. Using this broad definition, a cultural group includes people who identify themselves as belonging to:

- A country or nationality: French, Sudanese, American, etc.
- Specific regions in a country: South, North, West Coast, USA; North Korea
- Generations: your grandparents, parents, and your age group
- A lifestyle: air heads/pot-heads, emos, jocks, dramas, preps, hippies, gangsters, etc.

- Race/ethnicity: People of different racial groups can be seen as distinct cultural groups if you consider that racial groups share cultural history and present-day life experiences.
- Socio-economic status: poor, middle class, wealthy
- Gender: male, female, lesbian, gay, transgender

Obviously, we each belong to multiple cultural groups, all which influence the way we see the world and communicate with others.

Components of Culture

So far we have discussed intercultural communication and cultural groups, but I have not yet defined culture. ***Culture*** is a set of beliefs, values, attitudes, practices, traditions, speech patterns, and norms that is passed down from one generation to another and sustains a particular way of life. In short, a culture is a way of life—a guidebook for who you are and how you should relate to others. Your cultural groups form the basis for who you are by providing a ***worldview***, or a way of thinking about the world and the people in it.

Cultures are by no means static—they can and do change—though they tend to be relatively stable. Listed below are some components or influences on culture:

- History (slavery, colonialism, etc.)
- Religion (core values and principles for living)
- Geography (temperature, climate, food availability, etc.)
- Institutions and organizations (education, the justice system, media, etc.)
- Major events (9/11, a tsunami, etc.)

Though cultures can differ widely, there are a number of orientations or values that can be used to compare and contrast cultures. As you read the following list, try to think of examples to share with the class.

- Individualistic vs. collectivistic orientation . . . Is the focus on the individual or the group?
- Values equality for all people vs. accepts power inequality.
- Definitions of work and play and the balance between them.
- How conflict is managed . . . overtly? Covertly? Directly? Indirectly?
- How time is viewed . . . Is the focus on the past, present, or future? Is time measured by a clock or by other means, like the cycle of the day or season?
- How the ideas of "progress and change" are viewed . . . positively or negatively.
- Gender roles vary greatly across cultures, as do attitudes toward homosexuality and transgender people.

Our cultural orientations provide us with a basic understanding of the world and with challenges when we attempt to communicate with people who have different cultural understandings. You can be a more effective intercultural communicator just by being aware of these basic differences in worldview.

Language and Culture

Language and culture are interconnected. We learn about culture through language. When we listen to others' stories, we learn about their cultural understandings. One of the best ways to learn about a culture that is different from your own is to listen to the narratives—the fables, myths, news, histories, and other stories. You can also pay attention to the popular culture (like music, fashions, media, etc.) and artifacts (items or things).

In addition, language actually shapes culture as well. For example, the structure of language provides a framework for understanding. In some romance languages like Spanish and French, there are two different verbs for "to be": one indicates a temporary state and the other indicates a permanent state. In English, we only have one verb. Also, some cultures use a lot of non-verbal communication to transmit meaning, while others rely primarily on words.

A professor of mine used to say: "My enemy is someone whose story I do not yet know." What he meant is that our conflicts often come from a place of cultural misunderstanding. If we listen to the stories of others with an open mind, we might find our commonalities beneath the difference in culture.

Non-Verbal Communication and Culture

Just as with language, non-verbal communication is also culture-bound. What this means is that non-verbal signs and signals can be interpreted differently across cultural groups. Eye contact, gestures, physical distance, turn-taking practices, sounds, and other body movements can be understood differently based on cultural context.

Business Communication and Culture

In the business world, as in all contexts, there are rules for how people are supposed to communicate. In a typical American business interaction, we shake hands to greet the other, keep a foot or two of distance between us, make direct eye contact, smile, and exchange business cards. However, this code of conduct is very American! Other cultures have their own rules for conducting business, and your success in **intercultural business** is dependent on your knowledge of the cultural practices and norms. A friend of mine was asked to work in an office in Japan for a few weeks, and he was required to study the Japanese "way" before he went. His company wanted to make sure he would not inadvertently offend his new coworkers.

Words of Caution

As with most ideas, understanding culture and intercultural communication strategies have both benefits and limitations. The obvious benefit is that you can be more effective in your interactions and experience richer relationships with others from distinct cultural backgrounds. However, you need to be careful not to oversimplify or over-generalize the cultural characteristics of individuals you meet. While cultural groups strongly influence who we are, they do not determine who we are. Individuals have the ability to change, create, and re-create themselves, and we need to keep an open mind about the possibilities.

While having categories for people makes a complex world easier to understand, it can also exaggerate the differences between people, rather than focus on the similarities. In the end, human beings do share the common experience of being human! Our shared fields of meaning are often larger than we might initially think.

The major problem with fixed or rigid views on culture is stereotyping, which can lead to prejudice and ethnocentrism. **Ethnocentrism** is the belief that your culture is superior to others. Often, our ethnocentric tendencies lead us to avoid interacting with others who are culturally distinct, or we become intolerant and reject them. Everyone deserves the chance to define himself or herself and be seen as an individual.

Developing Intercultural Communication Competence

Sometimes **intercultural communication** goes well with little effort. When there are shared fields of meaning, then intercultural understanding is easy. However, more often than not, when intercultural communication is successful, it is because one or more of the people in the transaction has intercultural communication competence.

Communication competence refers to the ability to communicate effectively with others. Intercultural communication competence is the ability to communicate effectively with others from different cultural backgrounds, and it is a skill that can be developed.

Self awareness is the first step toward becoming an effective intercultural communicator. Remember, we have all been socialized to see the world from a particular point of view and to communicate in a particular way. How has your cultural background shaped who you are? How might others have been shaped differently?

The next step in becoming an effective intercultural communicator is to develop a **dual-perspective**, or empathy toward others. This is the ability to temporarily step outside your own worldview so you can try to understand the worldview of another person.

Developing good listening habits is another way to enhance your intercultural competence. *Active listening* is a process where you really attend to the messages of another person and interact with them to check your understanding. This involves your ears, eyes, body, and mind!

Finally, remember that effective intercultural communication is based on the **recognition of cultural difference**s and a respect for cultural differences. Just because someone or something is different, it does not have to be judged as "bad." Try to adopt an "I'm OK, You're OK" approach to others, and you'll be amazed at the connections you can make with people from a variety of cultural groups.

Activities:

1. Select a scene from a movie or novel that depicts intercultural communication. Discuss how well (or poorly) the characters managed the transaction.
2. Write an "I am from . . ." poem. The only guideline is that the first line has to start with the words "I am from . . ." This exercise will help you to see how your cultural background has influenced who you are today.
3. Create a list of the cultural groups you identify with and some that you do not identify with. Are there any commonalities between the two lists?
4. Imagine what your life might have been like had you been born into a different cultural group. How might you be different today?

....

The Japanese Business Card Exercise

....

by Daniel Richardson

When discussing intercultural communication, you may find some unique differences in areas of communication that may seem very small with little impact. Simple etiquette is one of these areas. To demonstrate this to my students, I have them participate in "The Japanese Business Card Exercise." The exercise is dramatically acted in my classroom as follows:

1. I ask two student volunteers to leave the room with me. I explain the exercise to them.
2. When we return, I explain to the class that these two students are two Americans attending a business-networking event. The two students meet and exchange business cards (I provide the cards). The students glance at each other's business cards, have a short conversation, and one student mentions their company has a new website. The second student pulls out a pen, crosses out the original website on the face of the business card, and writes in the new website address before putting the card into their pocket. (All this behavior would be considered acceptable [not polished perhaps] in our western culture.)
3. For the second scenario, I explain to the class that one student is a Japanese businessperson and the other person is an American businessperson at this same networking event. The two students meet and exchange business cards. The American glances at the Japanese card and waits while the Japanese businessperson takes time to read and absorb the information on the American card. A short conversation ensues and the Japanese businessperson mentions their company has a new website. The American whips out a pen and starts to write across the face of the business card. The Japanese businessperson protests and the American responds, "It's okay. I do this all the time." and proceeds to write in the new website before stuffing the card into their pocket.
4. The epilogue is that the Japanese businessperson excuses himself/herself and does not speak to the American again or take their phone calls after the event. The American is puzzled and asks a friend who is more knowledgeable about Japanese culture if they did anything wrong. The friend explains:
   a. Merely glancing at the business card without reading and absorbing the information is considered rude.
   b. Stuffing the business card into your pocket is considered extremely offensive.
   c. Writing across the face of the business card is viewed as a direct insult.
5. When the American businessman says they don't understand why making an important correction on the face of the card would be insulting, the friend says, "Permit me to demonstrate the equivalent behavior in our culture." He takes out a pen and starts writing across

the face of the American businessman (I make sure the students don't actually touch each other).

6. "Now do you understand," the friend begins. "Would you do business with me after I just wrote across your face?"

7. "Heck no!" the American businessman retorts.

8. "Well, in Japan, the business card is an extension of the individual and writing across its face would be like writing across your face," states the friend.

I like the experiential component of the exchange because my students are able to understand the level of insult being offered in a way that is difficult to grasp with mere explanation. Sensitivity to intercultural communication and nonverbal messages across cultures will help minimize such misunderstandings in real life situations.

Cultural Perspectives of Political Understandings

by Regina Williams Davis

In the field of Communication Studies, the interview is a **qualitative research** tool for data gathering to uncover beliefs, attitudes, political views, and worldviews. The questionnaire may be used as a device to initiate an experiential focus of where understandings or misunderstandings of culture, politics, and diversity in terms of race, social class, ethnicity, culture, alternative life styles, religion, gender, exceptionality, and the "other" intersect; and how these understandings are communicated and transmitted across generations.

People who are perceived as different are likely to experience bias and differential treatment as well. Most people do not realize they perpetuate bias through communication. What better time in life than being a college student to grapple with these complex notions of culture, communication, and politics.

For many who study issues of racism, social class discrimination, misogyny, and other forms of bigotry, they often believe that ineffective communication (verbal and nonverbal) exacerbates these long standing problems. Effective communication must be adequately addressed when seeking to reduce misunderstandings about culture and its impact on politics. Most political issues may seem simplistic because they are communicated in a 10-second sound bite to persuade or dissuade the listener quickly; when the essence of the issue is much more complex than a 10-second sound bite or even a 140-character tweet.

Using an interview for promoting the understanding of how people may communicate the manifestations of "isms" in conjunction with the political discourse of race, social class, gender, special needs, religious differences, and alternative life-styles is an assertive approach toward "staring these issues in the face;" looking at one's self in the mirror; and effectively learning the intensity of the deep-seated roots of cultural incompetence. This exercise is a critical component of cultural communication and learning to see where the student interviewer has misunderstandings. The student interviewers should and must feel something from this experience and should be prepared to write about it.

The interview has statements that express variations in culture, religion, and language to help demonstrate how individuals can be perceived as self-contradictory in their understandings. Some examples may be:

1. "I believe in a women's right to choose; yet, I do not believe in the right to bear arms."

2. "I don't believe in big government. Government needs to be small and less regulatory; yet, I believe that a constitutional amendment should exist to ensure that marriage is only recognized between one man and one woman."

Hopefully students will gain insight and understand effectively what marginalized populations all too often experience in America. Preparing future voters and public servants to represent a more varied population than ever before in the history of this country is the impetus for encouraging college students to interview individuals, tabulate their data, and discuss the results in class.

When conducting these interview sessions, individuals are often reluctant to share their true feelings and beliefs when in group settings. Therefore, it is essential that individual meetings are conducted in a quiet and comfortable environment. The person you are interviewing should feel relaxed and that they can trust you. Please keep your personal opinions to yourself and minimize facial expressions that may convey a nonverbal message. Remember, we all have bias and personal preferences. The potential for future success of today's college student can be impeded by allowing the baggage of racism, sexism, social class bias, or other prejudices to continue and manifest.

Using the data collected from the interview to start hard conversations about culture and politics will only be the beginning. Self-talk will continue as students, professors, and the individuals interviewed reflect on their initial responses to some of these prompts. This exercise may be life changing.

Key Terms:

Bias

Culture

Cultural Groups

Communication Competence

Diversity

Dual-perspective

Ethnocentrism

Intercultural Business

Intercultural Communication Competence

Fields of Meaning

Encode

Decode

Globalization

Political Views

Qualitative Research

Worldview

Key Concepts:

Intercultural communication is transactional, a process, systemic, dynamic, contextual, and symbolic.

The steps towards developing intercultural communication competence include self-awareness, developing a dual perspective, active listening, and cultural difference.

Application Activity: *Curious Cultural and Political Communication: An Interview*

Objective:

- This assignment will help you realize that communication behaviors and beliefs across ethnicity, race, and culture have heavy influences on the direction of the political climate. As future voters, public servants, and leaders, you will be responsible for interacting with a wide variety of people. It will be your responsibility to develop cross-cultural skills in communicating with them.

Directions:

Conduct **two separate** interviews (each separately). Please be sure to conduct one interview with someone who is ethnically similar to you and a second interview with someone of a different ethnicity. You will ask your interviewees a series of questions listed on the following Questionnaire. Record their actual responses. Do not change their words. What the interviewee says is what you should report, regardless of the harshness of the content. Your task is to record their responses, organize the results, and then prepare a narrative to reflect the data that you've collected. The data, tabulations, results, and narrative must be typed and double-spaced. Charts and graphs are encouraged!

INTERVIEW:

Section I. Question on **American Culture**

1. What is your understanding of our social welfare system?

    _____

    _____

2. What group do you believe receives the majority of services?

    _____

    _____

3. Name two minority groups in the United States.

    _____

    _____

4. Name two minority groups in Canada.

    _____

    _____

5. What is the largest minority group in California?

    _____

    _____

Section II. Cultural Practices (You select a minority for the interviewee)

1. What types of foods do you commonly eat? What types of foods do you perceive are an untrue stereotype for your ethnicity?

    _____

2. What types of music do you commonly listen to? What types of music do you perceive are an untrue stereotype for your ethnicity?

_____

3. What types of clothes do you commonly wear? What types of clothing do you perceive are an untrue stereotype for your ethnicity?

_____

Section III. Personal and Political Responses

1. What is your understanding of liberalism? (Explain)

_____

2. What is your understanding of conservatism? (Explain)

_____

3. Should a naturalized citizen be allowed to become President of the United States?

   a. Why?

   _____

   b. Why not?

   _____

4. Should an American born Muslim be allowed to become President of the United States?

   a. Why?

   _____

   b. Why not?

   _____

INTERVIEW: *(continued)*

5. Should a person with a physical disability be allowed to become President of the United States?

   a. Why?

   _____

   b. Why not?

   _____

6. Should an atheist be allowed to become President of the United States?

   a. Why?

   _____

   b. Why not?

   _____

7. Should a racist be allowed to become President of the United States?

   a. Why?

   _____

   b. Why not?

   _____

8. Is there any group in particular that irritates you?

   a. Why?

   _____

   b. Why not?

   _____

9. Demographic Information on Interviewees (Please record the information requested below for each interviewee)

   a. Age of your interviewee _____

   b. Sex of your interviewee _____

   c. Ethnicity of your interviewee _____

   d. Level of education of your interviewee _____

   e. Social class of your interviewee (according to interviewee) _____

   f. Range of geographic experience of your interviewee _____

   g. Has been outside of the state _____

   h. Has been outside of the region (southeast) _____

   i. Has been outside of the country _____

MINI QUIZ

10. True or False: Nonverbal communication is the one aspect of communication which is consistent across cultures.

11. Multiple Choice: Cultural groups share
    A. Values and beliefs
    B. Attitudes
    C. Traditions and norms
    D. All of the above

12. Fill in the Blank: _____ is a process where you really attend to the messages of another person and interact with them to analyze your understanding.

13. Essay: Think about your future career goals. Explain how your understanding of intercultural communication, your personal political view, and personal bias may influence your ability to communicate with others.

CHAPTER 7

Nonverbal Communication

Nonverbal Differences Exist Between Women and Men

Although men and women may share a common culture, their nonverbal behaviors tend to differ. Research concludes that gender differences exist between the nonverbal behaviors of men and women. Each statement below characterizes the differences between the nonverbal behaviors of American men and women. Check yourself! Make the statement true by circling the correct gender.

1. Women/Men are less likely to return a smile than women/men.
2. Women/Men use fewer gestures than women/men.
3. Women/Men use fewer one-handed gestures and arm movements.
4. Women/Men are not more attracted to others who smile.
5. Women/Men exhibit greater leg and foot movement, including tapping their feet.
6. Women/Men more frequently use sweeping hand gestures, stretching the hands, cracking the knuckles, pointing and using arms to lift the body from a chair or table.
7. Women/Men establish more eye contact than women/men.
8. Women/Men use more facial expressions and are more expressive than women/men.
9. Women/Men do not convey their emotions through their faces.
10. Women/Men smile more than women/men.
11. Women/Men tend to keep their hands down on the arms of a chair more than women/men.
12. Women/Men do not appear to be disturbed by people who do not watch them.

Answers:
1. Men/Women 2. Women/Men 3. Women 4. Men 5. Men 6. Men 7. Women/Men
8. Women/Men 9. Men 10. Women/ Men 11. Women/Men 12. Men.

Adapted from Judy Cornelia Pearson, Lynn H. Turner, and William Todd-Mancillas, *Gender and Communication*, 2nd ed. Dubuque: Wm. C. Brown Publishers, 1991. As in Wilson, Gerald L. Groups in Context: Leadership and Participation in Small Groups 5th ed. Boston: McGraw-Hill College, 1999: 123–126.

You Don't Have to Say a Word!

by Regina Williams Davis

© Yayayoyo, 2012. Used under license from Shutterstock, Inc.

My teenage daughter loves to use *emoticons* to help explain her text messages. At her emotional age, she seems to be fully aware that I tend to receive messages from her facial expressions and other nonverbal behaviors more than anything she says. I will see her dreadfully sad, "my life is over . . ." look on her face often, and hear her words, every time I ask her, "Are you okay?" respond to me with, "I'm fine!" All of her nonverbal behaviors say otherwise. Therefore, in spite of the digital way we communicate, it is apparent that some method of reinforcing a text or an email with an emoticon symbol, be it ☺ or ☹, is a valued part of nonverbal communication.

Different textbooks and studies in communication will suggest there are more nonverbal categories, but the following eight are consistently addressed: aesthetics, artifacts, chronemics, haptics, kinesics, oculesics, paralanguage, physical appearance, and proxemics. These categories are broad, with sub-categories included. Figure 7.1 provides the behavioral emphasis that clarifies the nonverbal category.

Nonverbal behavior typically accompanies our verbal messages, but not always. Often we send nonverbal messages unintentionally. **Aesthetics** includes atmosphere and ambiance. Having your boyfriend over for dinner, setting your table with candles lit, playing soft sultry music, and dressed

Nonverbal Category	Behavioral Emphasis
Aesthetics	Environmental Factors
Artifacts	Personal Objects
Chronemics	Time
Haptics	Physical Touch
Kinesics	Body Movements
Oculesics	Eye Movement
Paralanguage	Vocal Variations
Physical Appearance	Personal Presentation
Proxemics	Physical Space

FIGURE 7.1

From *Communication Voices*, 3/e by Myra M. Shird. Copyright 2007 by Myra M. Shird. Reprinted by permission.

slightly provocative can send an intentional message. However, folding your arms across you chest, in concert with a serious look of concern, may send a message of judgment unintentionally.

When my students hear "artifacts," they immediately think of ancient artifacts. **Artifacts** are as simple as earrings or a belt buckle. **Chronemics** is the use of time. Arriving to an interview for employment, ten to fifteen minutes late, sends the interviewer the message that you either have no respect for another's time, or that you are not truly interested in the job. On the other hand, arriving early to the same interview will send a message that shows interest and eagerness for the position.

Haptics deals with physical touch. If a male brushes against a woman's body and she perceives it to be inappropriate, then negative interactions can result. Waving a fist purposefully through the air until it touches another person, hitting them sends a belligerent message. Nonetheless, the human touch is powerful, and a genuine hug or a congratulatory handshake can take positive messages a long way.

Kinesics is body movement and includes hand gestures. It can enhance or hinder a message. It can simply be walking away from the podium to become more engaged with the audience. However, pacing can annoy your audience and excessive gestures can be a distraction to your audience. Most people are not always conscious of their body movements. Becoming aware of it will aid in effective communication.

We can send nonverbal messages using our eyes. **Oculesics** is eye movement. Did your mother ever ask you to stop "rolling your eyes"? If or when you did this, it sent her a message that you had a negative attitude about something. In **neuro-linguistic programming (NLP)**, the study of eye movement and its meaning posits that when eyes move up and to the right, the person is trying to recall or remember an event. If their eyes move up and to the left, the person is constructing a new idea. Some people who ascribe to this philosophy suggest that this is a way to tell if a person is telling the truth, or not.

Paralanguage is considered nonverbal communication even though words are stated. It is not always what you say, but how you say it. For example, the way I say, "Whatever" and the way my teenager says, "Whatever" seems to provide two completely different connotations. Practice all of the different ways you can state the same sentence and see how many different meanings can be understood.

Physical appearance is a major form of nonverbal communication; hence, "dress for success." Your "self" presentation will speak to your knowledge of appropriateness and respect for others. Physical appearance will include your hair or hair cut. So many college students are disappointed that they may need to cut the dreadlocked hair they had grown fond of over the four years they were in school in order to land that first job after graduation. Fortunately, many companies currently are less judgmental about such things than they have been in the past.

Proxemics is really nothing more than respecting personal space. However, I do recall living in Europe and felt that my personal space was violated. It was common for individuals in Germany to ask you questions or dialogue with another with less than five inches between you. In this country, the United States of America, it is important to respect each others' personal space.

There are times where words are not used because we believe that actions will speak for themselves. However, it is important that an effective communicator not assume that their audience or the individual you are in dialogue with will comprehend nonverbal messages the way they are intended. Please be mindful of your words, actions, and nonverbal behaviors.

WHAT MESSAGE CAN YOU GET FROM THE TATTOO?

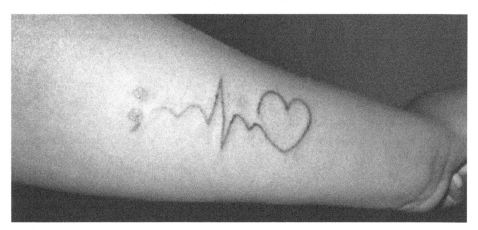

Key Terms:

Aesthetics
Artifacts
Chronemics
Emoticons
Haptics
Kinesics
Neuro-linguistic Programming
Oculesics

Paralanguage
Physical Appearance
Proxemics

Application Activity: *Nonverbal Awareness Exercise*

Objective: Nonverbal Communication
- Nonverbal communication conveys meaning or feelings consciously or unconsciously.
- Nonverbal communication may reinforce verbal communication.
    - Nonverbal communication can substitute for spoken words.
    - Nonverbal communication is culturally defined.
    - In a direct conversation between 2 people, up to 65% of the social understanding is sent through nonverbal means.

Directions:
1. Class is divided into small groups.
2. Each group makes a list of symbols used in our culture.
3. Some examples may be:
    - greeting someone by tapping the top the other's head
    - turning your back to the audience during a speech
4. Each group shares their list of gestures or symbols.
5. Discuss how some of these strange gestures may be appropriate or inappropriate in other countries and cultures.
6. Discuss why we know what these symbols mean.

MINI QUIZ

1. True or False: Nonverbal messages may be sent unintentionally.
2. Multiple Choice: This form of nonverbal communication is concerned with body movement and hand gestures.
   A. Oculesics
   B. Proxemics
   C. Paralanguage
   D. Kinesics
3. Fill in the Blank: The form of nonverbal communication that is defined by the use of

   time is referred to as _____.
4. Essay: Discuss how nonverbal communication may replace the meaning of verbal communication during communication interchanges.

CHAPTER 8

Ethically Speaking...

by Regina Williams Davis

Have you ever heard that there's always someone waiting to be offended? Often they are offended by something said or done by another. Most of us have a set of standards that we live by—and we tend to expect others to live by our same standards. There are things that you believe with all of your heart are right, and there are things that you strongly believe are wrong . . . what we have learned growing up in a particular environment . . . society and family values that become transformed into our individual ethics . . . our set of values which guide us in our daily decision-making. We usually (not always) live up to our personal standards and govern ourselves according to our value system. Moreover, it seems to be a natural desire to act in an ethical manner.

A loose definition for ethics may be moral principles for living and making decisions. A more comprehensive meaning may include morals, beliefs, norms, and values that societies use to determine right from wrong. Now it gets more complicated because individual ethics may not always be aligned with the ethics of our society. Hence, there are multiple and competing views on what is considered right and what is wrong. Our thought patterns tend to govern our behavior, thusly, what we believe to be true or what we believe to be right will often determine what we will do or say. Since everyone does not share the exact same morals, beliefs, or principled reality, our actions and expressions may pose potential conflicting views on ethical speech acts. When I stated earlier that most of us have a set of standards we live by, these standards may be strictly guided by the law, religious beliefs, social group acceptance, or just personal values. It seems like everyone should be able to make the right and ethical choice at all times because of these standards and values we supposedly live by.

Although I believe most of us want to do the right thing, "the right thing to do" becomes convoluted in today's society. Individuals and society are forced to be confronted with challenges of choice and action. This is evident in speech acts on a daily basis. Essentially, when we choose to express ourselves, we may offend another because of this fragmented societal perspective on what is right. Therefore, it may help to quickly perform an ethical audit before acting. But before we develop our ethical audit (which may be slightly different for each one of us), let's look at the highly valued right in our American society to freely express ourselves, the freedom of speech.

The Highly Valued Freedom of Speech

I alluded in the last section that ethics is a gray area in this postmodern era, where it is difficult to find a clear set of rules. However, the very first amendment to our constitution, located under the title of "The Bill of Rights," is the freedom of speech. The first amendment provides that, "Congress shall make no law . . . abridging the freedom of speech or of the press. . . ." This might suggest that you can say whatever you want at any time, in any place. However, there are times when the highest courts intervene with restrictions to the freedom of speech. Understanding that "speech" includes other mediums of expression, there are four conditions for assessing the degree of the freedom of speech we have (Fraleigh 1997).

1. Freedom to communicate without fear of government sanction
2. Freedom from compulsory speech
3. Freedom of access to effective channels of communication
4. Freedom from government domination of the free speech environment

The "freedom to communicate without fear of government sanction" suggests that the government will not censor information. However, there are times when the government must exercise prior restraint after proving it is justified in doing so for the protection of society. Similarly, the "freedom from compulsory speech" means that we should not be required to say certain things. But again, there are exceptions to every rule. For example, there are times when students who attended public schools were required to salute the flag and recite the pledge of allegiance. The "freedom of access to effective channels of communication" seems to be restrictive based more on the socioeconomic means than anything else, although the Internet is swiftly becoming an effective channel for most people to access.

The "freedom from government domination of the free speech environment" is important and it is the reason Europeans wanted to make the continent of North America their home. They were fleeing the domination of their government of their time, desiring the freedom to speak of religious doctrine contrary to the dominant theology in their European countries. However, there are messages our government will send that may dominate the free speech environment. Examples may be recruitment for the armed forces or the "Just say, 'No!' " anti-drug campaign. We will discuss a case later in this chapter that highlights controversy pertaining to this freedom from government domination of the free speech environment.

What Makes The Freedom of Speech So Significant?

We defend and substantiate our right to the freedom of speech because it is critical to our system of "self-government" and it promotes "the discovery of truth." (Fraleigh 1997) Likewise, it encourages free will, independence, and freedom while affirming the premise that one person does not necessarily possess the moral right to stifle or suppress the ideas of another person!

Even though we highly value this freedom in terms of our individual rights, we also value the rights of the collective. There are many times when individual rights and the concern for the good of society may clash. Even our laws cannot guarantee ethical behavior in terms of the freedom of speech. Why? Speech acts are just too complex and situational!

There is a popular school of thought that ethics in communication should be thought of in terms of the collective, as opposed to the individual.

Do the Courts Control the Freedom of Speech or Protect our Safety?

When I suggested earlier that you may not say whatever you want at any time, in any place, I wanted to point out that the safety and welfare of our society often takes precedence in the courts when the freedom of speech is in question. If someone were to yell from the top of their lungs, "Fire!" in a crowded nightclub, initiating a mass of people running to an exit, and causing injuries, they have compromised the safety and welfare for that group of people. This is the classic example of time and place being variables that may restrict freedom of speech, thus, an ethical concern for the collective.

Additionally, there are many questions about the responsibility a speaker has when provoking or encouraging an audience to perform an illegal act. Consider the effects of a Black Panther leader during the 1960s, a Ku Klux Klan leader during the 1950s and 60s, or a Communist politician during the 1940s. Leaders in each of these factions held meetings and gave speeches on a regular basis. There were some gifted speakers in the art of persuasion and they incited members of their audience to commit questionable acts or illegal acts of violence. In some of these cases, the courts ruled the speaker guilty for inciting the audience. Arguably, many psychologists believe that only individuals who are predisposed to wanting to commit such illegal acts would actually follow through.

Another argument advocates the concept of "free will." How could a speaker make someone do something wrong if we all possess free will? Of course, these arguments may or may not apply to children.

The Morality of Communication

Inevitably, there will be a debate among those who ascribe to a moral absolute and those who recognize moral relativism. The moral absolute determines right and wrong from their perceived absolute truths. This "absolute" is considering only one standard, yours, and no one else's; whereas moral relativism is the notion that we may consider that there are other ethical systems that others choose and their choices are equally respected.

Moral relativism, however, brings difficulty to an already complex study of ethics in communications. And if that isn't challenging enough, ethical communication suggests we are simultaneously expected to be able to respect others, affect another's behavior, and maintain our own psychological health. Therefore, you can understand why a study in ethical communication, albeit very interesting, may also promote an ongoing controversy for speech acts.

An Ethical Audit

What are some of the ethical questions in terms of the role and function of communication in society and for individuals? There are many, but the few I generally ask are, "Is it right?", "Is it fair?", "Is it restrictive or deceptive to others?", "Who does it affect?", "Who does it serve?", and my personal favorite, "Is it something one might become ashamed of when it comes to light?" I use these questions when I perform ethical audits.

An ethical audit is simply an appraisal of a situation or a potential situation that may challenge the morality of actions. I have noticed with my students that I rarely have an entire class agree on the ethical standing of a case study. What are your thoughts on the following case?

Recently, the *USA Today* reported that "Armstrong Williams . . . was paid $240,000 to promote President Bush's No Child Left Behind Act on his talk show . . . provide media access for the Education Secretary, and . . . persuade other Black journalists to talk about the law as part of a $1 million . . . contract with the Ketchum [PR] firm."

A liberal interest group strongly believed that Williams should return the money given to him illegally. Williams was ultimately fired and refused to return the money. This issue became controversial because Williams did not disclose that he was working for the government. It was believed that he was a journalist reporting a human interest story. President Bush stated that he was unaware of the situation.

What do you believe the ethical questions are in this situation? How much responsibility to society does one have with regard to expression or speech acts? As I was preparing this chapter, two other cases that are similar to the Armstrong Williams situation were reported:

The Department of Health and Human Services (HHS) paid three conservative columnists to assist in promoting a Bush administration policy. Mike McManus said he received $10,000 and Maggie Gallagher says she was paid $21,500 to promote a conservative view of marriage—an initiative promoting that only marriage between a man and a woman can build strong families. The Armstrong Williams case had already been exposed. All three columnists failed to disclose to their readers their relationships with the administration. The new director of HHS has since implemented a rule to prohibit the use of outside consultants or contractors who have any connection with the press in an effort to restore public confidence that taxpayers' money is not being used to pay journalists (columnists or commentators) to use their positions of influence in the media.

Federal law bans the use of public money on propaganda. There are two major ethical questions:

1. Did these journalists violate general ethical standards for not disclosing their relationship with the government?
2. Is this an illegal use of taxpayer dollars?

Many of my students stated they would have taken the money, not returned it, and just apologized for not disclosing—no harm, no foul! They really could not see much wrong with the actions of these journalists. Even some of my non-traditional students (those who are over 25 years of age) seem to feel the same way. Living in a tight economy, I suppose there are many people who may relax their ethical standards if they believe it will not cause harm to anyone.

Ethical Communication Theories

I want to highlight just a few communication theories that may shed some light on why we continue to have controversy regarding the choices we make concerning our speech acts. There are three theories in particular that I believe we can use in our ethical audits for communication: Virtue Ethics, Taoist (pronounced /DOW-IST/) Ethics, and Dialogic Ethics (Anderson 2002).

The first theory (and the most noted historically) is the Aristotelian idea of the management of rhetoric and virtue ethics, which emphasizes the unity of acts and reasons. **Virtue Ethics** advocates that speakers communicate in a way that is not manipulating another. Aristotle was concerned with the advancement of societal virtues like freedom, justice, courage, temperance, fairness, gentleness, and wisdom. In an effort to be true to these values, Aristotle's view would strongly suggest the ethical goal in communication would be to choose to find mutuality, middle ground, or a central point.

The second theory is referred to as **Taoist Ethics**, an ancient philosophy. Taoist ethics is becoming more popular in America as it embraces the vogue-ness of "organic" culture. The premise in Taoist ethics focuses on a vigorous ecology of values that promotes the concept of natural balance. It suggests that nothing exists alone. Everything should exist only in harmony with someone or something else, hence the "yin-yang" concept. Yin and yang are comparative opposites, interdependent, supportive of each other, and can transform into one another. In this light, the communicators are unique and will clearly define their views, yet require themselves to defy their egos and use empathy to understand the views of the other.

The third communication theory, **Dialogic Ethics**, is an understanding of how important it is not to devalue others by avoiding rhetorical manipulation and objectification. Without realizing it, a speaker might begin to think of his/her audience as merely valuable objects. For example, a candidate may not see their audience as human beings as much as they may see them as potential votes. There are six characteristics of dialogue developed by Richard Johannesen (1990) that fit in this dialogic ethical theory: authenticity, inclusion, confirmation, present-ness, spirit of mutual equality, and a supportive climate.

Consideration of all three of these theories can help when creating your own ethical checklist or can become a useful tool to use when auditing communication.

The Basis of Our Ethical Guidelines

We started this chapter discussing the fact that we all have our own ethical standards based on society, family values, and what we have learned growing up in a particular environment. However, there are underlying philosophies that have existed across the ages that are the foundations upon which we have built and structured our value system. Three of these philosophies include **egalitarianism**, **teleology**, and **deontology** (Anderson 2002). Consider the following scenario:

You are the team leader working on a major project. One of your team members, Terry, is not doing her part and causing concerns for everyone else on the team. You are concerned that Terry is not taking this assignment seriously. You do not want your grade to suffer because of Terry. Which philosophy would you use?

Egalitarianism is primarily concerned with the goal of social equality, fairness, and justice. In this philosophy, an ethical speaker will be more concerned with fairness and equality than any other goal in their communication efforts. When involved in speech acts, the desire is to know that the information communicated did not infringe upon the rights of another, but also that conditions of equality for all are protected. This suggests that someone does not commit an act of good just to gain recognition. Using an egalitarian philosophy, what might be your ethical response to the slacker team member scenario?

The **teleology** philosophy has a focus on the end result. An ethical communicator grounded in a teleological philosophy is governed by the best possible outcome from their choices of speech acts. The communicator will weigh the different outcomes and decide what will be the best of all possibilities and govern their speech act accordingly. Considering a teleological philosophy, what might your ethical response be to the slacker team member scenario?

Deontological philosophy suggests that the ethical speaker will do what his/her individual commitment to a faith or guiding principles will support and will not deviate. The ethical speaker has pledged to uphold certain principles, and the speech act should be governed by those principles. Ideally, both parties in the communiqué would be guided by the same principles—articles of faith, for example. What would be your ethical response to the slacker team member scenario under the deontological philosophy?

Usually, we can find ourselves considering one of these philosophies when selecting our ethical behavior. However, it is evident that we shift from one philosophy to another depending on the situation; although, we tend to think only about ourselves, often before others. Remember what my students thought about the Armstrong Williams controversy?

Space Then – Facebook Now . . .
Email Then – Twitter Now . . .
What's Next? Cyber-Ethics?

Most of us were taught that we live in a country that was built on the ideals of liberty and the pursuit of happiness, which in essence is the freedom to pursue how we want to live. There are morals and standards that we live by, but the United States is a pluralistic society so we tend to live in a moral relativistic manner as opposed to the moral absolute. What I mean is that moral codes and standards have differences from one person to the next or from one company or organization to the next. Therefore, when we become an employee, we are made aware in advance of the company's code of ethics. This "code of ethics" is the pre-set guidelines (a deontological philosophy) for the behavior of the employee.

Communicating in the public sphere is a concern with social media today. We represent our *selves*, our families, and our employers. We are all grappling with judgments made based on the information you, as an individual, share in cyberspace.

A very interesting case took place last year regarding what I refer to as **cyber-ethics**. According to Wikipedia (the free encyclopedia online), the Anthony Weiner Sexting Scandal, which is also called *Weiner-gate*, started when Democratic U.S. Congressman Anthony Weiner used the social media website Twitter to send a link of a sexually suggestive photo to a twenty-one-year-old woman. He denied having done so, but admitted to posting other sexually explicit pictures to women before and during his marriage. Former Congressman Weiner seemed forced to resign because of his social media faux pas and, in my opinion, his poor judgment in ethical communication. There is so much more to read about this story (Wikipedia online) that includes the fact that "evidence later revealed that a group of self-described conservatives had been monitoring Weiner's Twitter communications with women for at least three months. Two false identities of underage girls had been created by unknown parties to solicit communication with Weiner and the women he was contacting, one of whom Weiner followed until he was tipped off that it was a false account." (http://en.wikipedia.org/wiki/Anthony_Weiner_sexting_scandal) Ethical communication in cyberspace is a must.

When working for congress or a small public school, one must make a decision about his or her moral code. If your company's moral code is in conflict with yours, there are decisions to be made. The employer has a moral responsibility to inform the employee. Read the following ethical dilemma and determine who is right and who is wrong and why.

1. I taught in the Fulton County School System for three years with all satisfactory evaluations and no write-ups when this injustice took place. On February 21, 2007, I went to work as usual and at 8:45 a.m., right after I called the roll, my assistant principal entered my room and requested that I turn in my laptop. Of course, wondering what the hell was going on, I did as I was told. I figured that maybe they were going to install updates or something. (Wow, was I wrong!!) Anyhow, around 12:30 p.m., my principal stopped me in the hallway and told me I needed to report to human resources by 3:00 p.m. By then I knew it was some drama.

2. I went down to the Human Resources Office and a guy took me into the office and stated that Fulton County had received a phone call from a concerned citizen. They complained that I had an inappropriate Myspace page. When the assistant principal picked up my computer, he took it so that they could determine if I accessed my Myspace page from the school laptop.

3. We were required to take our laptops home every day. From my understanding, there is no policy against using the laptop at home for personal reasons, as long as you are not accessing inappropriate websites. So yes, they would have seen that I accessed Myspace, Facebook, Hotmail, and Yahoo.

4. My Myspace page had been up for about a year now and it promotes me as an actress and model. None of the pictures were inappropriate and I didn't think it was a crime to model and act part time. Hell, every teacher I know has a part time job. You would be amazed at what some of them do!!! (But, yet, they still have a job in the school system.)

5. I was told that I was being terminated because of Code 10, which discusses moral and ethical issues (I have yet to read Code 10). Of course, I asked the dude if he was serious.

6. Could it really be that deep because of a phone call? No warning? No simple request to take the page down?

7. I was given the option to resign. I told them that I would come back tomorrow with my decision of whether or not I would resign. I asked if I would be allowed to report back to the school. The answer was, "No, I'll set up a time for you to meet with the principal and collect your classroom items." You know I am looking at him like he lost his mind, right? They were treating me like a straight up criminal. I was still in shock from it all. I couldn't even say goodbye to my students. To this day, the principal still has not offered an explanation to the students or parents about my whereabouts. That's just tacky and unprofessional! Parents and students are wondering where I am.

8. I immediately left the Human Resources Office and went back to the school to get all my things. It was like 5:30 p.m. by this time, so no one was there but the janitors. I took four trash bags and cleaned my whole room out in thirty minutes, loaded my car up, and left the key with my name on it in the principal's mailbox. I wasn't waiting to meet with him about SHIT!!!!! Mission already accomplished.

9. The next day I returned to Human Resources with my letter of resignation. I have never been terminated from a job and I didn't want that on my record, so I did resign.

10. The lady I turned the letter of resignation into had the nerve to tell me, "Next time, don't mix business with pleasure. And make sure you don't discuss this with anyone because it might be bad for your image as an educator."

11. I laughed in her face. I hadn't done anything wrong and I will back that until the day I die. My image is just fine.

Ethical Discussion

   a. Evaluate the ethical dynamics in paragraphs two through four.
   b. After reading paragraphs three and five, what do you believe would bring clarity to this situation?
   c. In paragraph six, the teacher was offered an opportunity to set up a time to meet with the principal. How do you think the teacher should have handled this entire situation?
   d. Which of the ethical philosophies did each person tend to base their decisions or choices?

Is It Ethical?

by Zakeya Renay Mitchell

Discuss in small groups of three or four and reach a unanimous decision, if possible, about whether the following statements are ethical or unethical.

- Advising someone on a situation you have never experienced.
- Exercising loyalty to a friend that exhibits bad behavior with no hope of active change.
- Turning your head when you are present for something illegal.
- Not telling someone the truth to preserve their feelings.
- Loving someone that is abusive to you.
- Only telling someone parts of the truth, but not the details that have the potential to change their perspective.
- Committing illegal or degrading acts for money.
- Bringing a gun to someone else's homecoming.
- Women are the only ones with authority or accountability in respect to having sex, because men cannot help themselves.
- Women are gold diggers if they marry a man who is going into a major league sport (i.e., NBA, NFL, PGA) before he is famous.
- Men who are in professional sports are expected to cheat, so the wife should have expected it or known what she was getting into before marrying him.
- Getting rid of the 14th and 15th amendments.
- Same-sex marriage.

Family- or Foster-Care?

by Zakeya Renay Mitchell

A Question of Ethics?

Kerri, an 18-year-old freshman in college and Kay, a 19-year-old sophomore in college went home to visit with their mother, Gwen, in Washington, D.C. One morning Gwen called a family meeting to discuss some of the things that have been occurring while the two elder sisters were away at school. Gwen states, "Your uncle Richard and his girlfriend, Denise, have been fighting. The police were called and they filed a report on the matter. The rules were that they had to live in separate places for six months without any contact—visual, oral, or physical—until the period was over. Afterward, they could resume being together. However, if they break the agreement, the children will be taken from them and separated." This is not the first time these two have been reported, or is it the first time Richard has seen the inside of a police station or a jail cell. Nevertheless, they took immediate action to obey the arrangement.

Two months passed and Gwen calls another family meeting to discuss the fact that she spotted Richard's car in front of Denise's house, and she presumed that they were together in their house. So she files another report to have the children taken away from them. Two of their six children were Richard's children biologically. The other four were separated across the country to live with their fathers' families to avoid the foster-care system. However, the youngest two children were placed into the foster-care system because their father, Richard, and his family have not made arrangements as to who will be responsible for them. Additionally, Richard is not allowed guardianship because of his domestic violence record. So anytime he sees his children, it will be a chaperoned visitation.

During the third family meeting that was called by Kerri and Kay's grandmother, the discussion was who will be responsible for caring for the two younger children. Kerri and Kay's mother, Gwen, would automatically be voted responsible for caring for the children because she is perceived as having a stable home, stable job, and a stable car. During the meeting, the grandmother opened the floor for everyone to express themselves on the matter. Kerri and Kay expressed that they felt their mother should not be responsible for taking care of the two children because she does everything else for the family and cannot take the responsibility of two small children. Their grandmother said, "That isn't very nice to say." She rudely stated, "Remember, someone took care of you," which was true! Kay and Kerri's grandmother took them in while their mother, Gwen, was trying to get a divorce from her abusive husband. However, the difference was the level of responsibility and accountability Gwen always exhibited, and she paid her mother handsomely for her assistance with her children.

The next morning Richard goes over to Gwen's house because there was something he wanted to discuss with her. He was invited in and after some small talk, he asks Gwen if she would be the permanent guardian for his two young children. Gwen responds by saying, "Richard, I don't think that's a good idea. I am financially strained right now with my own children and my responsibilities, and I cannot afford to care for your children on a permanent basis. However, I will take them in through the foster-care system until we can figure out more permanent arrangements." Enraged, Richard tells Gwen, "You know what, I don't care about your excuses. If you don't want to do it then don't do it! Damn, whatever." Then he stormed out of the house. Shortly after, Gwen took the children in for a while, but eventually returned them to the foster-care system because the cost of child care in respect to what she was receiving from the system was not sufficient. So, currently, the two little girls live with a seasoned foster-care guardian that is able to care for them appropriately.

Discussion Questions

1. Do you think it was right to report the couple to the police the second time?
2. What are your thoughts of the mother of the two young children (Denise)? The father (Richard)?
3. Did Kerri and Kay have a just reason for NOT wanting their mother to take the responsibility of two more children?
4. Was it ethical for the grandmother to address Kerri and Kay in that manner at the third family meeting?
5. Would the ethnicity of the characters change your opinion in any way? Why or why not?
6. Why do you think Richard was upset with his sister, Gwen?
7. What do you think would be best for the young children?

Key Terms:

Authenticity
Cyber-ethics
Deontology
Dialogic Ethics
Egalitarianism
Ethics
Ethical Audit
Freedom of Speech Confirmation
Morality
Present-ness

Spirit of Mutual Equality
Supportive Climate
Taoist Ethics
Virtue Ethics
Dialogic Ethics Teleology
Authenticity Deontology
Inclusion

Application Activity: *Ethical Choices and Decisions*

Objective:

- To learn about others ethical choices.

Directions:

Read to your class the following list of activities. Allow them to respond to each one determining if they believe it is ethical or unethical.

1. Purchasing bootlegged movies.
2. Taking minor supplies home from work.
3. Lying about your age to purchase an alcoholic drink.
4. Cheating on your income tax.
5. Exaggerating about your work experience in a job interview.
6. Flirting your way out of a traffic ticket.
7. Surfing the internet during work hours.
8. Cheating on a test.
9. Splicing cable from your neighbor.
10. Exaggerating about yourself to influence someone of the opposite sex.
11. Calling in sick when you really are not sick.
12. Reporting to your professor about someone else cheating on a test or plagiarizing a paper.
13. Telling a child to lie about their age in order to pay the price for a child's ticket or children's meal.
14. Telling someone to say you are not home when they call and you do not want to talk to the person on the phone.

Vignettes are portrayals of a brief evocative description, account, or episode that will illustrate an important lesson.

VIGNETTE B: INTERCULTURAL COMMUNICATION

The United States is a diverse nation and it is likely that you will work, live, and/or socialize with individuals whose culture is uniquely different from your own. One of the common intercultural college scenarios involves instructors with heavy foreign accents. Students will complain of not understanding and react in ways that the instructor may find culturally offensive. How would you manage effective communication in a delicate situation where the cultural communication barriers may affect your grade in your class? Create a vignette that will demonstrate this lesson.

MINI QUIZ

1. True or False: Based on the rights given to U.S. citizens by the first amendment in the Bill of Rights, individuals have the legal right to say whatever they want, without legal repercussions.

2. Fill in the Blank: The questions: "Is it right?", "Is it fair?", or "Who does it affect?" are all examples of questions one may ask when conducting a(n) _____.

3. Multiple Choice: This communication theory values the concept of natural balance.
   A. Aristotelian Ethics
   B. Taoist Ethics
   C. Dialogic Ethics
   D. Buddhist Ethics

4. Essay: Discuss how egalitarianism may influence a speaker's aim to be a more ethical communicator in cyberspace.

UNIT III
HyperRelationship

Communication with Self, Relationships, and Groups

UNIT OBJECTIVES:

- *Understanding intrapersonal communication: Awareness of self-concept and self-scripts*
- *Advancing healthy relationships through communication*
- *Understanding gender, family, and friendship communication*
- *Awareness of communication clues that may lead to abuse*
- *Developing positive group communication climate*

. . . .

You may discover your intrapersonal communication, the importance of self-awareness, your self-concept, perception, and the importance of the relationship between self, others, and with the greater society with questioning social media as a tool or a veil. You will practice interpersonal and group communication to learn to recognize when another does not understand your message and how to manage misunderstandings. Interpersonal communication will include recognizing when it is appropriate to speak, when to listen attentively to questions and comments from other communicators, friends, and family communication, and how to work on collaborative projects as a team.

. . . .

CHAPTER 9

Who Am I? Really?

by Regina Williams Davis

As we evolve and grow individually, we gain an understanding of self discovery and **self-aware-ness**, but we do not always take the time to examine the messages we send to ourselves. The messages that we send to ourselves are a form of communication**: intrapersonal commu-nication.** So what is it that we tell ourselves? Why do we unconsciously meditate on certain messages? How can we gain control of the messages we send ourselves and initiate an internal mind intervention to initiate rein-vention of self? How powerful are our minds and can we strengthen them, thereby enhancing our **self-concept** without promoting egocentric view or narcissism?

We have a sense of who we are based on the identity we have been taught from our families and the socialization we experience from our environment. Our interpretation of **self** is somewhat re-stricted by the language we have available to describe the "self." For example, my three-year-old grandson can only define himself through his understanding of his relationship to others. He knows he is a boy and can point to himself as he says that. He also knows to refer to himself when he hears his name. He will state that he is a big boy when I accuse him of acting like a baby. However, he is quite limited in his ability to communicate his identity, although I believe that his mind has a greater comprehension of self than he can express. Most of us begin to understand self in terms of being the central point of reference for communicating with others.

Intrapersonal communication is the series of messages that you send to the "self." It is important to explore what you tell your "self" on a regular basis. These messages may be viewed as internal monologues or self-talk. These internal monologues have a major impact on your "self-concept." I define the self-concept as personal acknowledgement of your manifestation of your **multidimen-sional identity** constructed from environmental stimuli. Let's break this definition down . . . Per-sonal acknowledgement simply means an acceptance of who you are. Manifestation is the demon-stration of who you are.

The construction of your multidimensional identity from environmental stimuli suggests that you respond to your environment, which helped to shape who you are today. You and I are probably nice, kind, and thoughtful individuals because we were exposed to positive environmental influences. As good as most of us are, we can all be better. Hopefully, your experiences were ALL absolutely wonderful! But we know that is not true for any of us. However, we can intervene by strengthening our minds so that we can be better.

So what kind of **self-scripts** do we have? To hear internally in your mind, "Boy, I am fat!" suggests a form of a negative self-script. Are *your* self-scripts negative or positive? Are your internal monologues more negative than positive? Later in this chapter we will discuss ways to improve the messages you send to yourself, your positive self-talk, and the self-scripts you rehearse within your mind.

When I am teaching a unit on intrapersonal communication, I include a lecture about two psychological concepts that are helpful in acknowledging self. The first is Maslow's Hierarchy of Needs. See Figure 9.1.

FIGURE 9.1   © iQoncept, 2012. Used under license from Shutterstock, Inc.

The American psychology professor, Abraham Harold Maslow, created the popular "**Hierarchy of Needs**" pyramid. The pyramid is a pictorial display of what is needed by individuals before they can achieve other goals. The base of the pyramid is referred to as physiological needs. These needs are food, sleep, stimulation, and activity. The philosophy suggests that these needs must be met prior to achieving the next level of the pyramid, which is safety needs. The safety needs are security and protection from harm. Safety needs must be met before having the ability to fully achieve the third level of the pyramid, which is the need for love and belonging. Love, friendship, and feeling valued by others and/or another are desired and necessary before getting to the second highest level of the pyramid. The second highest level of the pyramid represents esteem needs: the need for self-respect, personal worth, and having personal autonomy. The highest point of the pyramid is the most difficult to achieve, but it is doable once all of the other needs are met, which is the need for self-actualization. Self-actualization is when an individual believes that they have reached their full potential. I am not certain that we all know what our full potential is exactly, but it is worth striving toward.

The second psychological concept I discuss with my students to promote personal awareness is the concept of the **Johari Window**. The window provides a vehicle to compare how we see ourselves to the way others see us. It was created by American psychologists Joseph Luft (1969) and Harry Ingham (1955).

The Johari Window is used to examine self from a unique perspective. There are four panes. The first pane is called the "Known Self." It consists of personal characteristics and attributes that are known to you and are known or can most likely be known to others. This information is biographical, like where you live and where you work. It includes your name and physical characteristics like height and the sound of your laugh. The next pane is called the "Blind Self." The Blind Self are those characteristics and attributes that are seen, observed, and recognized by others but are unbeknownst to you. This might be a pattern for when you raise your left eyebrow, or how you sound when you snore. The third pane is the "Hidden Self." These are those personal characteristics, traits, or behavior of which only you are aware. Only you may know that you still suck your thumb at night at twenty years of age. The fourth or last pane is referred to as the "Unknown Self." The unknown self will remain unknown until a significant event or a traumatic experience forces a new behavior or unusual out-of-character response. It may be important to recognize that there are personality traits that may not exhibit themselves until they are highly provoked. I often ask my students to ask their significant other if they have information that might help them learn about their Blind Self.

As I progress in the intrapersonal communication portion of my course, I encourage my students to seriously use this time for personal growth and reflection. We begin with the articulation of the self concept and the internal monologues of "who am I?" and self-defining. I lead my students through what I referred to as a "Self-Concept Workshop." After I requested each student to have a pen ready and six clean sheets of paper, each one labeled at the top as Page 1, Page 2, Page 3, Page 4, Page 5, and Page 6, I would turn the classroom lights off and play soft, smooth music to set a peaceful mood. Next, while the music is playing, I have the following instructions projected on the screen for my students to read and complete:

1. Write on page 1, a list of five or more reasonable statements you would like to change about yourself.
2. Write on page 2, a list of ten reasonable statements or more about yourself that you like about yourself and would never want to change.
3. Write on page 3, a list of five reasonable statements or more that you believe others would like you to change.

4. Write on page 4, a list of ten reasonable statements or more that you believe others really like and appreciate about you.

It is okay for the lists to have some overlap. After about thirty minutes, I assume the lists are complete. For the next fifty minutes, I project on the screen the next set of instructions:

1. Review pages 1 and 3. Determine which of the statements are doable for you and mark them with a check. Cross through the statements that are impossible to do or those that you emphatically do not agree.
2. Review pages 2 and 4. Circle the statements that you believe are doable for you. The statements that you believe are impossible, please note why you think it is impossible in the margin.
3. On page 5, rewrite the statements circled on pages 2 and 4 as well as the statements checked on pages 1 and 3 in the form of a list.
4. On page 6, describe how you would define yourself without using biographical data. (Biographical data are statements like where you were born, who your parents are, etc.) Incorporate the lists on page 5.

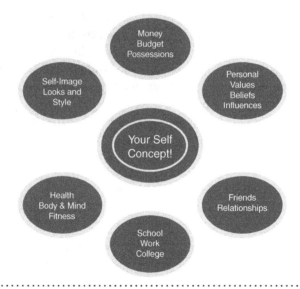

SELF CONCEPT

I ask my students to use this data to work on their self-concept paper. The Self-Concept Paper is an opportunity for my students to analyze the idea they have of who they think that they are. The assignment requires at least five type-written pages plus a cover page. The cover page should be a pictorial display of something that represents how you see yourself. The papers are always amazing, emotional, and the beginning of a journey of self-growth and self-improvement.

Key Terms:

Intrapersonal Communication
Multidimensional Identity
Self
Self-awareness

Self-concept
Self-scripts
Self-talk

Key Concepts:

Hierarchy of Needs
The Johari Window

Application Activity: *Self-Perception Art*

Objectives

- To become self-aware through understanding intrapersonal communication.
- To be able to develop a self-concept.

Directions:

1. Students use small poster boards, markers, crayons, magazines, and glue or tape. Students may bring these materials to class.
2. Students creatively use magazine clippings, drawings, and color combinations to represent a pictorial display of how they see themselves.
3. After the posters are completed, each student shares their artwork with the class and explain it's representation of self.

From *Communication Voices: Instructor's Manual* by Myra Shird and Regina Silverthorne. Copyright © 2007 by Myra M. Shird. Reprinted by permission of Kendall Hunt Publishing Company.

MINI QUIZ

4. True or False: Another word for self-talk is intrapersonal communication.
5. Multiple Choice: According to the Johari Window, this windowpane lists information that is known to others but not to ourselves.
   A. Open
   B. Blind
   C. Hidden
   D. Unknown
6. Fill in the Blank: According to Maslow's Hierarchy of Needs, the _____ level is an individual's ultimate goal.
7. Essay: Briefly discuss how your *self*-concept governs your daily communication interactions with others.

CHAPTER 10

Family Communication

Family Communication: Where It All Begins

---

by Deana Lacy McQuitty, Carl McQuitty, and Claretha Lacy

The study of **interpersonal communication** focuses on understanding how and why people behave and communicate. This includes aspects of both verbal and non-verbal communication, as well as the influence of **frame of reference**, medium, context, and culture on communication interactions. In addition, knowledge of **pragmatic functions** (i.e., the ability to determine the appropriateness of communication) is critical to effective communication. For example, the ability to appropriately participate in turn taking, eye contact, and social greetings during communication interactions are pragmatic functions. Fundamentally, interpersonal communication involves the process of exchanging messages between two or more individuals. These communication exchanges include communication between family, friends, and romantic partners, the effectiveness of which is influenced by the nature of our relationship with our communication partner(s). As we consider the concept of interpersonal communication, we must first explore our early interaction with those individuals that are closest to us: Family!

Our Earliest Interactions

How does a person begin to understand communication interactions? Early on, an infant learns specific strategies through interaction with family and those persons that are closest to them. As I reflect on my own children's infancy periods, around the age of 3–4 months old they began to develop a frame of reference interacting with family members. It is during this time that family members and the infant participate in **social engagement** activities. Social engagement activities are games such as "Patty Cake," "The Wheels on the Bus," and "Peek-a-boo." During these interactions, interpersonal communication is taking place. Let's think about this! As we play patty cake what do we do and say? We initiate the exchange with "Patty cake, patty cake baker's man, roll them up, roll them up and put it in the pan." The mother/caregiver is introducing interpersonal elements from a pragmatic (social) context such as turn taking, topic maintenance, and anticipating the next step. The young child will begin to imitate this social engagement. Through repetition, modeling and as a child's chronological age increases (around nine months of age or sooner), you can observe a child being able to spontaneously complete these social engagements that may include anticipating the exchange and utilizing an increase in eye contact to engage the parent in **joint attention** tasks. Joint attention is referred to as the child's ability to be fully engaged with the parent/caregiver through a learning experience. The child's early experiences with basic communication activities play an essential role in their receptive language ability to understand the pragmatic rules needed to have effective interpersonal communication. So I ask you: Where is the foundation for such skills? Family communication and the relationships established within the family unit provide the foundation for later relationships.

During the preschool years (3–5 years of age), experiences within the family continue to shape the child's belief system, values, and understanding of the world in which they live. As I think about my 5-year-old daughter, the values shared and reinforced within our family unit are portrayed daily. For example, I am a member of the Delta Sigma Theta Sorority, Inc. and speak of the sorority often on the telephone, in the mall, and when visiting other family members. In my home, I have a "Delta" room that is full of "Delta" paraphernalia. The other day, my daughter said "Mommy look"! OMG . . . she greeted me with the sorority's hand signal "pyramid"!! This is a prime example of how children internalize those verbal and non-verbal communication patterns that are portrayed within the family unit. They are consistently organizing their thoughts into cognitive schemata and adapting those skills in appropriate contexts as discussed in Chapter 1. Examples similar to this can be observed from infancy and beyond. Although we do recognize that peer communication and social communication are important, it is the early experiences with the family unit that provide the foundation for effective interpersonal communication.

CHILDREN FORM THEIR VALUES, BELIEFS, AND INTERESTS BASED ON FAMILY COMMUNICATION PATTERNS EXPERIENCED IN THE FORMATIVE YEARS OF LIFE.

New Age of Families: Effects of Family Communication

In today's society, the term family no longer connotes a mother, father, and children. In 2012, the nuclear family may or may not have children, may consist of a single-parent household, domestic partnerships, people living together before marriage, extended family members, and the list goes on and on. Although there are many facets to the family unit, there are still definite characteristics within the family that shape the communication values. These definite characteristics include defined roles, recognition of responsibilities, shared history, and future, as well as, shared living space. Each person within the family has his or her defined roles that may be very different depending upon the dynamic of the family unit. For example, a close friend was raised in a single-family home, therefore the children had to assume many adult roles and responsibilities. He often talks about his oldest sister having to assume many parental responsibilities because his mother worked during the evening. He further explained that his mother would (when her schedule would allow) come to programs at school or would come and see him play football. However, for the majority of the time when he was growing up, the oldest sibling was the disciplinarian and authoritative figure. She would *play school* with him so much that when it was time for him to go to kindergarten, he was already reading on a 2nd grade level. His sister would also cook, clean, and help him and his younger brother with their homework. In this family, the oldest sibling clearly recognized what her responsibilities were. He further revealed that what was important was not necessarily for his mother to show affection or say "I Love You"; it was understood. The primary focus was the necessities of life . . . food, clothes, and shelter!! My friend and his mother have a very close relationship to this day. Although she did not consistently say "I Love You," she used nonverbal communication by providing for the family to express "her love." On the contrary, such experiences may not exist within more traditional family structures where the man and a woman function within a partnership to address the welfare of the family together. In this family unit, the roles and responsibilities are traditionally shared between the adults to ensure the safety, security, and needs of the family.

Self-Reflection: As you think about your family unit, how would you describe it? What are some characteristics of the family? Who would you say was the authority figure? What family communication patterns do you think are portrayed (nonverbal versus verbal communication patterns)?

The shared history within a family unit can be influenced by cultural communication, values, and a belief system. Culture is learned from birth in the context of family, community, and environment. Interestingly, by the time children are five or six years old, they have internalized many of the basic values and beliefs of their native culture, including rules for social interaction, appropriate behavior, and learning style.

The above collage of pictures was taken from a visit to an attraction that celebrates the first English settlements in America during 15th–16th centuries. Historically, the family unit was comprised of the father, mother and children, all of whom had defined roles.

Whether the family consists of a traditional unit or unconventional unit, it is important to acknowledge the importance of early experiences and how they shape our values, beliefs, and moral standards.

The Close-Knit Family

by Alexis Haynes

To me, family communication refers to the way feelings and ideas are verbally and non-verbally exchanged between family members. Coming from a large, close-knit family, family communication is, and has always been, very important to me. Especially verbal communication. I grew up in a two-parent household until my parents divorced when I was eight years old. My sister's name is Ashley, but she is six years older than I am and we have two completely different personalities. She has always been very athletic and uninterested in school, while I have always been interested in fashion and my grades. Ashley is extremely passive, while I am more aggressive. Although she is older, I find myself acting as the big sister and defending her most of the time. Ashley and I would role play a lot when we were younger. I would pretend to be a cook, a salesperson, a preacher, you name it! My absolute favorite thing to do was play school. Since Ashley is older, she would pretend to be the teacher and I would be the student. I loved it because she always taught me "big girl" math and how to write like a "big girl." That's what my mom would call it. My mom has always been the authority figure in our household. Even when her and my dad were together, she always had the upper-hand. I remember asking my dad for permission to go places and do things, and his response would be "Go ask your mom." At an early age, this type of communication caused me to believe that the woman of the house always has the final say-so in family decisions. As I got older, I always heard about women being housewives. Once I found out what a housewife was, I realized that term shared many characteristics with my mom, but she had so much more going for herself. Although she cooked and cleaned, she also had a full-time job and took night classes to pursue her nursing degree. Now that I'm almost 20 years old and considered an adult, I believe that a woman, married or single, should always have a foundation of her own and strive to be more than just a "housewife." This proves that a lot of your beliefs and values come from childhood experiences and how you were raised. It also supports the statement that "family communication and the relationships established within the family unit provide the foundation for later relationships." Being that most my family live in the same city as me, I've always looked forward to family dinners and other family celebrations. I love the "kitchen talk." It makes me feel good when we sit around the table together, eat, and discuss the different endeavors taking place in our lives. As stated in this chapter, "good communication skills are essential and critical for positive and fruitful family relationships." Everything is not always peachy, but we make sure we find a way to compromise. As a child, I remember my mom would wake me up every morning before school and put bows or beads in my hair to match my outfits. She always painted my nails and toes the same color, and she made sure she gave them a touch-up whenever the polish started to chip. My room was painted pink and I had every new Bratz doll that came out. These gender-specific communication patterns played a critical role in how I viewed myself and the world around me. As I got older and a little more independent, I always bothered her about doing my hair and I had to have ribbons to match my outfits! I had to have my nails polished and I ran to her for her to fix them if they started to chip. I don't need ribbons to match my outfits anymore, but till this day, I still worry my mom about my hair and I hate chipped nail polish! The statement mentioned by the authors that "During the preschool environment, you readily see gender communication among peer groups" is also true. My grandmother used to run an in-home daycare. She watched all my cousins until they were old enough to go to school, and then there was only me. When my grandmother started watching kids I did not know, I had to try to communicate with them. These kids were Hispanic, Caucasian, Vietnamese, etc. Since I was not old enough to attend school yet, this was my first introduction to diversity. This helped me further develop my speech, language communication skills, and socialization skills. I was taught to say hello and goodbye in different languages. When we would play, the boys would always play trucks and car, while the girls played dress up and played with baby dolls, just as the chapter stated. In conclusion, "culture is learned from birth in the context of family, community, and environment."

A father's love needed no words

by Dwight Davis

"*My father never told me he loved me.*

He never told my brother he loved him, either.

Not ever. Not once. And Dad lived to be 80."

Of course we knew he loved us. He just did not communicate his love through words. Doing so was not a dimension of his social self.

This was never a distressing issue for my brother and me. In retrospect, we only find it odd and a quirky part of his complex multidimensional self. It was not something on which my brother and I dwelled because the narrative of Dad's life was unquestionably one of morality, dedication, unrelenting resolve, and frugality. In the aggregate sum of his various selves, we saw a rather admirable man who was a strict disciplinarian, a good father, neighbor, friend, and loyal husband. He and Mom were married some 50 years and only by death did they part.

I never found that my brother or I ever suffered from anxious or ambivalent **attachment styles**. Attachment styles relate to how parents communicate with their children. A child may form an anxious or ambivalent attachment style when they perceive communication from their parents to be inconsistent. This may result in children who struggle to form relationships as adults. Dad's work habits defined much of who he was to us, his nuclear family, and to others who knew him well. Amazingly as our primary provider, he carved out a comfortable middle-class life for the four of us by working two jobs. Nothing in Dad's life, however, seemed easy. He was a furniture upholsterer and tobacco farmer; one left his fingers aching and bloody, the other his skin burned and his back bruised.

Various aspects of our multidimensional selves sometimes seem to be at odds with one another. For example, Dad mostly held the conventional beliefs of his generation. Yet, he was way ahead of his time in thinking the use of tobacco was harmful to one's health. He proclaimed many times that alcohol never touched his lips, but he was unrepentant about profiting from one of the most-vile plants known to humankind. He was a staunch Democrat, but offered conservative views. He was quiet and outspoken. He believed in his Bible but was often unmerciful with his belt. He had a 10th grade education, yet he was highly intelligent. He was knowledgeable of etiquette, but not refined. A nonsmoker who died of lung cancer, he was a man of incongruities to the end.

He was a ***quintessential son*** of the rural South, yet unique in so many ways. We did not see imperfections in Dad. We saw **idiosyncrasies** or odd habits, many of which we found amusing. During his last days in the hospital and when he was still relatively lucid but not mobile due to an IV in his arm, Dad took a seat on his portable potty when I was visiting. There was a knock at the door and I answered to find three of Dad's friends wanting to visit. I told them Dad would be a minute, but Dad insisted I allow them in. So I did. Dad remained in that position—his hospital gown gaping down his back and barely covering his thighs—for the duration of their visit. None of the three acted as if they found that strange.

Dad was reared in harsh environs; therefore, it is not surprising he became hard-bitten and a bit bitter. His childhood home—a porous clapboard structure perched precariously off the ground on four piles of stones—consisted of only four small rooms. The family had no indoor plumbing, running water, or electricity. The house was heated by a pot-bellied stove and fueled by wood cut from the small farm. It was cooled by whatever breeze stirred through open windows and two screened doors. On many scorching Carolina summer days, I'm told, it was much more pleasant to be under the shade of a tree than in the house.

In the fall of 1930 when Dad was 7-years-old, his mother died in childbirth and left his father with seven children. During that decade, the situation only got worse. They were not only motherless children, but also children of the Great Depression.

I would imagine Dad followed the "tough-love" **identity scripts** of his father, his primary **particular other**, or one who was a close individual who influenced him greatly in his childhood. Identity scripts are figurative life maps or written scripts we follow that our parents communicate as to who we are and who we should be. Evidence of this comes from a story Dad related later in his life. When he was about 16-years-old, Dad stayed home from school one day because he was sick. When his father saw him lying on the floor he said, "If you're not going to school, go out there and cut those logs." He pulled himself together and obliged. There were no sick days in his household.

Most of Dad's life was void of a nurturing other, which likely accounts for his stern nature—one that fashioned his survivalist's mentality.

Those of us who study communication know the self develops over time and is always in a process of change. To some extent, Dad mellowed in his later years. In retirement, he did take some time to enjoy the fruits of his arduous labors.

We once took a trip with Mom and Dad to Grandfather Mountain, the highest point in North Carolina. While perusing items in the gift shop, we noticed Dad was missing. After a brief search, we found him at a summit where he was among a group of young men helping to stabilize a hang-glider for the pilot as strong winds buffeted the craft.

Dad also exhibited a caring nature late in his life. He attended many of his relatives in their last days. He physically cared for an uncle and three of his brothers, just to name four. When his eldest brother became bedridden from Alzheimer's, Dad spoon-fed him for months in the nursing home.

It was not until his passing that my brother and I confirmed that Dad never said he loved either of us. We never thought that was important. We can reflect on the communication model and its **shared field of meaning** or messages that are communicated within a communication model.

We never doubted he loved us. Not ever. Not once.

Discussion questions:

1. Why do you think the author and his brother did not suffer from anxious or ambivalent attachment styles?
2. Why do you think the author saw idiosyncrasies in his father instead of imperfections?
3. How do you think the culture of the era influenced the identity scripts of the author's father?
4. Why does the author say he never doubted his father's love?

Family Communication: Another Interesting Perspective on Group Dynamics

by Regina Williams Davis

© Lorelyn Medina, 2012. Used under license from Shutterstock, Inc.

There are many interesting dynamics that can complicate family communication. I remember how much I dreaded going to the Thanksgiving family dinners and other family celebrations fearful of the "kitchen talk." Who were they going to talk about this time? Why did they judge other family members so much? And if I were not present, would they be talking about me? I know they hate my outfit and I heard them whispering about my hairstyle. Communication in families can be very challenging. However, communication in families resemble the challenges small groups and teams have in their interpersonal dynamics. Nevertheless, good communication skills are essential and critical for positive and fruitful family relationships. I am always disturbed when I hear about someone who has not spoken to their sister or brother in years.

We have all had experiences where we felt disrespected or that we were misunderstood and ignored. These actions hurt family relationships to the extent where family members are wounded for years and sometimes across generations.

Within the immediate family, there are challenges when trying to meet the specific needs and desires for each individual person. It might be trying to make a decision about which movie or channel to watch on television, or whose turn it will be to clean the doghouse. At my home, I am accused of being sexist because I always asked my son to take out the trash. These conflicts arise often and may bring stress into a household. However, there are ways to reduce these kinds of conflicts within a family or any other small group.

Families have to learn to compromise and develop a skill set that will be conducive for positive relationship building. The family leader or the "head-of-household" should create an environment for all opinions to be heard.

All family members should feel valued and take the time to show that they value others by listening and being empathetic. The family leader may encourage suggestions and ideas. They also will attempt to have family ground rules that refrain or eliminate name-calling and other negative behaviors. The entire family unit should be committed to the win/win solution to issues.

Initiating family meetings can be a tradition for decision-making. These types of gatherings allow children and adults to experience how choices affect others on the household. The meeting environment—with stated ground rules—should be in an inviting, respectful setting that promotes an atmosphere of trust.

These strategies for supporting authentic, respectful communication in families strengthen family bonds. And, of course, taking time to have fun and to laugh will undoubtedly advance happy, healthy family relationships outside of the immediate family, as well.

Family Communication and the Influence of Mother Interactions Based on Socioeconomic Class

by Deana Lacy McQuitty

Heath (1983) studied the interactive behaviors of African-American caregivers and their young children from working-class families or lower socio-economic status (SES) families in rural communities in the South. The interactive behaviors included behaviors such as shared reading and responding to story retelling. Farran and Ramsey (1980) provided information on mother-child interactions of 60 children (three to five year olds) from the southeastern region of the United States. Within the participant selection process, all children considered high-risk were African-Americans of low socio-economic status (SES) and the remainder of the sample was middle income status. "High-risk mothers seemed to withdraw from the interactions whereas middle-class mothers interacted more" (254).

A replica of Heath's 1983 study was conducted by Vernon-Feagans (1996). Vernon-Feagans indicated African-American children who were poor had adequate vocabulary and narrative skills compared with middle-class Caucasian children. Their method included a natural environment in which the children participated in storytelling activities. The middle-class children were more likely to relate a story they had been told or to provide more abstract problem-solving skills to discuss events in their lives and make associations, than their African-American counterparts.

Similar findings were identified in study conducted by Farran (1982). She revealed middle-class mothers (White and African-American) were considered the prime communicant for the child. The mothers communicated with their children during routine nurturing activities. They were also the prime caregivers for transmitting cultural norms and linguistic behaviors to their children. Recent writings that involve the cultural interaction styles of families living in the United States supported conclusions drawn from these studies.

Hammer and Weiss (1999) took current research findings a step further and examined the play and interactive behaviors of African-American mothers and their children who were of low and middle SES and living in an urban area in the South. Hammer and Weiss examined 12 African-American mother-infant dyads. Findings revealed varied language goals, expectations, and communication patterns from the two socioeconomic classes. Specifically, interactions between middle-class dyads—dyads representing parent and child interactions—were characterized with numerous language goals when compared with interactions between dyads from the lower SES. For example, the middle-SES mothers verbally initiated play more frequently than low SES mothers. Furthermore, children who vocalized more frequently tended to produce a higher percentage of spontaneous words and phrases, and mothers responded more to their vocalizations.

Scholars reported on the interaction of African-American mothers and their 1-year-old infants. The study focused on "the patterns of mother-infant interaction in African American mother-child dyads and the relationship between those patterns and the development of cognitive and communication skills during the first year of the child's life" (902). The participants included ninety-two 1-year-old African American infants and their mothers.

It is interesting to note that regarding language and culture the following similarities have been revealed:

1. Both groups of mothers engaged in book reading for the same amount of time.
2. Both groups of parents utilized shortened utterances, decreased percentage of different words, and produced similar amounts of nouns and verbs.
3. The children from both groups produced similar proportions of spontaneous and imitated words and phrases.

Differences in behaviors exhibited by the mothers were noted and the behaviors included the following qualities:

1. Mothers of middle SES engaged more frequently in book reading.
2. Mothers of middle SES included more modifiers in their utterances, suggesting more complexity in language use.
3. Mothers of middle SES varied in communicative intentions during videotaped sessions.

Recognizing cultural differences among linguistically different populations, Hammer and Weiss (2000) conducted a study of African-American mothers' views of their infants' language development and environment for learning. The participants consisted of six African-American mothers of low SES and six mothers of middle SES. The investigators wanted a clear understanding of mothers' perspectives of their child's language development and how they structured their child's learning environment. Hammer and Weiss (2000) reported that most mothers from both socioeconomic status groups "believed that children learned to talk by listening to and watching others or by imitating more competent language users" (128). The authors noted two differences between each group of mothers: (a) only one of the low-income mothers discussed discourse strategies and more middle-SES mothers reported a systematic teaching agenda, and (b) all middle-SES mothers discussed verbal and vocalization abilities when discussing their child's current communication system. The authors posited that such information (although the parents interviewed provided a small sample) provided "valuable information for speech-language pathologists regarding differing culturally interaction patterns exhibited when assessing for comprehensive speech and language skills" (140).

Dollaghan et al. (1999) addressed the importance of analyzing maternal education and measuring early speech and language. The researchers believed it was important to focus research efforts to provide additional empirical studies that analyzed environmental and educational factors of the family as a predictor of speech and language acquisition. The scholars selected 241 three-year-old children drawn from a prospective longitudinal study. The children selected for the study had a diverse **socio-demographic** profile and included both African-American and Caucasian participants.

Socio-demographic components consisted of many variables, which included family income, parental education, and racial-ethnic backgrounds. Although Dollaghan et al. (1999) recognized the challenge of independently determining the most critical variables for language development and because of a larger longitudinal study, they were able to examine maternal education as it related to spontaneous language production. Dollaghan et al. (1999) investigated the relationship between maternal educational level and four measures of children's spontaneous speech and language: MLU, number of different words, total number of words, and the percentage of consonants correct and measures on the Peabody Picture Vocabulary Test (PPVT-R).

According to Dollaghan et al. (1999), children whose parents had the most maternal education demonstrated significantly higher mean scores on four measures of spontaneous language production, which included mean length of utterance (MLU), number of different words, and total number of words, as well as on the standardized vocabulary tool. In addition, vocabulary-testing results indicated a significant difference and favored children whose mothers were high school graduates over children whose mothers had not graduated from high school.

Dollaghan et al. (1999) cautioned the use of maternal education as the sole socio-demographic variable to assess speech and language acquisition skills in the present study. Dollaghan et al. further noted, "Both norm referenced and conversational language measures vary across socio-demographic groups and complicate efforts to specify the prevalence of language impairments" (1439). Tomblin, Records, Buckwalter, Zhang, Smith, and O'Brien (1997) further supported the recognition.

Tomblin et al. (1997) acknowledged in an effort to obtain a comprehensive understanding of speech and language acquisition in culturally diverse populations that other socio-demographic variables such as socioeconomic status and ethnicity are associated with quantitative and qualitative differences within conversational discourse and norm-referenced assessment batteries. The claim is critical considering the findings of Rice, Wexler, and Hershberger (1998) who determined that "maternal educational level does not predict rate of growth in acquisition of the grammatical forms by which tense is marked in English" (1413). Therefore, Dollaghan et al. (1999) acknowledged future research must investigate maternal educational level in addition to other socio-demographic factors that affect speech and language acquisition skills. Furthermore, participant selection for future investigations should consist of homogenous ethnic participants that may provide generalization within the culture.

Several research studies have addressed the critical link between socioeconomic status of families (specifically families with low income) and language acquisition skills. Vernon-Feagans, Miccio, Manlove, and Hammer (2001) supported the correlation and examined the link between early language and literacy skills in African-American and Hispanic children whose families had low incomes. However, implications for African-American children were only discussed because they were the focus of the present study. Vernon-Feagans et al. noted the environment in which children live to be a possible cause of their low school performance so this received the greatest attention in the research.

Much of the research focused on the literacy performance of the low-SES African-American children (Snow et al. 1998; Vernon-Feagans 1996). The authors supported the notion that such socio-cultural variables as ethnicity, as well as socioeconomic class, must be considered when determining speech and language acquisition factors during early literacy experiences, which will influence the child once he or she reaches school age.

Prominent scholars have examined storytelling and book-reading skills of Africa-American and Hispanic children as a prerequisite skill in early literacy. Various studies conducted on book reading supported the claim that children representing low-income and culturally-diverse backgrounds are read to less frequently than their White middle-class counterparts (Anderson-Yockel and Haynes 1994; Hammer 2001).

Both low and middle-income African-American children experience book-reading activities with their mothers; however, the interactional style differs. Such differences include African-American mothers producing relatively fewer questions and exhibiting four book-reading styles described as follows: (a) ***modeling-*** the mother labels the pictures in the book and that serves as the model; (b) demonstrating ***different styles for different text-*** with picture books mothers tend to model and with textbooks mothers tend to combine reading with providing their children models; (c) ***reading text from the text;*** and (d) ***limiting periods of joint attention***. As demonstrated in a previous study, African-American mothers tended not to engage in question-asking routines, a style commonly seen in White middle class mothers (Hammer, 2001). The authors contended that socio-cultural variables, such as ethnicity and socioeconomic class, must be considered when determining speech and language acquisition factors during early literacy experiences, which will influence the child once he or she reaches school age.

Ethnographic examinations of families as they interact with young children learning language are important as they examine differences in communication in natural family environments. Scholars posited that each family has its own **cultural norms** of behavior in child rearing which influences the normal development of language regardless of the SES of the family (Anderson and Battle 1993, 2002; Hill 2001).

The use of the language system by African-American children indicated socio-cultural, as well as socioeconomic bases. During the language-learning process, children simultaneously learn the social system of their respective culture. Battle (1996) noted, "The social system refers to concepts such as values, expectations, rules, and regulations of a culture" (29). The interactions provided within the social unit are a critical foundation for language acquisition.

According to Battle (1996), such cultural variables are transmitted within the micro-culture of the mother and child through daily interaction in a variety of situations. The interactions form the basis, and are influential in the quantity and type, of communication patterns children acquire. Many prominent authors (Anderson and Battle 1993, 2002; Battle 1996) posited that future studies should examine how socioeconomic status, parenting styles, and interactions affect African-American children's acquisition of morphological, phonological, and semantic structures over time. In addition, Anderson and Battle 2002; Battle 1996; and Hecht et al. 2003 advocated that additional studies should focus on larger sample sizes, provide studies that are consistent in cultural sample selection, and examine children from varied communities across the United States.

Formation of Initial Communication Patterns: The Emergence of Gender Communication

by Deana Lacy McQuitty

Communication is the essence of human beings as we have learned in Chapter 1. It is the ability to communicate through both nonverbal and verbal communication patterns that sets us apart from any other forms of existence. Communication skills are specifically the ability to understand aspects of both receptive and expressive language skills, which begins earlier than you think. In fact, during an optimal maternal interaction during this period signifies the initial milestone that the mother recognizes the very young child. It is during this momentous occasion that parent interaction and attachment patterns begin. Interestingly, this signal is not only recognized in the Western culture, but similar patterns of maternal attachment styles have been noted in other cultures as well. At this point, mothers begin those early communication styles that may include activities such as recording her voice, the father's voice, or perhaps a sibling and placing headphones across her stomach in an attempt for the young child to hear the voices of caregivers for association.

During this period, mothers have been reported to play classical music to the unborn child in an effort to stimulate brain and neural development. Furthermore, such activities as reading to the unborn child enhance later cognitive development and maturation. It is during the pregnancy period that the idea of our self-scripts and self-concepts begin to emerge. Around 18–19 weeks of the pregnancy, a mother is anticipating knowing the sex of the baby. This becomes a very anticipated and exciting time for the mother and all family members. Once the sex of the unborn child is discovered, **gender communication** develops.

Is It a Girl or Boy?

by Deana Lacy McQuitty

If a mother is told that the sex of her unborn baby is a girl, perhaps she begins to rub her belly and gently whisper: "Hi little girl.", "I wonder how pretty you will be?", or "You will be a doll baby and my little princess." Likewise, dad is experiencing the same gender communication styles by stating "You are going to be daddy's little girl." On the contrary, the views of "You're having a boy." may be communicated to the unborn by statements such as "You are going to play football." or "I wonder if he will be tough?" As early as before birth (or the first trimester of a pregnancy), these gender specific communication clichés are evidenced. As families prepare for the arrival of the infant, provisions are being made to gather gender specific toys, paint the room pink or contemporary colors of aqua and brown for girls and blue and red for boys. These acts signify the early parental contribution to communicating gender differences, thus establishing those societal boundaries. With the arrival of the infant, the gender-specific communication patterns persist, thus contributing and playing a critical role in the formation of the young infant's self-concept and how they view themselves within the world around them.

During the infancy, toddler, and preschool years of a child's life (birth–5 years of age), parents and caregivers are recognized as the primary communication models. The child acquires his/her role in society based upon the communication models that are provided by caregivers, peers, and the media. I often reminisce about the development of my 5-year-old daughter, Camille. I can remember that very early on I dressed her "picture perfect." I would often sing a song to her as early as five months of age that was sung to me as a child. The words were as follows: "Here she is Miss America." I always put dainty bows in her hair, bought her dolls, and called her a princess. She recently celebrated her 5th birthday and was crowned Miss May Day at her childcare center. During both events, I observed her with her friends singing, "Here I am Miss America." Often in my childhood, I laughed at my parents singing this but later realized that those early communication patterns influenced my own gender style (communication) and are shaping my daughter's in the same way.

Likewise, the same gender communication was manifested with my husband and son. As referenced earlier in this chapter, parents tend to relate gender-specific communication patterns to the child. My son is nine years old and plays football with a local recreational tackle football team. This truly delights his father because as I interacted with my daughter, he did the same with our son. He would often go outside with my son as a youngster and play catch, throwing the football to him and saying "One day son I will coach you." Furthermore, Sundays were spent watching football and learning the fundamental principles and rules of the game. Cheering for the Dallas Cowboys was a must!!! So what happened? Once our son was cognizant of the rules and concept of the game, he was eager to play football and has adult-like discussions with his father about the game.

During these gender-specific communication actions, children learn who they are, their preferences, and social acceptable behaviors based upon gender specific routines. Not only do these opportunities offer a positive attachment style between parent and child, they also offer a glimpse into what society views as the norms for gender behaviors.

Self Reflection: As you begin to think about your parents and/or caregivers, what early recollections do you have about the gender-specific messages you received? Do you feel as though these early experiences helped shape who you are today? Why or why not?

Peer Modeling and the Continued Development of Gender Communication

by Deana Lacy McQuitty

Once children reach the preschool period, they not only communicate with their parents and caregivers, but to their peers, as well. Children begin to value the interaction with peers. The experiences with peers continue to foster gender communication dynamics. The early interaction with peers in **structured settings** plays a role in the continued development of the self. Structured settings include environments such as Head Start programs, child development centers, and day care settings. In these settings, the primary premise is for the young child to further develop speech, language communication skills, and socialization skills through formalized instruction and interactions with others.

During interactions with their peers, children reevaluate and reconstruct their understanding of the world in a social manner through collaborative processes with their peers. It is important to remember that children live in a diverse society, which consists of varied social complexities. It is important to recognize that the interaction between peers is different from those with adults because of their egalitarian stature. This concept can be observed in a typical preschool/day care environment. During the preschool environment, you readily see gender communication among peer groups. Such gender communication styles are evidenced in the kitchen center, block center, dress up, and seating arrangements. The young girls tend to engage together in activities that involve "motherly" roles such as the kitchen center, dress up, and baby dolls. You often observe them dressing the babies, feeding, and consoling them. Likewise, you can observe the young boys rough housing with each other, playing in the block center, or playing with trucks and cars. Children's activities are always embedded in a social context and involve children's use of language and interpretive abilities.

Children interpret, organize, use information from the environment, and use the knowledge they gain from these actions to acquire skills and knowledge. The initial foundation that is set by the initial communication partners (parents and caregivers) provides the foundation and/or constructs for these shared contexts. They develop a fundamental social understanding that helps shape their understanding of the cultural values in which they exist.

GENDER COMMUNICATION IS ALSO COMMUNICATED WITH PEER GROUPS IN THE EARLY YEARS OF LIFE.

Key Terms:

Attachment Styles
Cultural Interaction Styles
Frame of References
Identity Scripts
Idiosyncrasies
Joint Attention

Modeling
Multidimensional Selves
Pragmatic Functions
Socio-cultural
Socio-demographic
Socio-economic

Application Activity: *Your Attachment Style*

Identify your attachment style and be prepared to share what it is and why when requested by your instructor.

MINI QUIZ

Essay: Based on your individual family structure, how would you describe the communication dynamics in your childhood home? How have those interactions with your family carried over into your adult interactions?

CHAPTER 11

Romantic Communication

By Marissa Dick

HERE, FIRST COUSINS, AGE 3, AND AGE 2, USE ROMANTIC COMMUNICATION TO GREET ONE ANOTHER THROUGH PHYSICAL TOUCH AND CONFIRM THAT RITUALISTIC ACT BY SHARING QUALITY TIME.

What is Romantic Communication?

What do you think of when you hear the words **Romantic Communication**? Perhaps you think about a significant partner or even passionate utterances you have while being intimate. In actuality, romantic communication can refer to all of those aspects and more. When we speak in terms of romantic communication, we are talking about relationship building and how what we are saying is perceived and received during that dialogue. We are assigning meaning to our emotions.

We can consider the term Romantic Communication as a verb—an action word that involves more doing than being. Romantic communication is closely related to Verbal and Nonverbal Communication. Romantic communication consists of five tenants whose attributes consist of action, such as words of affirmation, quality time, acts of service, receiving gifts, and physical touch. Each of these tenants' help people speak and understand emotional love when it is expressed through verbal communication. Gary Chapman, author of *The Five Love Languages* (2010), argues that words of affirmation, quality time, acts of service, receiving gifts, and physical touch are indeed languages and are enjoyed to some degree by all people. In essence, your love language exemplifies the way you feel most loved and cared for. Further, Chapman (2010) concludes that one of these languages will be more dominant than the others for each person.

Keep in mind that there are well over three thousand languages and dialects that are in use in the world today. This means that interpretation and concepts of any given word can vary from culture to culture. Because words are often manipulated from generation to generation and from culture to culture, they do not have meaning of their own; instead, people assign meaning to a particular word as it relates to their cultural perspective. It is incumbent upon the receiver of the communication to seek clarity. For example, a teenager may use the word "wifey" while speaking to a peer. In this definition of "wifey" the teenager is actually meaning "girlfriend." A grandparent overhearing the conversation may interpret the meaning of "wifey" as a female spouse or wife. Clearly, in this instance, there is a distinct difference of generational communication, even within the same familial space and community.

In essence, *The Five Love Languages* are incorporated into our daily conversations with our family, friends, and within our community. Based on two key life experiences, I have concluded that my dominant form of communication is Physical Touch while Acts of Service and Words of Affirmation come in a very close second.

Two Key Life Experiences

After realizing my romantic communication form, I began to reflect upon my daily interaction with people. When teaching, my main focus is to create a holistic learning environment so my students can feel comfortable and learn the lesson plan that I have prepared for the day. According to Richmond (2002), "The role of the teacher in educational systems is to create learning environments in which the probability of the desired achievements is enhanced" (65). This is what I thought I was doing, creating a learning environment where students could gain knowledge and apply that knowledge to their lives and enhance their community. Unknowingly, what I was actually doing was gaining some students' trust with immediacy (creating an environment of closeness) while losing creditability with others who probably needed my immediacy the most.

I have come to realize that there are just some students that I have a natural chemistry with and speaking with them is as easy as talking to my nieces or nephews, while others share my immediacy because they exhibit a strong academic attitude. Also, I tend to interact less with those students who do not engage in class or display an unattractive attitude toward education. Mehrabian (1971) says, "People are drawn toward persons and things they like, evaluate highly, and prefer; they avoid or move away from things they dislike, evaluate negatively, or do not prefer (66). Nonetheless, as a teacher, I must find a way to deal with all of the students who enter my classroom.

I believe the primary function of teachers is to improve classroom engagement and discover ways of disseminating the subject matter so that the student desires to learn more. Effective classroom communication reinforces effective teacher-student relationships. Cheseboro (2002) describes immediacy as "the degree of perceived physical or psychological closeness between people" (68). I have long known that I do not like to be touched by people that I do not have a relationship with. So if I feel this particular way, then I incorrectly assumed that other people or in this instance, a student, would feel the same. I have some students who may see me outside of the classroom and they will run over and embrace me and I willingly respond to their affectionate enthusiasm. Yet these are the students who I have chemistry with. For certain, I am not quite sure if it is morally appropriate to touch a person let alone a student that I have not developed a relationship with; therefore, most often I will take a posture of disassociation and choose not to embrace. Ambady and Rosenthal (1992) suggest that, "teachers should be made aware of the possible impact of their nonverbal behavior and perhaps even trained in nonverbal skills" (69). I am probably one of these teachers who should have attended one of these seminars because I absolutely do not like to be touched by those with whom I do not have a relationship.

KEY LIFE EXPERIENCE 1: Physical Touch: A Teacher/Student Perspective

A couple of years ago I designed and taught a course for students who had been placed on academic probation due to unsatisfactory classroom performance. In this class, I had a student who routinely entered my classroom late, would leave my class to answer her telephone, and would text in my class. When called upon during discussion, she would not engage and would actually give me a look as though I was wrong for expecting her to participate in class. Her attitude was less than inviting; therefore, I did not want to address her openly because I believed that conversation would not lead to a positive experience. I gave great consideration to Richmond (2002) when describing the decrease in nonverbal immediacy. She describes it as,

> Verbal immediacy decreases the likelihood of a positive relationship. Therefore, if you have not built any affinity or liking and you use verbal avoidance statements, then you have distanced yourself from

the other person and virtually guaranteed that there will be no significant relationship or the relationship that exists may be a negative one (68).

This is exactly what I did not want to happen; however, I also knew that I had to say something because I was not going to allow her actions to change my behavior or dictate my classroom.

In preparation for mid-term exams, I gave my students the option of taking an exam, performing a presentation, or writing a three-page paper on why they were on academic probation and what measures they had in place to improve their academic success. To my surprise, this particular student chose to present a skit on how she ended up on academic probation. I found that interesting because she did not engage in class so I was really curious to see what her skit entailed. As fate would have it, she did not show up for the mid-term exam nor did she contact me to let me know that she would not be present. The following week she came to my office with a paper and an attitude. I invited her in, offered her a seat, and then proceeded to inquire about her missed presentation. She explained that she relied upon her roommate for transportation to campus and the car was not working on the day of her presentation. I nodded with understanding and then asked why she did not follow protocol by calling or e-mailing me regarding her non-attendance. Furthermore, she came one week later. She immediately became defensive, stood up from her seat, and shouted at me that it wasn't her fault that she couldn't come for her mid-term presentation. I was non-responsive to her behavior. Richmond (2002) advises that, "Clearly we would like to avoid the person who wants to use physical violence or be verbally hostile or aggressive with us" (67). Calmly, I pushed away from my desk, out of her reach, and asked her to lower her voice and sit back down. I knew it would be futile to feed into her behavior as I felt my own "pressure rising." Instead of acting on my feelings, which was to treat her as though I had given birth to her and shake some sense into her; instead, I instructed myself to remain calm and find a way to gently calm her down. I remember Richmond (2002) saying, "One of the most important ways of increasing immediacy in a relationship is sending verbal messages that encourage the other person to communicate." Such comments as ". . . This is a team effort." and "Let's talk more about this." creates increased **immediacy**.

I inhaled deeply and reminded myself to be aware of my own posture and tone. I fixed my face so it would not be distorted. Instead of transgressing to attack her with a verbal assault, I simply asked her if she felt better now that she had released her frustration. I invited her to sit back down again and reminded her first that it was not my fault that her roommate's car was not working; second, I reminded her that she did not communicate with me regarding her absence; and finally, I reminded her that she was bringing me a paper that had not been approved one week after mid-term presentations were due. I also told her that I did not appreciate her tone and posture toward me and that she was being extremely disrespectful and I was not going to tolerate her behavior.

After my little soliloquy, she plopped down in the chair and began to cry. I offered her some facial tissue and gave her time to gather her emotions. I asked if she was okay and she said, "No ma'am." Excuse me, but did she say, "No ma'am"? She began apologizing for her behavior and acknowledged that she had not been the best student. The problem was that she was ashamed to be on academic probation. Furthermore, she had not divulged this information to her parents and she believed that her peers would perceive her as being "dumb." As a matter of fact, her exact words were: "I just don't like being in this class. I'm not dumb. I shouldn't be in this class." OMG, the first sign of intelligent engagement! Mottet and Richmond (1998) have shown that "In relationship development, working with verbally immediate or approach-oriented communication strategies are a much more powerful communication tool in relationship formation than avoidance or verbally none-immediate communication strategies" (68). I cannot explain how happy I was that this incident happened. It was in this space that I was able to gain an understanding of how she perceived herself academically, as well as, appreciate her emotional condition. Because of this exchange I was able to toss my inaccurate judgments about this student out of the window. Ambady and Rosenthal (1995) also reminded me "impression formation takes place very early in a relationship" (69).

While she was in my office, we engaged in productive dialogue. I explained more about the course and advised her not to see it as punitive, but to know that the course was actually designed to help her put positive academic behavior measures in place so she could be successful. We also roll-played the conversation she would have with her parents informing them of her current grades. Due to her low grade point average, her financial aid was definitely going to be affected and her parents needed to know so they could have the opportunity to put other financial measures in place for the following semester. While having this dialogue, we laughed and built a student-teacher relationship. I actually retrieved a record of her grades and saw that she graduated high school an honor student. She apparently had allowed her new social life to influence her academic life. In reviewing her grades, I used "Words of Affirmation" for her prior academic success and that made all the difference in the world for her. It was at this moment when she shyly stated she thought I did not like her because ***I did not touch her*** like I touched some of the other students. Okay, wait a minute, hold up! This student was actually watching me to see how I responded toward the other students. She was looking for acceptance from me through Romantic Communication—Physical Touch. As previously stated, I know that I have some touch-avoidance anxieties and I am still working on those issues. Since we were in a safe and productive holistic milieu, I was honest with her and explained that her negative attitude caused me to be reluctant to embrace her. Gorham (1988) explained that "Touch is a form of communication that can be very useful in establishing and maintaining an effective teacher-student relationship" (74). I was glad that she understood. After our dialogue, I accepted her paper and before she left my office we genuinely embraced one another.

When she came back to class, she held true to her word and was engaging. I watched her participate with her group. I even heard a member in her group say jokingly, "Auh, who are you?" The group was silent for a second, but when she laughed they joined her. She actually apologized to her group members for not participating earlier in the semester. They accepted her apology. When I walked by her, I laid my hand on her shoulder as I did all of the students in her group, hoping to reassure them with Romantic Communication—Physical Touch that they were on the right track.

As a teacher, I asked myself why I didn't incorporate the five love languages inside of my classroom. For the remainder of the semester, I watched this student blossom in my class and even today she comes to visit me with open arms. I greet her with a big hug and a genuine smile because she could have been the one that got away from me. She is off of academic probation and is performing well academically in her major. She could have been lost in the academic cesspool of students who feel as though education is not for them when, in fact, all they need is Romantic Communication. I thank God that I did not allow my own behavior or social misgivings to dictate my treatment of this student. I am so glad that I was able to critically reflect about the scholars that I have studied and implement their theories. For that reason, I was made aware that students want and need Romantic Communication from their teachers. Furthermore, I have had to face and come to terms with my own touch issues. By incorporating Physical Touch and Words of Affirmation as a part of my curriculum, I have been able to enhance the lives of my students by making them feel a part of me.

There is an element of Romantic Communication that involves marriage and/or relationships. Thus, I will provide yet another personal testimony from the standpoint of Acts of Service. Keep in mind that Acts of Service denote a service, which is performed without any expectation of result or reward for the person performing it. I would like for you to think about your own relationships where you seem to be the one constantly giving. Here I will discuss how often married women or women in relationships adopt a prescribed social-gendered role. Over time, Acts of Service can be taken for granted and if not carefully monitored, they can lead to an oppressive marriage or relationship as described below.

KEY LIFE EXPERIENCE 2: Acts of Service – A Divorced Woman's Perspective

The Dream . . . I remember walking down the aisle in a beautiful white wedding gown and smiling with pride behind a sheer white veil. While I was walking, I tried to concentrate on my short rehearsed strides to the rhythm of the music, *Here Comes The Bride*, but I was distracted. I could not help but notice that the moaning and groaning was penetrating the harmonious melody. I remember looking to my right and wondered where my father had gone. I could not believe that he was not at my side walking me down the aisle. When I was midway down the aisle, I could see the water coming from the sides of the pews. I quickened my pace because it seemed as though the water was chasing me. I tried to lift my wedding gown to protect it from getting wet, but it felt like lead. Panic struck me and my pace hastened toward the altar. The closer I got, the more the water began to rise and the moaning intensified. Right when I reached the altar, a well-groomed hand extended and I grabbed for it right before the water rose above my head. . . . I had this dream every night for two weeks before I actually got married. Additionally, I was fitted for my wedding gown twice and each time I put the gown on my body, I had to literally take it off in haste and race to the bathroom to empty my stomach and my bowels. I remember clearly hearing the Hispanic seamstress stating to me with a thick rich accent, "Mommy, are chu sure chu need to do this? Que? Every time chu put this on chu get sick. Maybe this is a sign chu no need to do this. Eh, Mommy?"

Five years after I said "I do", I was in the bathroom combing my hair when I realized that I saw a stranger staring at me in the mirror. I remember leaning forward to inspect the image somewhat hesitantly. That reflection couldn't be me. The person I was looking at didn't possess signs of life. There was no smile where one used to be. Instead, there was a nervous twitch. Instead of the once sparkle in my eye, I was actually using makeup to hide the minor bruise from where I had been slapped to the hardwood floor the night before for disagreeing with my ex-husband in front of our company. I believe the only reason I stopped long enough to even notice this stranger was because I couldn't do anything with my hair. I was so frustrated because I was running late for work and my hair would not cooperate with me. Where my hair was once shoulder length and thick, it was now broken off and thinned. As I combed my hair, I could actually see it falling into the bathroom sink with every stroke. "Who *is* that woman?" I asked myself. "I know that's not me! It can't be me!" I don't know how long I cried. All I know is that I did. I also know that I asked God to forgive me for being disobedient. He told me not to marry my ex-husband. God warned me with the dreams and the wedding dress. I had no clue until I heard myself moaning and groaning on the black and white checkered bathroom tile floor that those disturbing sounds in my dreams actually belonged to me. The water rising above my head drowning me was a representation of the river of tears that I would cry the majority of my marriage.

According to society, a **marriage** is a union between a man and woman who promise to love and cleave to one another until death do them part. In a physically abusive marriage, it's the *"until death do them part"* that becomes more realistic than they know that leads marriages toward divorce. Initially when a man and woman enter into holy matrimony, it is because the relationship is harmonious and love flows fluidly between the individuals. Often, relationships operate at their best before these vows are established. It was my experience that once the marriage vows were stated and the license came in the mail, my marriage took a turn for the worse. My ex-husband felt as though he owned me. I remember being in shock when he literally shook the license in my face claiming, "You're mine now!" as though I was his property. I remember feeling the bottom fall out of my stomach as I watched him walk away. My sister held me tightly in her arms as though she were protecting me, assuring me that everything would be all right, but that could not have been further from the truth—everything was not "all right."

In retrospect, I realize that I married into the myth of marriage. You know—believing in a widely held fictitious story in spite of the overwhelming evidence that it is not true. In the beginning of my marriage, it was my assumption that I had married my knight in shining armor. I had mistakenly thought that I would live happily ever after in a loving and non-threatening relationship because this is what society described, this is what my family portrayed, and this is what I wanted to believe. In wanting or needing to believe that I could indeed attain the house with the white picket fence, I ascribed to the social roles that society had subliminally implanted into my thought process. The man was supposed to be the provider and protector and the woman was supposed to be the nurturer and caretaker of the home. Though I had a full-time job, I was somewhat confused and bewildered as to why my ex-husband was unable to remain employed or obtain employment on a regular basis.

His inability to maintain employment played a profound role on my mental and physical well-being. Initially, I took it upon myself to help him find employment, but somehow it became my responsibility to seek out and find him employment by combing through the job listing section in the daily newspaper. Whenever I found an advertisement that seemed appropriate for him I would contact the employer, set up the actual interview, and give him the information. As Stephanie Coontz (2005) points out in her new book, *Marriage, a History: From Obedience to Intimacy*, achieving equity in marriage is less a problem for couples and more from policies in a society where traditional roles are valued. She writes,

> The big problem doesn't lie in differences between what men and women want out of life and love. The big problem is how hard it is to achieve equal relationships in a society whose work policies, school schedules, and social programs were constructed on the assumptions that male breadwinner families would always be the norm. Tensions between men and women today stem less from different aspirations than from the difficulties they face translating their ideals into practice.

Society had not hinted to nor prepared me for playing the social triple role of mother/wife/provider.

While growing up, the ethos in my home was that my father worked and performed the majority of the "household chores" (in particular, cooking). He did all this while my mother worked and practiced the art of being a professional student. My father never once attempted to oppress any desires she had. In fact, he went out of his way to support her, especially when it came to her education. My mother has three undergraduate degrees and she's back in school yet again because she's addicted to academia. I expected my ex-husband to help me around the house especially when he was not working. I also expected him to cook since he was certainly a much better cook than me. I expected him to take control of the kitchen just as my father had. My mother's father even dominated in the kitchen so it was practical for me to assume that my ex-husband would do the same. Additionally, he appeared to enjoy cooking; however, it never once occurred to me that the only time he would lift a finger to cook would be when we had company so he could receive all of the accolades. I expected him to support me when I wanted to return to school just as I had witnessed my father do so many times for my mother, but my ex-husband refused.

After being married for a few years, my ex-husband and I had developed two different ideologies regarding marriage. For him, "Marriage is a quintessentially gendered institution embodying expectations of male dominance and female subservience" (Hill 2006). For me, "Dear God, please forgive me for being disobedient" (Dick 2009). It was not until we were arguing one day that out of anger he screamed, "You want to be smarter than me!" did I understand why he would tear my books apart or toss them down the incinerator. In his opinion, we were equally educated because we both had two years of college. For me to surpass him in education would make us inequitable academically. The inequality in labor was often more than I could handle as I worked long hours. After working nine or ten hours as an engineering secretary at a major insurance company, I would come home and start working all over again. My second job as housekeeper, cook, entertainer, and mistress began as soon as I crossed the threshold of our apartment. I welcomed his yawn because I knew then I would finally be able to lie down and go to sleep.

When payday came I brought my money home for distribution. After the bills were paid we would split what was left. More often than not I would still have to split my half with him because he would lavish my hard earned money on his friends, which left him with no money to go job hunting or to purchase his personal vices. I was not allowed to make decisions about purchasing anything for our home or myself. I never did understand why I was not allowed to spend the money I earned. All I knew was that doing so was not worth the altercation that followed. Every now and then I would risk buying myself a new dress or a new pair of shoes only to lie and tell him my mother bought it for me to keep an argument from ensuing.

These role attitudes were so hard for me to prescribe to when I saw my parents share so much in their marriage. There were no designated gender roles in our family; however, my ex-husband had the notion that he was entitled to power just because he was the man,

> Men hold power in the outside world, and women hold power in the home, and are primarily responsible for the home and its work. . . . Men, responsible for financial support of the family, develop the more valued resources of earning power and prestige; this power, combined with their traditional patriarchal position of final authority, allow them exemption from many of the responsibilities of the day-to-day maintenance of family and home (Scanzoni, 73).

Because I mistakenly thought my marriage was constructed on traditional Christian values and ideologies, I believed that I should have some governing power somewhere. I did not want to feel as though I was merely a legal whore (wife), who brought her money home to her legal pimp (husband),

> While deference to the husband on many of the aforementioned issues might seem like just compensation for his financial contribution, it only serves to underscore the injustice women suffer in performing the bulk of unpaid labor in the family. The compromise arrived at means men contribute paid labor and women contribute the bulk of unpaid labor. One gender, by virtue of the social value attached to his contribution, is squarely in charge. Furthermore, in many instances the husband's exercise of power does not end at relatively innocuous decisions such as whether or not to buy a new television, or where the family will go on vacation. Many husbands are able to use their power as wage earners to abuse their wives or commit infidelity with impunity. Because dissolution of the marriage creates the most significant vulnerability for women, it is often enough for a husband to threaten to leave in order to perpetrate any number of abuses against his wife (Scanzoni, 73).

My father always told me that it took more than a man having a "third leg" swinging between his legs to qualify as a man. I never understood the significance of that statement until I married. I understood the family structure—based on what I saw in my childhood home—as a nurturing balance of power, not as an oppressive authoritative union.

After my divorce, I was able to return to school and submerse myself (like a salve) in its healing walls of knowledge, in particular, regarding Romantic Communication. Discovering that there is actual terminology related to my experiences is refreshing. I feel less alone. Instead, I feel as though I can be realistically tangible in my Words of Affirmation, Quality Time, Receiving Gifts, Acts of

Giving, and Physical Touch as I have experienced all of the five love languages in multiple and competing ways that have impacted me both positively and negatively. Education brought me out of an allegoric way of thinking. When I walked out of that cave, where I lived and viewed life through shadows, I was gently awakened to a new lens on life. Education gave my prior existence meaning. It was through education that I learned about Romantic Communication and was able to place it appropriately in my life. After my divorce, I had to constantly speak Words of Affirmation to myself to increase my self-esteem. For the first time in years, I was able to spend Quality Time on myself to nourish my body, mind, heart, and spirit. As weird as it may sound, I had learned to Receive Gifts from myself when for so long I was not allowed to shower myself with my most basic desires. In return, I was able to provide Acts of Giving to my loved ones without having to sneak and purchase them for fear of my pay check coming up short and having to provide an explanation of where the money had gone. And last but not least, I allowed myself Physical Touch from a man because I had to reassure myself that all men don't beat and intimidate.

Romantic Communication

I love studying interpersonal communication because of the unique twists that come when you put a male and a female together. Not only do you have to deal with the individual idiosyncrasies of each person, but you also have to deal with two different modes of relating and interpreting. I like to use the following scenario in my classes as I talk about the communication process and gender. To set the stage, the couple has been together long enough for HER to discover something that looks like a problem. She decides to talk to HIM about this "problem." The interaction goes something like this:

HER: I'd like to talk to you about something.

HIM: Okay.

HER: Well, I've noticed something that really bothers me.

(She pauses waiting for him to say something, but he just continues to look at her. She continues.)

Well, it just seems like I'm more concerned about the relationship than you are.

HIM: Why do you say that?

HER: Well, like now you don't seem to be bothered by the fact that something is bothering me. Why aren't you more upset? Or is it that you just don't care?

HIM: No, it's not that I don't care. I just don't see the use of getting all upset.

HER: See, that's exactly what I'm talking about. You don't care. If you cared, you would be upset. Since you aren't upset, then you must not care. So why am I wasting my time with someone who doesn't care about my feelings or our relationship?

(He begins to say something, but she stops him by holding her hand up like a traffic cop to stop him in his tracks.)

No, don't bother answering that question. It doesn't even matter any more. I bet I won't waste any more of my time.

Does this interaction sound familiar to any of you? If it doesn't, then you might be saying to yourself that the dialogue described would only happen with a woman who was a little bit off. Some of you women may be offended because you are saying to yourself that you would never act like that and that it is stereotyping women. I understand both responses, but let me share something with you. As a woman who has had the opportunity to interact with a lot of women of different races, religious backgrounds, and socioeconomic statuses, I have concluded that any of us can "go there" in the right situation. It doesn't mean that you are crazy. It just means that sometimes our logic can be illogical. Reading the previous scenario may have made you see the irrationality of HER responses, but can you see it when you are HER. I had a chance to be HER even as I was writing this chapter.

I became HER when I asked my husband if the interaction sounded real, to which he answered yes. I proceeded to ask him if he had ever had an interaction similar to the one I described, to which he promptly responded, "Yeah, with you." Of course, this answer rubbed me the wrong way. So I had to ask him if I was the only woman he'd had this type of interaction with because in my mind his response seemed to imply that there was something wrong with me. His response was "No, but if I had said yeah, with so and so, and so and so, and so and so, then you would have been upset." Needless to say, I had to laugh because he continued to point out just how real such an interaction is and how easily you can find yourself "going there."

I am a communication scholar with expertise in interpersonal communication. I am not crazy (although I will admit that there have been times that I have engaged in what even I would consider extremely irrational behavior in the name of love). Yet, I found myself responding to things my husband said in much the same way as HER in the example. Why would that be the case? Let's examine some of the factors that influence how we communicate and how we interpret the messages of others.

Research on interpersonal communication is extensive. However, much of this research does not include nor consider people of color. Duncan and colleagues (1998) embarked on a major study of interpersonal variables in African American, European American, and interracial relationships. For a more detailed discussion, see *Towards Achieving Maat: Communication Patterns in African American, European American, and Interracial Relationships* published by Kendall-Hunt. In a summary, Duncan and colleagues discovered that many of the traditional research findings did not hold up when African American relationships were included and considered. For example, the combination of race and gender combined affected the use of several communication variables and the intersection of the two. Although communication competence was positively related to interpersonal solidarity or intimacy for European Americans and African Americans, the relationship was stronger for African Americans. African Americans who perceived themselves to be more competent communicators reported higher levels of intimacy in their relationships.

In this book, differences were also reported on self-disclosure with African American males reporting less positive self-disclosure and less honest self-disclosure than European American males and females and African American females. Additionally, European Americans reported greater amounts of self-disclosure than African Americans. Why might that be the case? What societal factors might affect African American self- disclosure? These trends suggest that race and gender have a greater impact on some aspects of communication than others, but the assumption that there is no impact and no difference should not be made automatically.

Think about your relationships. Has your self-disclosure been positive and honest? How much do you disclose in romantic relationships? Do you disclose more in friendships than you do in romantic relationships? Why or why not? Does it make you feel vulnerable? Does it depend on how much power the other person has in the relationship? There are many factors that can influence whether or not we disclose information to others, allow ourselves to become intimate, and the role our communication competence plays in it all. However, the bottom line is that romantic interaction, like all of the other types of communication, requires that we work on being effective.

Diversity in Romantic Communication

by Jasmine Blue

Communication is a two-way process of reaching a mutual understanding, where participants exchange information, ideas, and feelings. Communication can be shown in different forms such as romantic communication. Romantic communication refers to communication between you and a significant other in terms of relationship building. This form of communication assigns meaning to our emotions. The words we say, the sentences we use, and the tone connected to those phrases play a part in how we communicate romantically. I consider myself a sucker for love. Communicating romantically is a big part of my love life. We must be susceptible to express our love by using verbal, nonverbal, and written communication. I find that expressing your feelings and emotions help build a foundation for communicating openly when one is feeling vulnerable, angry, sad, jovial, and more. Not all romantic communication will be constructive. There are times when we will find ourselves in disagreement with our significant other that's why effective communication is essential in romantic relationships. Disagreements give us a chance to come back to our focus point of expressing ourselves in romantic ways. If I am feeling some type of way, I will communicate those feelings with my significant other to correct those actions or prevent those actions from reoccurring. I find it easier to address those feelings at the time of the dilemma. Romantic communication finds its way to resurface which allows the couple to return to their romantic state. Setting up dates, leaving love notes, writing love letters, send or receive gifts, and a distinctive touch could be a romantic sign of communicating without verbal use. These gestures show appreciation of your partner and set the atmosphere to be willing and open to romance. Both partners may not be from the same ethnic group or background. Communicating romantically has different interpretations and concepts from culture to culture. Depending on your significant others background, words have different means and they may be perceived diversely.

Every generation possess diverse ways to communicate romantically. I am "old school" when it comes to levels of communicating. Texting is a fashionable way of communicating for the younger generation, whereas, being an older adult I prefer to communicate face to face. The younger generation is comfortable with expressing themselves romantically via-text. It's a difference in technology and generational curse. Showing up at a woman's house to request permission to her parents and herself was a way of being romantic. It showed respect and showed interest in the woman. I have male's friends who discuss their romantic lives with myself. I attempt to take them back when romance was real and alive.

Key Terms:

Acts of Service

Affirmation

Cross-Sex Relationships

Immediacy

Intimacy

Marriage

Physical Touch

Quality Time

Romantic Communication

Receiving Gifts

The Five Love Languages

Application Activity: *Love Language*

Determine your own love language by accessing the online link below and completing the one question assessment. Upon completion, you will be able to determine the love language with which you associate. **http://www.5lovelanguages.com/assessments/30-second-quizzes/love/**

MINI QUIZ

1. True or False: Romantic communication is best defined as a noun.
2. Multiple Choice: This form of love language is the transfer of something without the expectation of payment.
   A. Acts of service
   B. Physical touch
   C. Receiving gifts
   D. Words of affirmation
3. Fill in the Blank: Individuals in relationships characterize _____ friendships with the opposite sex. These relationships may be platonic or sexual.
4. Essay: Briefly explain how romantic communication is not limited to those engaged in sexual relationships.

CHAPTER 12

Intimate Partner Violence

by Ingram Land-Deans

© Lightspring, 2012. Used under license from Shutterstock, Inc.

Photo courtesy of Javon Robinson

"*Let communication guide every life-changing decision. Observe every "action" with a critical eye, listen to every "word" with a critical ear, analyze meticulously the intention behind the "hand-shake," "hug," "kiss," and "undertone." For these non-verbal and verbal clues will uncover the true personality of your prospective interest and/or future mate. And when it is revealed . . . BELIEVE IT . . . and use it as a compass to determine whether or not this "prospect" is best for you. Approaching dating in this way, will safeguard your future, preserve your mental and physical wellness, and even perhaps . . . save your life*" (original quote by the author, Ingram Land-Deans).*

Every semester, I open with this advice as I prepare to discuss "Relational Communication" with my students. Having personally experienced an abusive relationship; sadly, I am well familiar with the life-altering consequences that can result. In my case, ignoring "red flags" during the honeymoon stage of dating, progressed to verbal abuse that led to the death of my self-confidence and the abrupt end to a promising educational opportunity.

Verbal intimidation diminished a leading lady to a follower. For example, I caved into someone else's beliefs and philosophies, instead of standing my own ground. I often second-guessed myself, instead of respecting my intellect and trusting my intuition. "Name calling and character assassination," transformed the "DIVA" (fondly described by friends) into a depressed individual, who no longer embraced her uniqueness. As a result of the verbal blows, I lost interest in nurturing my appearance and gained excessive weight that disfigured my image (see Figure 12.1). Domination and control reduced a happy, vibrant, social butterfly to a bitter, resentful, angry loner. And lastly, manipulation canceled my faith and confidence in people and robbed an educational opportunity that would have offered career advancement. Shamefully, during that period of my life . . . "I lost my soul" . . . to verbal abuse.

Photo courtesy of Javon Robinson

Photo courtesy of Javon Robinson

FIGURE 12.1   Left picture shows the affects of IPV compared to right picture, recovery from IPV.

But years later, after graced with time to heal, forgive, learn, and re-build from this traumatic experience (as God worked through my family, friends, and church family to comfort and support me through this crisis), I got my "happy" back and am now motivated to take action against "abuse." Although a painful and embarrassing memory, it is the benefit of this experience that has motivated the writing of this chapter. I refuse to allow this "bully" to punk anyone else! By empowering my readers with knowledge, understanding, and advice, I believe this will enable wise selections in future dating or romantic partners, thus preventing the spread of Intimate Partner Violence (IPV).

To develop understanding, I will define IPV and give examples of the associated types of abuse. Next, I will develop awareness of the seriousness of IPV by reporting the incidence and identifying the cultures most affected. Following this discussion, I will reveal the health and emotional effects that result from IPV. Then, I will uncover "red flags" to observe and will suggest "safe" dating approaches. Lastly, I will conclude with a summary and will provide help-group information for students currently undergoing IPV. And throughout the chapter, my students from past and current

Speech Fundamentals classes and victims of IPV will share inspirational stories. So now we have our road map, as I say in my classes, five, four, three, two, one . . . let's launch our discussion!

Photo courtesy of Javon Robinson

WHAT IS INTIMATE PARTNER VIOLENCE?

Intimate Partner Violence is the cruel act of controlling and demeaning a current or ex-romantic partner or spouse (Humphreys and Campbell 2004). The abuser executes these actions strategically through unpredictable patterns of **physical, verbal, and/or sexual abuse** (Kwako et al. 2011; Tjaden and Thoennes 2000). **Physical assaults**—defined as purposeful physical force against the victim— typically involve hitting, pushing, shoving, slapping, and kicking, etc. Batteries such as these can cause injury, disability, or death to victims (Kennard 2007). **Verbal or "word" aggression** consists of, but is not limited to, threats, manipulative tactics, and belittling. These malicious attacks intend to humiliate and shame victims (Kennard 2007). Lastly, **sexual abuse**—defined as forcing the victim to engage in sex against their will—intended to destroy the victim's self-confidence and worth (Kennard 2007). Based on these descriptions, it is interesting how abusers—also known as persons with low-esteem (Kennard 2007)—work strategically hard to inflict misery on their victims to cause them to feel the same and to suffer more.

Photo courtesy of Javon Robinson

IS IPV REALLY THAT SERIOUS?

Prevalence:

Numerous studies describe IPV as a "national epidemic" in the United States. Approximately 1,200 deaths and 2 million injuries are reported each year among women and nearly 600,000 injuries per year among young men (Tjaden and Thoennes, 2000). Additionally, a study that examined the prevalence of physical assault in dating partner relationships on 31 college universities reported the incidence of physical assault ranged from 17% to 45% (Straus, 2004). Based on these findings, IPV does not appear to be an isolated, random event. The incidence is high, rapidly spreading, and infecting a range of dating cultures like a "virus."

Which Cultures Does It Affect?

IPV does not discriminate. Studies show IPV crosses a range of ages, races, ethnicities, genders, and classes (Woods 2009) and also exists in same-sex relationships (Breiding, Black, and Ryan 2008). However, the cultures with the highest IPV incidence are adolescents, young adults, and women (Halpern et al. 2001; Sorenson, Upchurch, and Shen 1996; Straus 2004).

YOUR WORDS

— J. J. —

Being with him, I thought I was finally in love with someone who loved me also. He was bold at first, flirting with me in public with his friends. Then, coming to see and spend the night with me as a lover. I thought things were going in the right direction until he spoke badly about me. His words of hatred haunted me, made me feel less of a person at the time, but then he would say kind words for the moment. Going from extremes of "mean to kind, then kind to mean" confused and made me miserable, not to mention it hurt. I begin to feel the man I fell in love with didn't love me but loved the things I did for him. After I broke up with him, I didn't want to see him. Flashes of misery would come again. So then I started back at square one with his words of before, "Hello, what is your name?"

In a study conducted by Halpern et al. (2001) that examined IPV prevalence in adolescents and young adults, some rather surprising findings were revealed. Researchers found that out of 7,500 adolescents, IPV not only existed in 16- to 18-year-old romantic relationships, but also in teen heterogeneous relationships as young as 12 to 14 years old, although not quite as high. This simply was amazing to learn. Despite the lower incidence, who would have thought that psychological (verbal abuse) and physical violence (although minor) would have ever existed at such a young tender age known as "puppy love."

SO WHY IS IPV HIGH IN ADOLESCENCE?

Halpern et al. (2001) addresses this concern by suggesting the influence of violent single or married family structures. Furthermore, Osofsky (1995) suggests that living in a "chronically violent" community or environment influences children, as well as, child abuse at an early age (782).

The actions of parents, influential adults, and people in the community teach children how to problem solve. In some cases, unfortunately, adult models can send the wrong message. According to Halpern et al. (2001), children who live with one or two biological parents and witness a spouse or boyfriend or girlfriend physically or verbally assaulting their mother or father are likely to repeat this cycle as they grow up and become involved in relationships. Osofsky (1995) agrees, but from the perspective that "violent" communities influence IPV. He suggests that children who grow up in and are exposed to "gunfire, fighting in their neighborhoods" are also likely to show this "ripple effect" (782). Chris Brown, a popular musical icon, is an example of this philosophy. Witnessing abuse against his mother and despite his earnest intentions not to repeat this cycle, IPV erupted in his relationship with the love of his life, Rihanna. "Donna" also agrees with this philosophy. She shares her experience in the story entitled "My Journey."

MY JOURNEY

— DONNA —

My name is Donna. I am a 39-year-old female. My abuse began as a child. Both parents came from abusive homes. Therefore, I became a victim as well. My father left my mother when I was 10 months old. I have seen him no more then 10 times my entire life. I have always searched for the love I should have received from him. By the age of two, my mother had remarried. At the age of three, sexual abuse began for me. It started with a Head Start worker. I was there until the age of five. From there a family friend began sexually abusing me until the age of 10–11. By the age of 12, I became involved with a 16-year-old boy and was introduced to drugs and alcohol. At the age of 13, I began dating an 18-year-old boy. By age 14, I was pregnant. I had my first child at the age of 15. After the birth of my son, it became evident my mother hated me. She had always been physically, mentally, and verbally abusive. She would tell me I was a whore and I was worthless. She had said for years I was the reason my father left her. She told me he never wanted me. Close to my 16th birthday, my mother beat me so severely I decided to leave. My son watched that last beating I received. He stood in the hallway as my mother broke a wooden broom over my back. When I left, I did not take my son. I felt as if I was nothing. How could I give him anything? My mother and stepfather adored my son. I thought he would be better off with them. Shortly after I moved out, my boyfriend's cousin raped me. I never told anyone. I felt no one would care or believe me. I lived from couch to couch. A friend introduced me to a cocaine dealer. He was 36. I began living with him and his girlfriend. Needless to say, the environment was horrible. I was taken advantage of in many ways. By age 18, I had met my next two children's father. He was a violent drug user and dealer. I had our first child at 19 and the second child at 20. During the pregnancy of our second child, he would make me sit on the couch and hold our first child in my arms. He would be holding his guns, alcohol, and drugs. He would tell me to stand up and try to walk away. He said he wanted a reason to blow my legs off. His abuse ended on Mother's Day in 1993. He shot me and another person with a sawed off shotgun. We had argued earlier. He left home and I went to my neighbor's house. When he returned and found I had left, he came looking for me. It ended with him shooting the neighbor and myself. That same year, he was sentenced to 15 years in prison. He served eight years. After he was released, he was in prison again within six months. He is currently serving a sentence for assault with a deadly weapon inflicting serious injury.

After his incarceration, I attempted to better myself. I enrolled in school and received my adult high school diploma. I began college as well. Then in 1995, I met my first husband. We began dating in November and in December, he choked me until I was unconscious. In February of 1996, I moved with him to his hometown. The abuse became worse. I was now in a town where I knew no one. Many nights my two children and I would sleep in my car in the parking lot of the local grocery store to avoid his violent outbursts. I began calling the police as the violence progressed. We left once and moved to a battered women's shelter. After one week, I had gone back to the man I thought in my mind loved me. In 1997, we were married at the local courthouse. I gave birth to my last child in 1998. In my mind, I thought if we had a baby he would be good to me. The abuse never stopped during the pregnancy. When I was eight months pregnant, I was picked up by my neck and thrown to the ground. Two days after giving birth to our child, I was beaten. I continued to accept the abuse for many more years. I worked at a well-known fortune 500 company. No one knew what I was going through. I did become friends with two women and began sharing with them. Many times they would help me cover the bruises. They even lied for me about the black eyes. I began going to church in 2001. I joined support groups and self-help groups. I listened to other women talk about overcoming abuse and how liberating it was. My ex-husband even went to church with me at times. This gave me hope he would and could change. I felt as though I was needed to help him with his drug addition. I thought I could save him. He began going in and out of rehab centers. Once again, this gave me hope. He would always tell me how much he needed me and how he would not make it if I were not in his life. He told me how much he loved me. All the while, I was still attending the various groups within the church. I was growing and I was getting stronger.

And I was starting to love me. I was starting to see I am worth more than what I have ever been given. December 2003, he was being released from jail for another one of his various crimes. I went and picked him up. Once we got home, I knew things were different. He began yelling and telling me to give him the car keys. In the past, I would plead with him not to leave. Not this time. I gave him the keys. I called my coworker and asked her to pick me up for work that morning. I knew his pattern and knew he would not return for a few days. After he left, I knew I was finished. I knew I was beginning to love my children and me more then I loved this unworthy man. By June of 2004, I had purchased my first house. I allowed him to think he was moving with us. I allowed him to move all my furniture and help me get organized in my new home. He came in my new home and sat in the recliner and began yelling and cussing and telling me I needed to pay him for his help. He stood up and demanded the car keys. I said ok; let me go get you some money. I went into the bedroom and called 911 and told dispatch my husband was becoming violent and to send an officer. Within 2–3 minutes, law enforcement was there. I told them I wanted him to leave because of his anger and I was a victim of his abuse for many years. They made him leave. He was given a bag of clothes and was told to start walking and not return to my home. February of 2005, I divorced him.

Today, I have a really good job and I am currently a full-time criminal justice student. All four of my children live with me. The 24- and 20-year-old are in college. The 19-year-old is a senior this year. And the 13-year-old is in eighth grade. In spite of all the adversities my children have been through, they are all well-rounded productive members of society. I am so proud of my children. Each of them has a story to tell about the impact the abuse had on them. I would be a fool to think the abuse did not affect them. Many women including myself are selfish while being involved in an abusive relationship. I know my actions were hurtful and disappointing to my children. My focus for many years was on the abuser. Although I never allowed my children to be physically abused, the psychological abuse was there. I am so thankful the cycle of abuse has stopped with me. My boys are caring and giving to me. Although I did not feel worthy for many years, I made sure I talked to my children about abuse and drug use. I never wanted any of them to become like their fathers or me. My daughter is a strong-willed young lady. She makes me proud each and every day. She has a bright future in nursing. My 19-year-old is a junior firefighter and has already been offered a firefighting job in the city we live in after graduation. The 23-year-old endured a lot of hardships. He was left in the same environment I escaped from. He has come along way and has a bright future ahead of him. He is majoring in psychology. He wants to work with children. Children like the both of us. The 13-year-old is an awesome caring and compassionate young man. His future is wide open. He has concrete memories of his father and the abuse. He gets very upset when he sees a female being disrespected. He vows to be nothing like his father.

My life was extremely hard. It took many years to realize I am worthy. I deserve to be treated with respect. No one has the right to hit me. No one has the right to call me names.

No one has the right to control me. No one has the right to abuse me in any way. It took many years to realize I cannot save a man. I can only save myself. The abuser typically will not change. The change only comes when we as women realize we are worth more. We have the power to stop this epidemic. Domestic violence will continue as long as women are suppressed and held down by their own negative thoughts. There needs to be more awareness and support groups offered for women in abusive relationships. So many times, we tell these women just leave. It's not that simple. As with me, abuse was all I had ever known. How do you leave? How do you walk away from what feels right? We as a society need to start reaching out to these women and offering support instead of criticism. My dream is to travel the country and talk to young women about their self-worth. Tell them even though your father or mother doesn't love you or believe in you, I believe in you. You deserve better and if you want better, it is out there. But first you must believe in yourself. No one has the right to abuse you.

WHAT ARE THE CONSEQUENCES OF IPV?

Now we have become more knowledgeable about IPV through facts and personal stories, let us uncover why awareness is so crucial, especially to adolescents and young adults.

For most students, the college experience is an exciting time. While receiving educational training for a prospective career(s), students enjoy and embrace the personal and social perks of the grand college life. Independence emerges at the first opportunity of living on their own and managing college-related business matters, without the watchful eye of mom and dad. "Self" is discovered, chiseled, shaped, refined, and matured by life's "highs and lows" and experiences with friends and acquaintances from various backgrounds. And not to forget, good times are created with lifetime friends and "love" is discovered after meeting "the one."

Photo courtesy of Javon Robinson

While meeting "Mr. or Mrs. Right" can be a wonderful highlight, it also can be detrimental if "red flags" are ignored and a potentially violent personality is allowed into your dating world. As mentioned previously, IPV does not discriminate. It affects a range of cultures, especially teens and young adults. The consequences of IPV are serious and not taken lightly. Safeguard your education and future aspirations by protecting yourself from the life-altering consequences.

If not death or injury, IPV can result in serious short-term or long-term physical, emotional, and/or neuropsychological (brain-related) disabilities that can alter a promising future (Coker, Davis, Arias, Sanderson, and Brandt 2002). Examples of physical health consequences that victimized women and men have reported include: a. migraines; b. chest pain; c. arthritis; d. gastrointestinal disorders; e. heart disease; and f. hearing loss (tinnitus ["ringing of the ear"]) (Breiding, Black, and Ryan 2008). Emotional complications associated with IPV that have been reported include: depression, anxiety, personality changes, and disturbance in sleep. **Neuropsychological** (brain-related) complications inflicted by **Traumatic Brain Injury (TBI)** (a blow to the head) and/or post-traumatic stress have led to long-term disabilities that negatively impact the following: a. memory; b. attention; c. processing speed; d. perception; e. learning; and f. language. Impairment in one or more of these skills can result in one or more of the following conditions (www.asha.org retrieved January 15, 2012):

1. Understanding and producing written and spoken language
2. Comprehending body language and emotional non-verbal signals
3. Problems with articulation and self-expression
4. Complications with intonation and inflection
5. Dysarthria (muscle weakness that can impact clear speech)
6. Aprosodia (an inability to produce or comprehend the affective components of speech or gesture)

In college, higher-order thinking and effective communication skills, such as those listed above are needed to master educational training for prospective careers. Clearly, inviting into your dating world or remaining with an individual with a violent personality "in the name of love" can lead to damaging or fatal health, physical, and cognitive consequences. Undergoing IPV simply is not worth the gamble on your education, your future, nor your peace of mind.

HOW DO I APPROACH DATING RESPONSIBLY?

After experiencing the emotional consequences of IPV, I have often said, "If I could rewind time and revisit my young adult years, I would date differently." But since that is not possible, I will share my knowledge and experiences to foster wise choices and help to avoid involvement with potentially violent partners.

First, if the former relationship caused emotional and/or physical wounds or stresses, I suggest dating yourself for awhile. Release yourself from the guilt often felt by IPV victims. Instead, use this time to learn "who you are" and allow yourself to fall in love with "you" all over again. This begins by standing in front of a mirror and realizing, appreciating, and every day announcing your inner and outer beauty (flaws and all). Confidence development statements can include: "I am not perfect, but I am perfect for me;" "I am handsome or beautiful and am awesome in every way;" "I am not worthless, my life has purpose;" "I love my smile, confidence, drive, and laughter, it is a gift I embrace;" and "I love and will protect me!"

Photo courtesy of Javon Robinson

Secondly, find a quiet place of solitude to write down and embrace your personal goals and ambitions, likes and dislikes, philosophies and beliefs, and personal style and interests. For example, you may list: "Before entering the work force and marrying, I want to graduate from undergrad, go to graduate school to earn my Masters, and later pursue my Doctorate;" "I love helping people succeed;" "I do not like feeling humiliated;" and "I believe any dream can be fulfilled as long as I have the desire to persevere and see it come true." By seeing this on paper, it helps to develop self-appreciation of purpose and worth. When these are (re)discovered and embraced, the will to advocate for you and to make sound selections in friends and romantic partners emerges. Additionally, journaling and releasing the "roller coaster" of emotions (i.e., anger, depression, loneliness, and shame) cleanses the soul that was battered by abuse. For me, this along with prayer, meditation, and finding a supportive church family placed me on a path to healing and forgiveness. When I became emotionally sober, my mind and heart were able to work together to make wise decisions when I finally returned to the dating world. And as a result, this time, I was able to clearly recognize my "Mr. Right!" whom I am happily married to today. Thus, I strongly advise to ensure time is taken to get to know and love yourself; it will empower your ability to choose emotionally "healthy" and stable friends and romantic partners who are moving forward with you.

Thirdly, before saying, "yes" to the date, I advise checking your "prospect's" personal background. This will uncover valuable financial, criminal, and marital information that can either positively or negatively impact your life. Two years ago, when I suggested this while discussing "Relational Communication" in a Relationship forum, some students agreed and others did not. The latter felt checking someone's background intruded on personal privacy. In fact, some students argued, "whatever is hidden in the dark" will one day come to light. While this wise tale may be true, with IPV steadily on the rise, I feel waiting on that "one day" is risky. A close family member of mine with interest in a young lady almost found out the hard way. If members of the family had not yielded to intuition and investigated her background to learn of her violent crimes and felony record, her manipulative personality and life of crime possibly could have destroyed his reputation and interrupted his promising educational future if they had been together in the wrong place at the wrong time. Therefore, for the purpose of IPV prevention, I strongly recommend consulting a reliable personal background research engine to gain this knowledge before becoming involved. What you know in advance can preserve your mental, emotional, and physical health and maybe even . . . save your life!

Fourthly, plan your date. Decide your location, driving arrangements, and prepare questions that will give information about your date. Remember, in most cases, you are meeting a total stranger. It is not safe for them to pick you up from your dorm, apartment, or home before allowing yourself time to truly become acquainted with them. Go slow. Meet your dinner date at a location where you dine often, at least until you have become more acquainted with him or her. This, for example, would be where the wait staff is familiar with you. With "missing persons case files" also steadily on the rise, dining places where the staff knows you works to your benefit. Someone can identify where you were last to help officials retrace your steps (in emergencies). It also can work favorably with helping you become more familiar with your "prospect." Coincidently, if someone on the wait staff has seen this individual at their restaurant, he or she can give you some personal background information, or as my students say, "the heads up!"

Fifth, treat your "dates" like an interview. Prepare questions and observe body language to learn the personality and intention. After learning yourself and embracing the things in life that are important to you (i.e., moving out of state in five years, going to graduate school, having a family or children, traveling, problem-solving versus violence, your style of dress, etc.), discovering your commonalities as well as differences are important. So why not ask an open question, "Tell me a little about your family?" And if he or she replies, "Nothing much to tell, I can not stand my mother or father." Wow, this clues into personality and reveals how he or she feels about intimate family ties, which does not appear to be high on the list. And if someday having a close family is important, this may not be a "right" fit for you. Remember the goal is to choose someone who compliments you. Job interviewers ask questions for the same reason—to ensure the person who is a "right fit." Is not "your personal happiness, mental wellness, and life" worth far more? So then, wouldn't it be in your best interest to ask questions to ensure the same?

Photo courtesy of Javon Robinson

Lastly, reading body language is important. Nonverbal cues such as punctuality, facial expressions, posture, hand positions, and undertone can reveal loaded messages about personality, philosophies, habits, and future interactions with you. Woods (2009) in her chapter, "Nonverbal Communication," indicates verbal communication is easier to control than is nonverbal. As much as we may try to control our body language, subtle "signs" involuntarily creep up that clue into truth(s) about our real selves. If this happens, pay attention, study, and "believe it." My grandmother often said, "The eyes are the window to the soul." On your next date, take a moment to look into his or hers. Then ask, what do they tell me?

A wealth of information that informs and suggests how to avoid IPV has been covered. This chapter defined IPV, gave examples of abuse, reported the incidence and cultures affected, shared inspirational stories from victims who experienced abuse, disclosed the emotional, physical, and neuropsychological health hazards, uncovered the "red flags," and offered tips for "safe dating." I hope this chapter increased your awareness and motivated your desire to apply what was learned to prevent this traumatic experience from occurring in your life. Years ago, when I went through IPV, I remember driving down the highway with tears streaming down my cheeks asking, "Why Lord? Why is this happening to me?" Now looking back, as much as I did not wish to go through that experience, I now know its purpose. For if I had not gone through it, I would not have been inspired or motivated to write this chapter. Additionally, I would not have had the understanding of IPV and how to advise others to avoid it. I firmly believe that persons going through a divorce, drug addiction, or in this case IPV, are best reached by those who share common experiences. So, for this reason, I embrace my experience and hope the facts and advice in this chapter inspire "victims" to get out and students to date with more precaution. I believe everything happens for a reason and I feel it is not by accident or for entertainment reasons that this chapter was included in this course text. I believe it was intended to "save a life" and I hope the information and the personal stories "saves yours."

In conclusion, if you are going through IPV, there are available support resources on college campuses, in your community, and nationwide to assist you. They include: Student Counseling Services, Domestic Violence Services in your local city, and The National Domestic Violence Hotline,

1-800-799-SAFE (7233). I encourage you to make the contact. Do not delay your "peace of mind" or "personal happiness" any longer.

The dean of my college conducted a seminar on domestic violence for the entire campus during the month of October last year. Most of my colleagues decided to have our students process what they learned from the seminar by including in our classes some dialogue and writing about intimate partner violence or IPV. Please read some of the student comments:

1.

"SHE LEFT NO BRUISES"

by Gregory J. King

She left no bruises,
Instead she found a way to hurt me with her words.
She put me down from day to day,
And sometimes I would ask myself "Why Did I Stay?"
She would constantly tell me that I was nothing,
And in my heart she was everything to me.
I tried to look at her heart, and not her past,
But then I would find myself wondering if this marriage would ever last.
I tried to put aside my pride, and leave my hurt in the past.
But it was like her words always seemed to come back and haunt me.
I always wondered if she realized that her words hurt me.
However, she was too blind to see that I was always the man that I was supposed to be.

2.   Domestic violence is said to be the patterns of behavior in any relationship that are used to gain and maintain power over an intimate partner. This, however, can happen to anyone of any race, age, religion, or gender. Domestic violence affects people in a number of ways. I have actually witnessed domestic violence that led to someone dying. This tragic situation took place Christmas night. My mother, sister, cousin, and I were in the car leaving from my aunt's house headed to where I reside, and while approaching the curve that is on the same street as my house, there was a white man and a black woman on the side of the road. The woman was laid on the ground while the man was standing over her portraying to help her up. Not thinking she was actually getting hurt we decided to keep going past them, up enough for the attacker not to see us ahead. But something then says look back, and that's what I did. To look and see one stomping her, and the woman with her hand up to him, crying for help was so sad and if only we could do more than just call the police. Frightened were we all, we could not even talk on the phone with the police without screaming the different things the man was doing to the lady. Shortly after, the

man was about to get in his car and drive off, but before he did he backed up and ran over her body twice. December 25th was then a night to remember. To actually see someone get killed put me at a state wherein I was scared to do anything. Also with it being not even five minutes away from my house, I was scared to even stay there. I would sit on the floor in the house, all because I was scared to stand thinking one would start shooting. I was also afraid to sleep by myself. This stayed like this for a while. Not knowing if the attacker knew who actually called the law on him or not made me think he would come back for the only car that he seen ride past in that area. Everything was going through my mind that night. Situations involving domestic violence stay with you forever; it is a challenge to overcome tragic situations such as that. Life would be great if there was an end to the abuse that others do to their intimate partner. It could save many lives and increase the way one feels about theirself. After being physically hurt, some begin to have a low self-esteem or negative self-worth. Life can be just as good without the domestic violence.

3. To me domestic violence is a frequent problem that occurs in many households, yet it is hardly acknowledged. Domestic violence harms more than the victim. It harms everyone involved—the abuser, the abused, and the witnesses. Growing up in an abusive household had tremendous effects on my life. I saw my mother get beat and talked down on a daily basis. As a child, I sometimes was the only thing standing between my mother and death. My father abused all of us. He used to come home drunk and high, and make me and my sister fight each other for his personal gain. Domestic violence is more than physical it is also emotional abuse, verbal abuse, and sexual abuse. My father never supported me in anything I did as a child. In my household it was required to maintain good grades, but my father never attended the academic awards programs. Growing up, my father never acknowledged that I was his. He never attended my school functions, and most of my teachers believed my mother was a single parent. I graduated class valedictorian of my eighth grade class and once again my father was not present at my graduation. I believe my father has a mental problem. Living in my household taught me a lot about life and people. I learned how to defend myself and even though the demon in my father tried its hardest to destroy me, I learned how to stand strong. I am not a victim but a survivor. I love my father and forgave him a long time ago. I forgave him not for his sake but for myself. I believe forgiveness is extremely important in moving on. I forgave my father for what he did, but I will never forget what he put my family through.

4. Domestic violence is when a person is in an intimate relationship or marriage and one tries to control the other person. This type of violence is not only physical but it is also psychological and emotional. Psychological and emotional abuse is not taken as serious as physical abuse, but that type of abuse can harm also. The main goal of the abuse is to control a person. No one is exempt from this type of abuse. All races, backgrounds, genders, heterosexuals, and homosexuals all participate in this kind of abuse.

5. Personally, I know someone who has been involved in domestic violence. This was a very sad story. Her husband cheated on her and harmed her in every way that he could. When the hitting, punching, and slapping got old he went to another level. He held her down and burnt her all over her face with cigarettes. She had first-degree burns as a result. That put the icing on the cake and she finally found the strength to leave him and never return again.

6. I can remember a time when domestic violence invaded my home life and has since affected me. I was six years old and my parents were having a heated argument, as was customary for them. However, nothing else was customary about this day. From the moment I heard the door to their kitchen slam I knew something was about to happen. Voices rose to decibels I'd never thought possible from either parent cut through air, punctuated by the slap of a leather belt and skin on skin contact. I sat rooted to my spot until it was over. When it all ended, I remember my mother coming out of the room with a black eye. The next thing I knew, my sister and I were both uprooted from our Oklahoma home and went without mother to live with her parents, eighteen hours away in southwestern Virginia. My parents soon reconciled and have been together for going on twenty-three years, but to this day I live in fear that every argument my parents have is one more closer to their divorce, which goes to prove that domestic violence impacts everyone around it and can have a lasting effect on not just the abuse, but also those who are witnesses to it.

7. My experience of domestic violence came when I was a freshman in high school. I had a friend named Patrick. He wasn't my friend for too long throughout the year because I was also cool with his girlfriend Ashley. The reason why we befriended each other is because Ashley used to come to me often towards the end of the year and tell me about the fights and arguments that they constantly get into. I would normally give her advice on how to go about the situation and I would also talk to Patrick to hear his side of the story. Every time I talked to Patrick, I used to always think that he was in the wrong, based on what he would tell me. Soon I decided to tell them both to leave me alone with their problems. A week later, Ashley came to me with a bloody bruise on her face crying after school was over. She told me that Patrick and she got into an argument and he decided he was going to shut her up by punching her in the face. I took her to the main office to see if the nurses were still in and to tell the assistant principle what Patrick had done. The reason I didn't confront Patrick myself is because he was nowhere to be found at the time and I would have gotten suspended for doing so. My friend Ashley came out ok and Patrick was expelled from the school. He and I never talked again and I have yet to see him since.

8. Domestic abuse to me means to hurt someone physically, mentally, and psychologically. When someone is the victim of an abusive relationship, whether they are a female or male, the person tends to have some type of bad end result in which they will be left bruised and scarred from the abuse that was tolerated. I myself have not experienced being in an abusive relationship, but my aunt was once in a very unstable relationship with two kids to also endure the suffering. During her teens, my aunt thought she was in love with the man of her dreams. They had two beautiful daughters together, not to mention they were both very young in age. My aunt's boyfriend would go crazy at times and began to beat on my aunt in front of the eldest daughter. He himself was not only abusive to my aunt but also everyone else around him, especially women. Today, he has unfortunately paid for his aggressiveness and my aunt is finally happy, but her eldest daughter suffers a lot from her childhood. She was mentally drawn by her mother being beaten by her father. Now she is a very big trouble maker, she has been in and out of jail, she's only 17, she never finished high school, she's been kicked out of many schools, and now she is currently pregnant. Many people do not understand that domestic violence does not only affect the person that its directed too but it also affects those that it is constantly presented in front of and it also takes a heavy toll on those that commit the act.

Key Terms:

Intimate Partner Violence (IPV)

Physical Abuse

Physical Assaults

Verbal Aggression

Verbal Abuse

Sexual Abuse

Incidence

Neuropsychological Disabilities

Traumatic Brain Injury (TBI)

Application Activities:

Group Activity I: "Can You Read Me Like A Book . . ."

Have students gather in small groups. Ask students to review the questions below and discuss the implications the answers reveal about their date.

QUESTIONS:

1. Q: Where are you from?
   A: *A small town named Bear Grass. Many people have never heard of it.*

2. Q: Tell me about your family.
   A: *There's not much to tell.*

3. Q: What is your major?
   A: *Criminal Justice.*

4. Q: Do you have brothers and sisters?
   A: *Yes, two younger brothers.*

5. Q: What do like to do for fun?
   A: *Dog fighting.*

6. Q: What are your thoughts about the roles of men and women in a marriage?
   A: *(male). I believe a man should take care of his lady. She shouldn't have to work.*
   A: *(female). I believe both should work and make their own money. I like to make my own money.*

7. Q: What are you looking for in a relationship?
   A: *I am not looking for anything serious. Just want to kick it.*

8. Q: What does it take to make a relationship successful?
   A: *I am not sure. I didn't exactly have the best role models. My parents fought constantly.*

9. Q: Who do you hang out with mostly?
   A: *I like to keep to myself. I don't have close friends.*

Group Activity II: "Actions Speak Louder Than Words . . ."

Have students gather in small groups. Ask students to review the actions below and discuss the implications body language reveals about their date.

1. You meet your date at a local restaurant. He or she already has ordered your drink.

2. When you walk over to your table at the restaurant where your date awaits, he or she remains seated, smiles, and says "Hello!"

3. As you engage in conversation with your date, he or she occasionally texts on his or her phone during the conversation.

4. On your first date, you meet your date at a local restaurant. And when you arrive, he or she embraces you with a rather tight hug and a forced kiss on the mouth.

5. A potential prospect investigates your Facebook page (without your knowledge) and asks questions about your friend list and pictures.

6. During conversation, your date sits with his or her arms folded.

7. During conversation, your date does not consistently deliver eye contact.

8. Your date frequently interrupts your conversation and talks about himself or herself.

9. Your date comments, "You need to thank me for this meal! I'm just joking . . ."

10. When you say "Hello!" to a friend of the opposite sex as they pass by, your date inquires, "Who is that?"

11. Over dinner, which by the way is your second, your date orders several alcoholic drinks.

12. Your date seasons his or her food before tasting.

MINI QUIZ

1. True or False: Verbal abuse is not a true form of IPV because it does not include physical violence.
2. Multiple Choice: This percentage represents the estimated number of people killed in the United States as a result of intimate partner violence.
   A. 120
   B. 1,200
   C. 12,000
   D. 12
3. Fill in the Blank: Several _____ disabilities may result from Traumatic Brain Injury sustained in IPV incidents.
4. Essay: How do you feel media may influence or distort issues related to IPV.

CHAPTER 13

Friends and Peers

by Tracey Booth Snipes

During our early years, much of our communication is shaped by our immediate environment and those we are directly in contact with on regular basis. These are usually our parents, caregivers, family members, and siblings. As we begin to interact more with those outside of this group, we have to develop skills for interacting with others who will bring to us new perspectives. We find ourselves developing our own individual likes and dislikes, outside of that which may have been taught to us by our families, as we start to form new relationships and friendships. In other words, we hang around people who are doing the things we want to do and like the things we like.

We are attracted to people that bring us joy, happiness, and positive reinforcement. Also, we can be attracted to people who present us with new and interesting ways of seeing the world. This is how we develop friendships as well as other meaningful relationships with our peers. These peer interactions ultimately shape and change not only our lives, but their lives as well.

Communication Similarities with Our Peers

So what initially attracts us to these people? Usually these **peer** relationships are formed through some mutual event or interest such as a class we may take, an athletic group or organization we may belong to, and so forth. As we become involved in activities with people, we start to pay attention to the things they say, as well as, their behavior. We identify with those people we like and who express themselves in ways that are similar to our own feelings. We may find it easier to interact with these people because we share a similar perspective. As we recognize commonalities in our peers, we feel more comfortable with ourselves. We are usually attracted to these people because they behave in ways that we are familiar and comfortable with. They affirm that "we are okay" and that there are other people like us. In other words, we find "our people." When interacting with these people, we understand the rules for communication and are comfortable being ourselves and expressing ourselves around them. We begin to develop our sense of how we see ourselves in our peer groups. Our desires to "fit in," and be "a part of the group" become more intense.

The communication styles used with these groups are often very different from those used with family. It is different mainly because the power structures and original expectations are removed. Our roles in our families are often defined not by us, but for us by others. For example, if we are the youngest member of the family, we may be "the baby." The definition of our being by others may bring with it expectations, out of our control, such as limited and varying power, control, and/or respect. Let's face it; if you are the youngest, there may be a group of people in line to tell you what to do and what to think. However, when we join our peers, our roles may change greatly. My life experience is a perfect example. I was born into the family as the youngest and only girl of three children. I had to be "obedient" and "respectful" not only to my parents but to my older brothers as well. I seldom made major decisions for the family and I felt as though I was obviously the "weakest" link. However, when I went to school, I was a leader. Because I was an older child than most of my classmates, by virtue of my birthday, I was a bit more mature. This gave me insight and understanding about situations that often put me in a position of power and adoration. And I loved it! My peers had no idea that I was "the baby" at home and I liked it that way.

A Dichotomy of Ourselves

Our peers also give us an opportunity to explore our individualism and similarities within larger communities. In western society, where individualism is celebrated and encouraged, it may be challenging to define ourselves. We often want the opportunity to be valued for our individuality, but we also have a human need to "fit in." We can be driven by this dichotomy of being an individual and fitting in the group.

The dichotomy might exist because we may become attracted to people who are very different from us, yet we are more comfortable with people who are "like-minded." Moving from our comfort zone, we may allow ourselves to explore. This is especially likely in today's pluralist society where we are more exposed to and engaged with people from various culturally diverse backgrounds. Maybe these people exhibit behaviors that we are drawn to out of curiosity or novelty. In other words, they are communicating something new and interesting that we have not experienced or understood before. This offers us an opportunity to explore and experiment with new ideas and "ways of knowing." In other words, a new perspective. This offers an opportunity to take some new and exciting risks. College students leaving home for the first time are frequently exposed to new and exciting adventures. For most of these young people, this will be the first time they are not under the full watchful eye of their parents and guardians. They are now in an atmosphere where they can express themselves more freely. Often college students find their **"voices"** and begin to express their true feelings openly with their peers.

At times these new experiences lead us to new and fulfilling expansions of ourselves. Sometime these new experiences bring us to conflict and questioning. Depending on the experience, we will leave the relationships feeling more fulfilled and enhanced or we may leave the relationship with great regret and remorse. When we meet new peers we have the opportunity to try new things. Sometimes this occurs when we are invited to attend events with our friends, become members of various teams, or just hanging out.

Communication Conflict with Our Peers

Sometimes our peers lead us in new, maybe not so comforting, directions that may cause us to make decisions that ultimately challenge us. This peer pressure can result in unpleasant experiences. A great example of this is the common practice of backbiting that takes place in groups. It has become commonplace for groups of people to sit around and make unfavorable comments about others, even members of their groups. This is compounded in modern society where media such as "reality TV" and social networking seems to encourage constant communication about "other people's business." It is almost expected that once someone starts a conversation about another that is mean or negative, all that are present should offer some comment to show that they are in the groups' consensus. But what if you don't want to contribute to this poisonous conversation? Maybe you are not comfortable with the discussion. After all, "If they talk about them, they'll talk about you." But we often get sucked into communication exchanges that are not healthy for us. It can be difficult to be the one who chooses to not participate in the "group activity" of gossiping.

Sometimes communication with our peers can be further challenging in terms of maneuvering risky behaviors such as alcohol consumption, sexual activity, and illegal activity. Young people often have difficulty separating themselves from their peer groups for fear of not fitting in. As a result, they may participate in dangerous behavior that they are not equipped to deal with. It is difficult to say "no" when the whole group is saying "yes." Our peers can, in a sense, silence our voices by isolating our opposing views and making those views seem irrelevant or unpopular. It is interesting how many students develop drinking problems, engage in sexual activity for which they are not prepared for, and participate in illegal activity, simply because they did not want to be alienated from their peers.

Ultimately, we will seek a healthy balance by looking to those relationships that will resonate with what is familiar as well as bring us new and challenging experiences. Hopefully, these relationships will lead to happiness and self-fulfillment.

Social Networking and Peer Relationships

Another important aspect of peer communication that bares discussion is not so much the "what" but the how. With the advent of such technological tools as cell phones and computers which utilize texting, social networking, online chatting, emailing, blogging, instant messaging and so on, the medium for communicating with our peers seems limitless. We can talk to others miles a way instantaneously . . . or not. We can choose a face-to-face conversation, a phone call, or simple commenting on our own time.

Let's examine the practice of texting, for example. I am often amazed by young people's use of texting as opposed to talking on the telephone with their peers. When asking, I usually get a response like this from my students: "Texting is quicker, to the point; I don't have to talk to you or carry on a conversation if I don't want to." In regards to instant messaging devises like "tweeting," students tell me it is the quickest and most efficient way to get a message out to a large group of people. These various social networking technologies allow us to keep up with our friends as well as keep our friends abreast of even the minute details of our lives. Sometimes we are able to communicate with friends whom we otherwise would not be able to because of this social networking.

While these methods of modern communication are quite efficient and convenient, they do seem to omit some vital components from the communication interaction. The verbal component of communication is covered, somewhat, but the nonverbal aspects are totally removed. This may often promote misunderstandings. These mediums, thus, leave out valuable information that we utilize when interpreting other's communication. This includes not only the facial expressions but the paralanguage that we depend on so greatly to help us fully understand the message. We may not hear the sympathetic tone in a comment and misinterpret it as rudeness, for example. Or we may find that we can be less concerned about our comments when we do not have to face the other person as they receive what we are saying. This might be a contributing factor toward "cyber bullying," which is a growing concern. I am amazed at how many stories I have heard of people using social networking to end relationships. I guess it is easier to break someone's heart if you don't have to witness the carnage.

There are some great examples, however, where technology aids the communication process by allowing for both verbal and nonverbal messages to be exchanged. This is clearly observed with face-to-face video conferencing in such tools as Skype, Google FaceTime, and ooVoo. These tools allow people who may not have an opportunity to interact in person, to do so "face-to-face." We have all heard and seen the stories of deployed military officers being "reunited' with their loved-ones utilizing their computers and smart phones. This technology is not only important for personal interactions, but professional as well. In our growing "global society," business is often conducted using modern technologies. Those entering and continuing in their various careers are more likely to conduct interviews and communications with coworkers in different parts of the world using their computers and smart phones, but that's another chapter.

However we choose to interact with our peers, be it in-person or through the use of modern social networking technologies, it is important that we utilize various modes of communication and interaction. We should find meaningful ways of expressing ourselves and supporting others in their expression. We must maintain communication environments which are healthy for ourselves and that allow us to feel comfortable with the familiar as well as explore new and exciting adventures in a safe and productive manner.

Key Terms:

Peers
Perspective
Dichotomy

Voice
Verbal Communication
Nonverbal Communication

Friends and Peers

by Jabria Jackson

Forming relationships can be easy for some and hard for many depending on the individual. For me personally, it is not as difficult communicating with my peers due to my personality. Since I am an only child, growing up I was very anxious and ecstatic to meet new friends. When I am afforded the opportunity to talk with my peers, I take advantage of it because I have come to notice it is pertinent for social development. As a speech language pathology student, I have also noticed communication is important to discuss ideas and experiences with classmates.

Furthermore, being able to communicate effectively with my peers led to the progression of healthy friendships. For example, I met my best friend at summer orientation. We had a great conversation and later figured we had more in common than we knew. Our friendship started with a simple smile, we then went on to discuss our high school awards and hopes for our college experience. With that being said, the way people carry themselves and what they talk about are great assets when deciding friendships. Friends are those who will be there for you when you feel you have no one else. To add, I have also come to notice through experience, choosing friends will tell you a lot about yourself as a person. When I became a freshman in college, I surrounded myself around many people that inspired to do what I wanted to do, and more. The passion to be successful academically and socially was mutual. Also, the morals and values my parents instilled in me, stuck very closely as I started to interact with others.

A college is a mosaic of people from different walks of life, different cultures, religions, attitudes and faiths. My strong upbringing helped me stand firmly behind my faith, while still being able to communicate with others that believe in different forms of religion. Morals and values are unique from person to person. But due to effective communication skills I am able to talk with my peers and or friends and agree to disagree.

Social media and reality T.V. shows has played a major role on my life and many others. Communication on social media has made many people less personable, and uneasy to talk to. Social networking can either enhance or hinder peer relationships depending on the person. Social media gives people opportunities to become someone they are not, which affects peer relationships because the impression they are giving on social media is not a match of who they are in person. Character is a distinctive attribute of oneself that displays the true meaning of who they are and who they want to be. If a person's character is not pure, their communication will be unpure as well. Which then causes conflict because social media gives a person a platform to be whoever they want and not their true self. It has been many instances when a person has become quickly disappointed when they were not able to see and talk to the "real" person. It is also difficult communicating online because you are not able to actually hear what the person is saying. There has been a case where I have direct messaged someone and used three exclamation marks after the statement ok. To my receiver, it was taken as if I was screaming, but honestly I was just excited. If the receiver knew me personally they would have known I have a bubbly personality, and I did not mean any harm by it. In conclusion, fostering friend and peer relationships are beneficial for development overall.

MINI QUIZ

1. True or False: Peer relationships can evolve from both similar interest and differing interest.

2. Multiple Choice: This aspect of communication is easily omitted in some forms of technologically based social interactions such as emailing and texting.
   A. Verbal communication
   B. Paralanguage
   C. Nonverbal communication
   D. Both B and C

3. Fill in the Blank: This technological method of communication allows people to interact utilizing both verbal and nonverbal communication in real time. _____ Essay: Reflect on a recent conversation with one of your close friends. What types of verbal and nonverbal communication did you all use that may be misunderstood or difficult to understand by others who are not familiar with your relationship?

CHAPTER 14

IntraCultural Communication: Within a Marginalized Group

Elocutionist Hallie Quinn Brown: Public Speaking and the Cultivation of the Whole Person

Faye Spencer Maor

In the late nineteenth and early twentieth centuries, the academic subject and discipline of **elocution** gained popularity and acceptance in the United States' institutions of higher learning. A prevailing notion regarding the value and importance of teaching and studying elocution was that it was one of few academic disciplines which developed the "whole" person, body, mind, and spirit. Noted elocutionist, Thomas Sheridan said once that through elocution, or public speaking and speech communication, "The mind in communicating its ideas, is in a continued state of activity, emotion, or agitation, from the different effects which ideas produce on the mind of the speaker" (Ward and Trent, et al.). Elocution textbooks of the day focused on the proper way of breathing and enunciating words and phrases. The proper control and exercise of vocal chords were also part of the training in elocution. More importantly, there was an emphasis on the term "culture" and its communication to members of the society through language. In the introduction to Hallie Q. Brown's text, *Bits and Odds: A Choice Selection of Recitations of School, Lyceum and Parlor Entertainments*,

Faustin Delany says, "By culture we are to find these perfections of nature, and by training we are to conceal the art by which we adapt ourselves to the creations of the author, and the creations of the author to ourselves" (6).[1] This point would have been of key importance to the students and teachers of the day and even today. One review of a Hallie Quinn Brown performance in the black press said, "She has a wonderful voice and a culture to match it" (*African Methodist Episcopal Church Review* v6, n3 ONLINE).

A lack of **culture** was, and still is to some degree, a charge against African Americans—"culture" being defined as the development or improvement of the mind, emotions, interests, tastes, or manners. The result of culture can be what some call refined ways of thinking, talking, or acting. What better way than through the mastery of an art, such as elocution, for an African American to prove and demonstrate his/her humanity—culture—intelligence? In the search for the social processes of African Americans in their quest for acceptance and equality, perhaps the scholar must understand the way education is tied to the general matter of social structure.

Hallie Quinn Brown was an elocutionist, political activist, club woman, and teacher. She was, by far, one of the busiest and most productive African American literacy workers of the late nineteenth and twentieth centuries. She was a woman who did what very few black women of her day could do—get people, black and white, to pay to see and hear her, not for her singing and dancing, but for her interpretation and skill with language. It is important to know who she was and why she is so important to students who study speech communication. Brown is a living example of how the art of public speaking and communication can change lives and be used for larger purposes and people.

An **elocutionist**, by definition, is a person who has perfected the artistic style or manner of speaking or reading in public; one who is able to capture the meaning and feeling of an author and communicate it naturally (Ayers, et al.). Brown, who lived to be approximately 95 years old, did her literacy work through public speaking and teaching. Her fame, in terms of literacy work, was gained through her performances of recitations, readings, and writings. In a handbill advertising one of her appearances, a testimony reads: "I know no English Elocutionist, man or woman, who recites with the naturalness and charm, the vivacity and power of Miss Brown. I never knew, until tonight, what the human voice could do" (Rev. C.F. Aked).

Life and Career in Public Speaking

Hallie Quinn Brown was overtly political in her teaching and personal life. She was a bright, energetic, and highly motivated woman who lived a very public life. Despite the social and economic circumstances of her day, she engaged in and accomplished extraordinary things. The guiding and unifying theme of her life and work was the improvement of the conditions of her people, especially through literacy, which she practiced and taught through elocution.

Brown's parents were Thomas Brown who married Francis Jane Scoggins. Her father, Thomas, was born a slave to owners who fought in the American Revolution. When Thomas and Frances

---

[1] The writer here (Delaney) refers to the relationship between "natural" talent and training with the dominant phenomenon of influence being "culture".

married, they settled in Pittsburgh, Pennsylvania. In Brown's unpublished autobiography, *As the Mantle Falls,* she asserts that the Brown's home in Pittsburgh was a station on the Underground Railroad (15). She tells stories of her mother always baking bread that would mysteriously disappear. One particular story she recounts is of her family defying slave catchers and authorities by escorting fugitive slaves openly from their home under an American flag. The Brown family dared the officers to touch the flags (15–16). Brown has a flare for the dramatic and even in her writing seems to be performing. At the very least, it can be said Brown was always aware of her audience and had a clear purpose for her message as it related to the audience.

Early in life Hallie Quinn Brown was exposed to prominent figures in the free African American community. One family friend and frequent visitor was Robert Delany, one of the first African American medical doctors in the United States. She also speaks of meeting the real Uncle Tom from the novel *Uncle Tom's Cabin*. Brown says, in her writing, that she was determined to set and reach her goals as a child. As a result of a visit to Canada by Queen Victoria, Brown vowed to meet her. In fact, she not only met Queen Victoria, but also performed for her some 20 years later (McFarlin 5). Needless to say, she was a determined and persistent little girl and woman.

At about age 18 or 19, Brown was told she would be sent to school in Ohio. That school was Wilberforce University, the school Brown would be associated with the majority of her academic career. At Wilberforce, Brown was given a home with Bishop Payne, who was the first president of Wilberforce, and his wife. As a result, her education was continuous, since reading aloud was a regular practice in the classrooms of Wilberforce and in Bishop Payne's home. He regularly made students read aloud, even hearing such recitations in his study. In Brown's unpublished autobiography, she gives Payne considerable credit for her early training as an elocutionist, and her love of literature (21). She felt Payne was ". . . carefully trained in articulation, enunciation, and pronunciation . . ." (20)

After graduating from Wilberforce, Brown took a teaching job in Mississippi and South Carolina. In South Carolina Brown accepted and completed her first public speaking engagements. It was in the woods of South Carolina, on a tree stump she says. "A hundred dark faces with searching eyes peered into mine. It seemed unreal, uncanny under the light of wavering torches" (34). This was a foreshadowing of her later years in public life as a public speaker. After South Carolina, Brown moved to Ohio. In Dayton, Ohio, Brown taught in a one-room school situated above a firehouse. While teaching in this school Brown began to pursue her elocutionary training and performing in earnest—training which began innocently at Wilberforce with Bishop Payne and furthered with her debut in the woods of South Carolina.

Brown's first step into public speaking in the woods of South Carolina and encouragement of friends turned her interest toward a more serious study of elocution. She says, ". . . having my friends say I had a little talent for elocution I determined to direct my endeavors in that line" (McFarlin 4). Her teaching was never separate from her elocutionary studies. In 1870, Brown was teaching in Dayton, Ohio when she met a professor from the Boston School of Oratory. As a result, she enrolled. As she learned her lessons in elocution, Brown taught them to her students in the classroom over the firehouse (36). No doubt her students recited orally. Her first invitation to speak publicly in Ohio was extended by Rev. T. McCants Stewart, the pastor of a New York African Methodist Episcopal church. She received her first large fee of $100 for her second engagement (41). From then on, Brown studied and taught elocution. While teaching full time, she took lessons and bought books on elocution. As her efforts resulted in more speaking engagements, her mentor from Wilberforce, Bishop Payne, asked her to travel with him through his diocese to do readings. It was on this tour that Brown "broke herself in". She toured in the South and met such African American personalities as Booker T. Washington and Madame Selinka, a famous singer of the day (41–42).

When the tour with Bishop Payne fell apart due to finances, Brown was abandoned in Arkansas. As a result, she sought teaching positions at Baptist and Shorter Colleges in Little Rock, Arkansas to survive. In 1882, she went back home to Wilberforce. There she began teaching elocution, and during her tenure, she interrupted it periodically with speaking engagements designed to raise money for the school. In 1884, Brown began work to go to England to raise money for a new library. She paid her way to the east coast and her passage to England by speaking along the way. She stayed in England for six years, returning in 1900. One review of Brown's public speaking said, "Miss Brown may be thought to gesticulate too frequently in some of her didactic selections; but right here is shown that she discards the rules of the books and follows nature, for she possesses an ardent temperament, and nearly every sentence she utters in private conversation is made emphatic, or impressive by a gesture, or variation of the facial expression" (9).

Brown would spend the majority of her life and career at Wilberforce University. Further, Brown was a tremendously active feminist who took every opportunity to further the cause of black women, specifically, and black people as a whole. She spoke against sex discrimination at every opportunity. Her feminism manifested itself through her work for, and in, the organization of black women's clubs. Among other activities, Brown helped found the Colored Woman's League of Washington, D.C., which was a predecessor to the National Association of Colored Women. She was at the forefront of the black women's club movement, supporting women's suffrage. In the twentieth century (1920's), she was a political activist serving as vice president of the Ohio Council of Republican Women (McFarlin 177).

Approach to Teaching Elocution

Because of her long and extensive public career, Brown left behind many documents and texts that reveal the diversity and depth of her interests, commitments, and activities. She is most remembered for her feminist activities by many historians. Her extensive performing was in an effort to raise money for the library at Wilberforce. Rejecting the conventional elocution texts of her day, Brown compiled and published a text book on elocution distinctly reflective and geared toward African American students, one which embodies her ideologies of social responsibility, uplift, and racial pride in and through literacy, *Bits and Odds: A Choice Selection of Recitations for School, Lyceum and Parlor Entertainments, Rendered By Miss Hallie Q. Brown, with Introduction by Faustin S. Delaney.* The scholar Susan Kates studied Brown in 1997, concluding that Brown's approach to elocution and her deliberate attention to the history and folk art of African Americans, as seen in *Bits and Odds,* showed evidence that she used elocution or public speaking to "uplift" African Americans. Brown made history an important component of her elocutionary curriculum. Brown foregrounds the relationship between the development of cultural pride and social political action" (67).

According to Hallie Brown, "The great and ultimate object of all education is to fit the individual for service. One may be endowed with superior gifts, yet by neglect, or lack of use, utterly fail in the race of life" (McFarlin 173). Racial pride and celebration of African American history were ideals Brown pursued. These ideals permeated her teaching, her performances, and her politics. Language was the fuel which powered and moved Brown's philosophy of racial responsibility. As a result of these ideas, Brown wrote her own book with which she taught elocution. It is titled Bits and Odds: A Choice Selection of Recitations for School.

Brown's selections in this book are purposeful in the intent to meet and serve the needs of her African Americans students (59). Her selection of readings encourages and demands a cultural literacy of the pupils and the audience. I believe the goal of Brown's pedagogy was an embodied rhetoric, a rhetoric located within and generated for, the African American community (59). Women like Brown felt an overwhelming responsibility for the improvement and uplift of the race. Their lives bear witness to this fact. This was especially important to African American teachers in the nineteenth century. The introduction to Brown's text on elocution says for elocution it is vital for the pupil to **feel** the emotions and thoughts of the author. "It is not essential for him (the student) to lose his individuality. The reader has more to do than to imitate. He must feel and then express those feelings. . . . It is the cultivation of our own (emphasis added) natures that is aimed at and not the imitation of the nature of another" (Brown 6).

This means that when a student reads and recites a piece from *Bits and Odds*, like the one entitled "Brother Watkins" (34) he/she must know something, or learn something about African American ministers. This humorous story of a minister's breaking the ice with a new congregation, embodies the dialect and mannerisms of black ministers from rural areas and limited ability to read and write. Brown demanded that the students feel the emotions and thoughts of the author, and that the reader must use his/her own knowledge and feelings to express those feelings.

In this text Brown not only uses selections which use black dialect, but also includes pieces which require the reader and reciter to speak with Irish, Yiddish, and German accents, or dialects. She calls for the reader to enter various cultures. For students of elocution, Brown's text forces them an awareness and feel for the cultures and experiences of other Americans. Brown's collection is radical, challenging, entertaining, and educational. These ideas were, perhaps, why Brown believed elocution was one of the primary ways a student could become literate, educated, cultured. Elocution challenged and educated its practitioner and audience. Further, through serious study and development of the discipline, the students would also come to an appreciation and pride in the diversity of the world.

Bits and Odds is a celebration of linguistic diversity way before its time. It was written in 1880, at the height of Brown's professional career as an elocutionist, and teacher. As she became both an experienced elocutionist and teacher, she believed more and more in the importance of the literacy and culture a student could gain through the study of elocution.

Inclusivity, Not Exclusivity, of the African-American Vernacular English (AAVE)

by Hope Jackson

I recently taught a freshman composition class in a traditional setting (classroom environment) for the first time in about four years. So, as I read the textbook my colleagues chose to adopt, I was only slightly impressed with the few African-American authored essays. Moreover, I knew my students would call the essays and stories that were included "boring." The essays didn't discuss topics they encountered on a regular basis and the writings didn't utilize the language they were used to hearing. Needless to say, I knew I'd have to make a few changes for these young men and women so they could "connect" with the readings to be inspired to write. So, I begin to find "alternative" ways to have them enjoy reading, and at the same time be excited about writing.

When teaching any English class, reading and writing are always expectations. The challenge is making both enjoyable. Students' minds must be stimulated. Since my class was all African-American men and women, I wanted to supplement the readings with some type of African-American literature. So, we watched controversial cartoons like "The Boondocks." We also examined prevalent issues in the African-American community by viewing documentaries such as "When the Levees Broke," "Good Hair," as well as "Tupac: The Lost Prison Tapes." These representations of African-American culture generated lively discussions involving stereotypes about class and race, what is "good hair," along with concerns about the United States' for-profit prison system. All of them featured language dialects of the African-American community to which they could relate, thus enabling the students to discuss issues relevant to them. They could see these concerns within their own personal experiences. Geneva Smitherman (1999) refers to this as a unique attribute in the African-American community known as "Concreteness." In her book, *Talkin that Talk: African American Language and Culture*, she explains, "The speaker's . . . ideas center around . . . the world of reality, and the contemporary Here and Now" (65). Therefore, by including a concreteness philosophy in my teaching, these students weren't as apprehensive about writing assignments.

Writing and Communicating with Self

Most people find writing difficult because it is so personal. Writing is a demonstration of our thoughts. Our thoughts are a description of self-talk or communicating with self. When someone criticizes our writing, we feel hurt because it feels like one is criticizing our thinking and in some cases, our values or beliefs. Not surprisingly, many African-American students are wary of writing because they've been hurt by previous teachers' comments. As an undergraduate student, I remember receiving papers that "had been bled on." At a recent Communication and Composition conference, one of the presenters did a study with community college students who confirmed this. She captured their responses in a film that was shown to teachers of composition. When given the opportunity, many students asked their instructors, "What exactly are you looking for?" "Why do you use red ink?" or "Why don't you give more comments because they seem to offer a solution?"

AAVE and Affinity in the Black Community

Such frustrations are common for African-American students because of their use of African-American Vernacular English (AAVE), sometimes called Black English Vernacular. Many feel that African-American students should be required to use Standard English in both oral and written communication. Yet, this belief doesn't value cultural capital. Within the African-American community, like many others, language is developed through stories, customs, and other oral traditions. Children learn how to communicate primarily from the people in *their* environment. Likewise, it is hard for many who have acculturated to the dominant culture to remember that as Smitherman (1999) states, ". . . all . . . black folks . . . do not aspire to white-middle-class-American-standards" (61). Accordingly, many children do not realize that something is "wrong" with their communication until they enter an acculturated environment, like school. However, in order for the child/student to "fit in" when he/she returns home, AAVE must be used. If not, then his/her position becomes questioned. In *Talkin and Testifyin*, Geneva Smitherman (1999) refers to this as, ". . . the push-pull syndrome . . . *pushing* toward a White American culture while simultaneously *pulling* away from it" (10–11). She continues with providing evidence about this "push-pull" within the African-American community:

> Historically, black speech has been demanded of those who wish to retain close affinities within the black community, and intrusions of White English are likely to be frowned upon and any black users thereof promptly ostracized by the group. Talkin proper (trying to sound white) just ain't considered cool. On the other hand, White America has insisted upon White English as the price of admission into its economic and social mainstream (11).

Such hegemonic practice of accommodation strips one's sense of culture and identity. So, why shouldn't cultural nuances like African-American English Vernacular (AAVE) be appreciated in education? Several dimensions of AAVE are common everyday expressions that involve styles like call and response or signifying. Many are highly emotive and should be acknowledged and valued to reassure African-American students that their experiences have cultural capital. "It is time that teachers realized that poor grammar doesn't equal poor reading skills . . . Nikki [Giovanni] said, that's why we always lose, not only cause we don't know the rules, but it *ain't* [my emphasis] even our game" (Smitherman, 58).

Many scholars of color are brilliant teachers who continue to use AAVE in both the classroom and in their writings. Several individuals like Dr. Geneva Smitherman, the poet Nikki Giovanni, along with politicians like President Barack Obama incorporate AAVE in their communication. In Smitherman's texts, she knowingly infuses Standard English with AAVE to add cultural capital to both, equally in oral and written discourse. This allows her to demonstrate to her audience that she puts equal value in both dialects no matter the reader. It not only allows her to incorporate this belief of "code switching," but it further suggests that she is conquering this "push-pull" conflict because of her conscious choice of comfortably using both types of language in a professional environment. By demonstrating this to other educators, she is resisting notions of accommodation. Likewise, we teachers should be able to do the same for our students. We should provide an academic environment that discourages a "push-pull" struggle, and instead, encourages all cultural dialects in a harmonious learning space.

Deconstructing the Negative Connotation Associated with AAVE

We must deconstruct negative connotations associated with "sounding different." I suggest implementing exercises that create an atmosphere of sensitivity for non-Standard English speakers. I witnessed this exercise by Karen Keaton-Jackson at the 2009 Southeastern Writing Conference Association's Annual Conference.

Statements from Keaton-Jackson's Exercise:

"I come heah today to testify what the Lord done did for me."

"It bees that way sometime."

"Not no mo."

"She caint an aint gon do nothing."

"How you doin?"

"She be deh e'ry day."

"I'ma go head an be real wit y'all."

"I be done did this already."

Accordingly, by completing the exercise, I've begun to deconstruct hegemonic beliefs of literacy. We define literacy and reconstruct what it means as a class. Students begin to learn that literacy is heterogeneous. Therefore, an atypical dialect doesn't indicate intelligence nor does it make someone illiterate. This also makes it easy to transition into my teaching practices of including what I call informal and formal writing. Informal writing includes journaling, blogging, etc. This discourse allows students to communicate using whatever language or dialect they choose (including the hybrid language of technology). This writing becomes a significant portion of their overall grade. Formal writing allows students to utilize Standard English along with AAVE, similar to the way Geneva Smitherman (1977) includes it in the title of her book *Talkin and Testifyin*.

Like Smitherman, students must learn to "code switch" in order to conquer the "push-pull" struggle that does exist for non-Standard English speakers. I believe that when educators create inclusivity for all cultures, not only do students feel valued, but we broaden our own perspectives.

African American Language Structure... Let's Explain and Think Further

by Deana Lacy McQuitty

Many African-Americans speak Black English in informal situations. Cole and Taylor (1990) posited that such language is thought to be spoken primarily by individuals of low SES without formal education. However, Black English vernacular is also spoken by individuals representing middle SES and highly-educated speakers as a code-switching device in informal situations. This language style is characterized by "differences in phonology, morphology, syntax, prosody, pragmatics, and discourse from the features of Standard English" (Cole and Taylor, 171).

Stockman (1996) conducted a longitudinal study of the stages of language acquisition in African-American children between 18 and 54 months old. The study described the process involved in acquiring the Black English vernacular. African-American children acquired the same semantic categories described for children acquiring other dialects of standard American English. Upon completion of the review of studies in the development of language form by African-American children, the scholar concluded that, as early as 18 months of age, early word phrases are emerging, which depend largely on the social class. Before the age of three, children who speak Black English use language to accomplish a broad range of pragmatic functions, which include comments or informative directives, requests, and social interactions.

> Anderson and Battle (1993) also stated that among socioeconomic groups after the age of four, children from low-income families use Black English more than children from middle-income groups.

Anderson and Battle (2002) acknowledged a marginal increase in published research regarding the phonologic contrasts between Standard and American English and Black English phonology. Phonology refers to the study of speech sounds and the speech sound system. Interestingly, differences were discovered within Black English and Standard English regarding the acquisition of /n/, /m/, and /ŋ/(pronounced "ing" as in swing).

Within the past two decades, prominent scholars continued to investigate African-American speech and language development. Although the amount of language addressed to young children by caregivers has an effect on children's lexical and semantic development, minimal research has examined the relationship between the development of African-American children's language development and mother-child interactions (Battle 1996).

Exercise in AAE: Phone Pass (take the test)

Visit the website http://www.mnsu.edu/comdis/kuster2/newbasics.html and click on Phone Pass, a 10-minute test of English speech by telephone, which tests your fluency, listening, and pronunciation. You may also explore the Multicultural Education link, which discusses ethnic diversity. After you have explored the information, form small groups within your class and discuss best practices for teaching individuals about cultural responsibility and effective communication skills.

Code Switching: The Communication Accommodation Theory into Practice

by Deana Lacy McQuitty

Can you repeat yourself? Has anyone ever been asked that question? The term **perception** as it relates to communication can be seen in both nonverbal and verbal communication acts. We have discussed how we make false assumptions based on someone's dress, hair, gestures, and facial expressions (all nonverbal communication patterns). Likewise, we make judgments about people through our engagement in conversational discourse. "Additionally, listeners make judgments about a speaker based only on hearing their speech, attributing social characteristics and assigning broad social categories in consistent ways" (Drager, 1).

Phonetic variation in speech production is now known to correlate with variables such as social characteristics of the speaker and the formality of a given situation (Bylee 2002). Speakers may not be consistent in their phonetic use, shifting depending on the style they construct in a given context. Case in point: a group of college students who attend a HBCU decide they are going to homecoming festivities. They discuss the events for the week—the comedy show, Greek step show, and the hip hop concert. Once they arrive at their chosen event they transform to their environment. Transformation of dress, hair, demeanor, and yes communication becomes evident. They are now immersed in this social context. Examine the statements in the table below and notice the differences in word choice.

AAVE	Standard English
"What's up?"	"Hello!"
"Girl, I like your hair . . . it is fly!"	"Your hair looks nice."
"She don't look like she's going anywhere, ha nails aren't done!"	"I do not think she was planning to attend the event."

African American Vernacular English (AAVE), a much studied variation of Standard English, is an example of how social variables may influence communication and ones perception of the speaker. Studies regarding this phenomenon date back with authors such as Daniel and Smitherman (1976) who investigated African American communication and its relation to traditional African World View. Findings revealed similarities to African American communication, culture, and religion. This style of communication is rooted in child-rearing practices as well as religious beliefs and customs. Such phrase as "it takes a village" is a value supported by this notion. Another unique aspect of the African American communication pattern is the **"negotiation of culture"** (Hecht, Jackson, and Ribeau 2003). The authors debate that African Americans observe their surroundings and learn from them. This simply means that in an intercultural interaction African Americans choose their cultural identity and aspects of themselves to be displayed. Most African Americans continue to communicate "comfortably" and peak with AAVE with interactions involving their own racial group with friends and family. It should be noted that AAVE is not the "wrong" dialog but is a language difference with its own "persona of speech" (Rahman 2008). The fact that Standard English is the norm in the United States means that this language style is what's written in textbooks, advertisements, and is spoken by most everyone. The case of the college students who are participating in the HBCU homecoming events have displayed and expressed those aspects of their culture based on the given social situation. Should this impact ones perception of their intellect or social class status?

Members of the larger society who exhibit knowledge of communication practices and theory and intercultural variables in communication can appreciate the authenticity and how contextual variables play a major part in communication and our perception of others. Just as these college students communicated at these HBCU social events based on the context, when they returned to the academic classroom and/or to part time employment so did their communication patterns. This idea of "negotiation of culture" presented by scholars Hecht et al. (2003) involves switching off the AAVE to a more "socially acceptable" communication pattern. A theory entitled the **Communication Accommodation Theory (CAT)** involves "modifying speech behaviors, language use, and responses to accommodate the other person in a conversation dyad" (Ayoko, Hartel, and Callar 2011). Speech rate, tone pitch, or volume may also be altered to fit the person. I am sure you are familiar or have heard of the term "code switching." This term is also mentioned in this text. **Code switching** is simply defined "as the use of two or more linguistic varieties in the same conversation or interaction" (Greene and Walker 2004). Most of the research on this concept report that code switching is situation based, which includes varied social arenas or conversation with mixed status individuals.

We learn that in forming our cognitive schemata we must consider many variables that contribute to how we perceive others. Such variables include gender, culture and ethnicity, social context, and age. Acknowledging these variables is paramount in decreasing false perceptions and helping our ability to understand and engage in the world around us. Ogbu (1999) noted a study that the attitude, perception, and belief of African American students led to communication barriers between them and their Caucasian American peers. The lack of cultural awareness from both ethnicities led to communication breakdowns, which is an example of no communication accommodation and code switching. Research reveals that CAT actually helps to integrate different dialects and language between groups in order to promote communication effectiveness (Ayoko, Hartel, and Callan 2001; Mazer and Hunt 2008).

Let's Think Further:

Think of a time when you and your friends experienced being misunderstood or false perceptions were evident. Describe what happened. In your discussion include the context of the event, people involved, and the nature of the interaction. Discuss if nonverbal and/or verbal communication behaviors contributed to this misinterpretation. Were you involved in the concept of accommodating your communication in order to increase your interaction with others? How did you accomplish this? What communication lessons were learned from this experience?

Communicating a Socially Acceptable Identity in the Workplace: Lesbian Passing

by Amanda M. Gunn

Sally leaves each morning for work following the same ritual day after day. She kisses her lover, Karen, good-bye, grabs her coffee, walks outside, gets in her Honda Accord, and leaves for an eight-to nine-hour workday as an executive at one of the top soft drink companies in the southeast. As she drives down the freeway, she begins her mental transformation into what she assumes is the only identity that is safe to possess in her position; she begins to pretend that she is heterosexual. When Sally arrives at work, Karen will become Keith. Her weekend with women will have the addition of men's names, and she will call her friend Mark to see if he will once again be her fill-in boyfriend Keith for the upcoming company golf tournament. Sally is just one of countless homosexuals who lives a professional life engaged in the phenomenon of "passing."

Passing relies on the social-construction and self-construction of identities that are deemed, or perceived to be, desirable by society. It is dependent on the norms of a society and the subjective interpretations of those norms. With an increase in diversity awareness and the implementation of programs designed to bridge diversity gaps in the workplace, one might assume that passing—as an alternative for homosexuals—would become obsolete. The current emphasis in organizational scholarship on worker satisfaction, inclusion, and involvement would suggest that organizational leaders would attempt to eradicate behaviors within the organization—such as passing—that inhibit those outcomes (Cheney 1995); yet, as Carnevale and Stone (1995) point out, "gay men, lesbians, and bisexual individuals are one of the 'new minorities' in the workplace and among the least understood" (415). The inclusion of sexual orientation in the discussion of organizational diversity is rare, and when it is included it is often mentioned in the listing of diverse groups with an absence of elaboration (Allen 1995; Chemers, Oskamp, and Costanzo 1995). The issues that face homosexuals at work are couched in the "erroneous stereotypes" that perpetuates a desire to remain silent and "invisible in the workplace" (Carnevale and Stone 1995, 416). This is a silence that works in direct opposition to ideologies that promote diversity and voice in the organization.

For many homosexuals, passing at work is certainly motivated by the desire to possess an acceptable identity; however, it is driven by more than that. Homosexual passing is about social strategies that are deemed necessary to survive in a heterosexually dominated society. It is affected by the expectations of a work environment that exist in a society that often discriminates against differences. Woods and Harbeck (1992) contend that the "workplace is heterosexist in the sense that it structurally and ideologically promotes a particular model of heterosexuality while penalizing, hiding, or otherwise symbolically annihilating its alternatives" (9). Taken together, these perspectives indicate that the only option for Sally and others like her is to pass to, as DPhil (1994) suggests, "homosexuals daily engage in an elaborate ruse about their private life" (188). This "ruse" is accomplished through conscious communicative practices. Figure 14.1 is a summation of how five lesbians that pass in the workplace carry out that ruse through communicative behaviors.

STRATEGIC SELF-PRESENTATION BY LESBIANS THAT PASS IN THE WORKPLACE

Gollwitzer's Methods of Strategic Self-Presentation	The Methods Employed by Five Lesbians that Pass as Heterosexual at Work
"Displaying material symbols"	■ Placing pictures of male friends on an office desk ■ Wearing a ring that indicates marriage or an engagement ■ Wearing feminine clothing that would not be worn otherwise ■ Maintaining a longer hairstyle to adhere to perceived gender norms ■ Wearing more makeup than usual to adhere to perceived gender norms
"Performing daily duties associated with a particular identity"	■ The addition or substitution of male names and pronouns in conversations ■ Bringing male dates to company functions ■ Utilizing traditionally feminine mannerisms such as smiling and crossing legs while sitting ■ Participating in office flirtations
"Verbal claim to possession of a particular identity"	■ Replacing the name of a girlfriend with a male name ■ Creating stories about nonexistent heterosexual relationships ■ Discussing intimate relationships with men ■ Verbalizing attractions for men

FIGURE 14.1

This is a summation of the findings. It is not all-inclusive; these examples are representative of the descriptive accounts (Gunn 1998). Sally spends her days at work in fear of being found out. She then returns home to a love that she has denied just one more day out of many. Employee protection based on sexual orientation exists in very few companies and is almost nonexistent at the state and federal levels. Sally can be fired in most employment situations because she loves someone of the same sex. These behaviors of passing take a gr eat deal of energy—both emotional and psychological. The time that it takes to create a heterosexual person is at once demeaning to the individuals engaged in passing, the partners at home that they are denying, and unproductive for the task and maintenance agendas of the workplace.

Sally and countless others continue to leave their voice at home. Organizational leaders must be made to see that this practice of passing undermines the goals of an organization. Once a foundational understanding is established of how all the factions of an organization are affected by homosexual passing, we can begin to work toward a true "democratic workplace." Perhaps then Sally will no longer have to lie. She will not live in a reality of continuous stress, and perhaps she can begin to feel the connection with her coworkers that she is missing. Ultimately, Sally will be able to answer "yes" when she is asked if there is someone important in her life.

Key Terms:

Acculturated

Cultural Capital

Dialect

Discourse

Elocution

Hegemony

Heterogeneous

Vernacular

Strategic Self Preservation

MINI QUIZ

1. True or False: AAVE is a substandard version of Standard American English.
2. Essay: Briefly discuss your personal feelings around the use of AAVE.
   A. Are you a user of AAVE?

   B. Have you ever felt isolated or discriminated because of its use?

   C. Are there other vernaculars you have heard and formed opinions about?

3. Essay: What is your view of Strategic Self Preservation? Do you feel students should conceal their sexual-orientation in order to preserve their professional livelihood?

CHAPTER 15

Groups: Understanding and Working with Others!

by Regina Williams Davis and Stephanie Carrino

As part of a final exam, and assessing an understanding for interpersonal communication, one of my colleagues collected the responses from her students about the benefits and challenges of working in groups. The responses were very interesting and candid.

Some of the comments were very positive. They said that they liked working in groups because it allows you to meet new people in their classes. Other comments were not so positive. Some students stated that groups can be dysfunctional because there are some members who choose not to do their part of the work, causing everyone else to pick up the slack. Evidently, working and managing groups can be complicated.

Group-Thread

Groups and teams are interchangeable terms. Individuals are brought together either by choice or directive to work together to accomplish a particular mission. In order to be most effective, it is important that groups develop a sense of cohesion. I choose to call this cohesiveness "group-thread." Just as threading pearls on the foundation of a strong filament will produce a beautiful pearl necklace, "group-threading" is a movement toward unity or a creation of a virtual adhesive for people to be consistent and committed to working together to produce their best product.

Barriers to Group Success

There are many obstacles to getting groups to operate at optimum efficiency. I choose to refer to these obstacles as group-thread spoilers. Some spoilers to group-threads are lack of trust or credibility, lack of respect for other's time, and incongruent messages. Lack of trust or credibility kills cooperation. If people dedicate time and energy toward something that they find out to be a false or disingenuous reason, they will be hesitant to do it again. Time is valuable to everyone. When meetings are called and do not start on time, or nothing gets accomplished, individuals begin to feel devalued and this will affect group productivity. Incongruent messages can create confusion and diminish the ability for the team to produce the best product. When group leaders choose not to lead by example, incongruent messages are sent to the team. It also can destroy the credibility of the leader.

Servant Leadership

© Ivelin Radkov, 2012. Used under license from Shutterstock, Inc.

Although group communication is challenging, it has enormous benefits as some of the students pointed out in their narratives. The key is to consider selecting a leader who has the attitude of "servant leadership." Servant leadership is the leader who strongly believes that their role is to give priority to needs of their colleagues. These leaders tend to practice shared-governance, listen to everyone's thoughts and ideas, seek utilitarian resolutions to problems, and put their own needs after everyone else has been assisted.

The servant leadership approach is to encourage, support, and enable everyone in the group. Servant leadership is a sharp contrast to an authoritative leadership style of management, and has some of the characteristics in the participative leadership style. Authoritarians tend to give orders and directives and discourage questions. Larry C. Spears of The Greenleaf Center for Servant Leadership reported that groups and teams that have servant leaders tend to be higher producers than those who do not. Ten characteristics identified by the Greenleaf Center for Servant Leadership are: listening, empathy, healing interpersonal conflict, awareness, persuasion, conceptualization, foresight, stewardship, commitment to people, and building community. Let's review these ten characteristics.

© nokhoog_buchachon, 2012. Used under license from Shutterstock, Inc.

Active listening was discussed earlier in this text, in Chapter 1. Empathy is taking the time to consider how it feels to be in someone else's situation. Healing is taking the time to help others through conflict and personal challenges. Awareness is when the servant leader is present and engaged with their colleagues.

Persuasion is the ethical manner of helping their team or group do things that they might not have done without some encouragement. Conceptualization is having a vision for the team or group and being able to articulate it well enough for all team members to have the desire to make the vision a reality. Servant leaders rely heavily on conceptualization and often depend on their foresight. Foresight is the ability to predict potential outcomes of various scenarios so that reasonable decisions can be made. Stewardship is having the willingness to sacrifice for the greater good. Commitment to people is maintaining your integrity as a leader by being sincere about ensuring the welfare of others. Building community, I believe, is one of the most powerful aspects of leadership. Individuals have a need for belonging. When the servant leader brings an interconnectedness feeling to the team, everyone feels as though they are representing the integrity of the group.

Teamwork – Group Work – Community Work – Rewarding Work

We are familiar with some of the popular statements about working with others, but take the time to read the collection of quotes below, select your favorite, and share it with your team.

Teamwork divides the task and multiplies the success. —Author Unknown

No one can whistle a symphony. It takes a whole orchestra to play it. —H. E. Luccock

Teamwork is the ability to work as a group toward a common vision, even if that vision becomes extremely blurry. —Author Unknown

Individual commitment to a group effort—that is what makes a team work, a company work, a society work, a civilization work. —Vince Lombardi

The nice thing about teamwork is that you always have others on your side. —Margaret Carty

Many hands make light work. —John Heywood

No man is an island, entire of itself; every man is a piece of the continent. —John Donne

Cooperation is the thorough conviction that nobody can get there unless everybody gets there. —Virginia Burden

Sticks in a bundle are unbreakable. —Kenyan Proverb

Coming together is a beginning. Keeping together is progress. Working together is success. —Henry Ford

None of us is as smart as all of us. —Ken Blanchard

Team means Together Everyone Achieves More! —Author Unknown

Teamwork is the ability to work together toward a common vision. The ability to direct individual accomplishment toward organizational objectives. It is the fuel that allows common people to attain uncommon results. —Andrew Carnegie

Regardless of differences, we strive shoulder to shoulder . . . [T]eamwork can be summed up in five short words: "We believe in each other." —Author Unknown

A chain is only as strong as its weakest link. —Author Unknown

Contrary to popular belief, there most certainly is an "I" in "team." It is the same "I" that appears three times in "responsibility." —Amber Harding

We must all hang together or most assuredly we shall hang separately. —Benjamin Franklin

Never doubt that a small group of thoughtful, committed people can change the world. Indeed, it is the only thing that ever has. —Margaret Meade

A single leaf working alone provides no shade. —Chuck Page

If everyone is moving forward together, then success takes care of itself. —Henry Ford

Teamwork is essential—it allows you to blame someone else. —Author Unknown

The ratio of We's to I's is the best indicator of the development of a team. —Lewis B. Ergen

Respect your fellow human being, treat them fairly, disagree with them honestly, enjoy their friendship, explore your thoughts about one another candidly, work together for a common goal and help one another achieve it. —Bill Bradley

I am a member of a team, and I rely on the team, I defer to it and sacrifice for it, because the team, not the individual, is the ultimate champion. —Mia Hamm

No member of a crew is praised for the rugged individuality of his rowing. —Ralph Waldo Emerson

A snowflake is one of God's most fragile creations, but look what they can do when they stick together! —Author Unknown

In union there is strength. —Aesop

A group becomes a team when each member is sure enough of himself and his contribution to praise the skills of the others. —Norman Shidle

Gettin' good players is easy. Gettin' 'em to play together is the hard part. —Casey Stengel

It is a fact that in the right formation, the lifting power of many wings can achieve twice the distance of any bird flying alone. —Author Unknown

Sure there's no "I" in "team," but there is a "ME"! —Author Unknown

Interpersonal Communication: An Exercise in Group Dynamics

by Daniel Richardson

Have you ever seen the movie *Chicago*? When I introduce this exercise to my class, I show an excerpt from the "Cell Block Tango" scene from the musical number from *Chicago* as a way of creating additional interest. I point out that the two ladies (Roxie and Velma) defended by Billy Flynn were acquitted even though they were guilty of the murder charges brought against them. I then compare and contrast their experience to that of the Hungarian ballerina who was innocent, but not defended by Mr. Flynn because she had no money and Flynn did not see how defending her would further his career. The Hungarian ballerina is subsequently hanged. The guilty ladies are represented by red scarves in the musical number while the ballerina is represented by a white scarf.

The scenario below is much less dramatic and much less clear cut in terms of right and wrong. This ambiguity makes it a great example for my students to examine and become engaged in as they argue for conviction or acquittal. "It's Not About Inherent Right Or Inherent Wrong. It's About How It's Argued!" Recall "The Cell Block Tango" – "He had it Coming" – *Chicago*

I. Consider the case of Trevor Madigan who:
   1. Was driving to work one morning in the left lane on Business 40 West near Kernersville, NC. He observed a multi-car accident that had recently happened across the median on Business 40 East.
   2. Mr. Madigan gazed at this accident for a few seconds and failed to notice a fire truck partially parked in his lane, blocking the flow of traffic.
   3. Mr. Madigan slammed on his brakes and steered his car into the right lane of Business 40 West, barely missing the fire truck.
   4. Unfortunately, however, Mr. Madigan's automobile struck a firefighter who was retrieving medical equipment from the fire truck to assist the people involved in the multi-car accident on the other side of the median.
   5. The firefighter sustained severe leg injuries, including a compound fracture.
   6. As a result of the collision with the fireman, Mr. Madigan was charged with a felony under a new North Carolina statute designed to protect emergency services workers.
   7. Even though Mr. Madigan had no prior arrest record and a driving record with only a few minor traffic violations, the District Attorney's office pushed for the maximum sentence of four years in prison, a $5,000 fine, and a two-year license revocation to be completed upon completion of the prison sentence.

8. Mr. Madigan, being extremely distraught and despondent over the accident, chose to plead guilty and not to offer a defense. The judge agreed with the District Attorney's office on the $5,000 fine and two-year license revocation, but sentenced Mr. Madigan to only 18 months in prison.

II. Now, consider the case of Trevor Madigan from a parallel universe who experienced the same incident. This Mr. Madigan, while feeling terrible about the firefighter's leg injuries, retained an attorney who pointed out, among other things, the following:
   1. The fire truck had no caution cones set up behind it to alert motorists of its presence,
   2. The sun was in Mr. Madigan's eyes which may have hindered him from seeing the flashing lights on the fire truck, if not the truck itself,
   3. No siren was sounding at the time Mr. Madigan approached the truck, and
   4. The firefighter was unsafe exiting the truck on the side of traffic to retrieve medical equipment. The firefighter should have exited the truck on the side away from traffic and walked around from the rear of the truck, which might have kept him out of harm's way.
   5. And finally the question should be asked: "What in the heck was a fire truck doing parked in the left lane of Business 40 anyway?"

III. The District Attorney's office responded:
   1. The fire truck had just arrived on the scene; therefore, there was no time to put out caution cones.
   2. The median guardrails made it impossible for the truck to pull off the road.
   3. It would have been unsafe to park the truck in the right side emergency lane forcing the firefighters to cross multiple lanes of traffic to reach the victims.
   4. It would have taken far too much time for the fire truck to have approached the accident from Business 40 East given the location of the fire station with the next exit being two miles further down the road, and with the traffic back-up happening on Business 40 East as a result of the multi-car accident.
   5. The District Attorney's office also noted the issue of Mr. Madigan having a cell phone with him and being a regular "texter," even though there is no evidence that Mr. Madigan was using his phone at the time of the accident.

IV. As for the firefighter, he recovered from his injuries after a few months and returned to work. All his medical bills and lost work time were compensated by Mr. Madigan's insurance, although the firefighter received a 20% disability designation, which could hinder his career or force early retirement down the road.

V. Two groups of students will "try the case," with one group representing the prosecution or District Attorney's office, and one group representing the defense or Mr. Madigan's defense team. Each group is to utilize Aristotle's' three pillars of persuasion by presenting logos, pathos, ethos, and concession/refutation arguments for conviction (prosecution) and acquittal (defense).

VI. The rest of the class will serve as the jury. In keeping with our *Chicago* theme, jurors will vote by holding up red cards for guilty and white cards for not guilty. Their decisions will be based on how well each team effectively presents its argument.

Key Terms:

Interpersonal Communication
Group Communication
Group Leader
Servant Leadership
Shared Governance
Listening
Empathy
Healing Interpersonal Conflict

Awareness
Persuasion
Conceptualization
Foresight
Stewardship
Commitment to People
Building Commitment

Vignettes are portrayals of a brief evocative description, account, or episode that will illustrate an important lesson.

VIGNETTE C: FAMILY COMMUNICATION

Sometimes communicating with family is more difficult than speaking with strangers. When we care deeply about someone, the way we say things seems to take on a different challenge. When we want to tell our loved one something that may help to improve them, it may be received as critical and disingenuous, yet who else would care enough to tell us ways we can be better. Think of a time when someone in your family told you something that hurt your feelings initially but you later realized they were truly helping you. Then think of those times when you feel it is important to tell a close family member something that they may not want to hear initially, but it is something they need to know and you must share it because you care. How would you handle this kind of communication in the future? Create a vignette that will demonstrate this lesson.

MINI QUIZ

1. True or False: Servant leadership gives priority to the needs of colleagues.
2. Fill in the Blank: Servant leaders tend to practice _____ governance.
3. Multiple Choice: This characteristic of Servant leadership is the ability to predict servant outcomes for the future for various scenarios.
   A. Stewardship
   B. Empathy
   C. Foresight
   D. Persuasion
4. Essay: As a potential group member, what aspect(s) of servant leadership do you feel you possess?

UNIT IV

HyperProfessionalComm

Persuasion, Argumentation, Business Communication, and Careers in Communication

UNIT OBJECTIVES:

- *Understanding methods for persuading*
- *Constructing and advancing arguments*
- *Awareness of appropriate professional communication goals*
- *Audience analysis*
- *Exposure to careers in communication and communication disorders*

. . . .

You will learn ways to develop and enhance a message with the intent to persuade, using supportive arguments with relevant and adequate evidence. You will learn how to bargain and negotiate and demonstrate competence and comfort with persuading audiences. You will be exposed to how to handle "good news" and "bad news" messages in business communication and various careers that individuals can pursue who major in communication and communication disorders.

. . . .

CHAPTER 16

Persuading with a Positive Purpose

by Regina Williams Davis

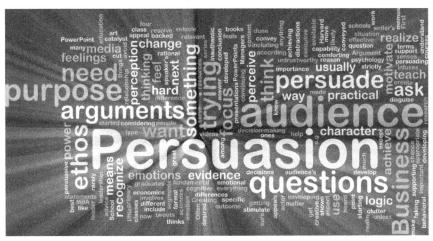

In the digital age, almost everything has signs and symbols associated with it. The competent persuader masters the ability to manipulate signs and symbols to convey and control a message. Politicians, media figures, religious leaders, and even pop stars rely on **symbol-manipulation**. Communication studies, persuasion studies in particular, find that symbol-manipulation addresses the creation of interpretable **symbol-sets** (particularly applicable to computing, advertising, and self-promotion) or **symbol substitution**. An example in war politics would be the term "collateral damage" which was used to replace "civilian casualties."

Other popular examples are usually easily identified in advertising.

The picture of the *apple*, which represents Apple Computers, needs no further explanation; nor does the Nike "swoosh."

Historically noted theorists in communication studies—Umberto Eco, Jean Baudrillard, and Nick Perry—define the **hyperreality** persuasive communication concepts. Notice that we entitled the units in this text with the prefix "hyper" to bring a level of multidimensionality and a high level of sensitivity. "Hyper" in mathematical terms means multidimensional. Hyperbole is the use of exaggeration as a rhetorical device or figure of speech. It may be used to evoke strong feelings or create a strong impression, but it should not be taken literally. Thus, we deemed labels for our units from the concept of **hypersensitivity.** Well, persuasive communication theory defines hyperreality as "the simulation of something that never really existed" (Baudrillard) and "the authentic fake" (Eco). Hyperreality describes a phenomenon of modern western consumer culture and its informational environment: the symbol, endlessly replicable and improvable, has come to replace the "real" object or idea it once represented. The map, as stated by Jorges Luis Borges, is sometimes substituted for physical territory. As we can see from the complex and deeply psychological impact of border-drawing in areas like the Palestinian Territories and the former Yugoslavia, this is often literally true; in the modern world, when a country ceases to exist on a map, it ceases to exist in reality. The *corset* that Madonna wore when she kissed Christina Aguilera no longer operates in the reality of which a corset was designed.

The dreaded foundational undergarment designed to mold and shape a waistline that was uncomfortable and always hidden from public view is now the desired sexy "outer" garment that women who have the body for it, will wear to a nightclub—hyperreality.

© Oleg Golovnev, 2012. Used under license from Shutterstock, Inc.

© MaxFX, 2012. Used under license from Shutterstock, Inc.

A related concept to hyperreality is hyperpraxis. **Hyperpraxis** is a means of altering public perception. An example that many Christians might be able to relate to is the fact that the symbol of the cross was a symbol of the practice of execution of thieves and other criminals. Today, the cross has a positive connotation and denotation because it represents the sacrifice of Jesus Christ and a significant event in the Christian religious faith.

Alan Monroe's "Monroe's Motivated Sequence"

Monroe's Motivated Sequence is a tool that has been used for persuasive speech writing for over seventy years. Among most marketers and communication strategists, it is believed to be a consistently successful method for gaining the interest of an indifferent audience to consider the speaker's point of view. Try testing the sequence on an audience one day. To be fair, you may want to survey your audience prior to your speaking presentation to find out what their feelings are on your particular topic. Remember that if your audience already has strong feelings in favor of your topic, your presentation will only reinforce their feelings. If your audience is indifferent, those are the individuals your speech might influence. The audience members that have a strong opinion against your topic may require multiple persuasive tools for persuasion (Monroe 1943).

After assessing the general opinion of your audience, prepare your speech using the following steps.

1. ***Attention Step. Get the attention of your audience.***
   - Detailed story
   - Shocking example
   - Dramatic statistic, quote, etc.
   NOTE: This is part of your introduction (thesis, preview, and credibility).

2. ***Need(s) Step***
   - Show the problem is significant.
   - The problem will not go away without the audience's involvement.
   - Support statements with documented statistics, facts, and examples.

3. ***Satisfaction Step***
   - Offer solutions for the problem addressed in the "Need(s)" Step.
   - These are solutions that the government or society as a whole can implement to satisfy the "need."

4. ***Visualization Step***
   - State what will happen if something doesn't happen about the problem.
   - Be graphic!

5. ***Action Step***
   - Offer alternatives that your audience can do *personally* to help solve the problem.
   - Be very specific and very realistic.

6. ***Conclusion***
   - Wrap up loose ends by giving a quick recap.
   - Restate your thesis.
   - Provide a powerful memorable statement.

Now that you gave your speech, take the time to survey your audience again. Find out if they were motivated by your presentation to consider exploring your point of view. If the general opinion of your audience leans toward your view of the topic, you have succeeded.

Aristotle's Persuasive Appeals

Hopefully, in your freshman English course, you were introduced to Aristotle's persuasive appeals. These appeals are used often in rhetoric and public oratorical expression. These are used in writing persuasive papers and crafting effective persuasive speeches. Most people have an innate ability to employ the idea Aristotle had in persuading an audience. I notice my children use the approach when they want something from me. My daughter, who is completely unfamiliar with Aristotle, and less concerned with the term rhetoric, used the three persuasive appeals on me the other day. Her first move was to attack my emotions. She used ***pathos***, an appeal to one's emotion. When engaged in a pathos appeal, words, pictures, personal stories, or a sharing of experiences are used to induce compassion, sympathy or empathy about your topic. My daughter will say something like, "Mom, may I go to Shay's birthday kick-back?" Of course, I said, "What's a *kick-back*?" She says, "It's when we hang-out at her house, watch movies, eat pizza, and just chill!" I said, "Will Shay's parents be there?" And she says, "No. It's no fun if parents are there!" I said, "Well, no! I don't think you may go." Then she says, "But, it's Shay's sweet sixteenth birthday, and I'm her best friend, and she will feel rejected if I am not there . . ." Can you explain how she is employing pathos?

Ethos is an ethical appeal. Because everyone has an idea about what they believe is right and wrong, good and bad, or fair and unfair, you may be able to connect with your audience in that manner. Going back to the example with my daughter . . . She would move into her ethical appeal with a statement like, "But, Mom, . . . I have straight A's; I have completed all of my chores; and I am already sixteen. It's not fair for you to deprive me of being with my friends." In my mind, I am more concerned with the fact that no responsible adults will be present at this "*kick-back*." However, she does make a reasonable argument for her perception of fairness.

The third rhetorical appeal makes an attempt to create a logical argument. Aristotle identified it as ***logos***. Your audience will want to make sense of what you are asking them to consider. If it makes sense to them, then there may be a possibility they will consider your point of view. My daughter made the following statement, "And, Mom, all of my other friends' parents will be letting their kids go to the kick-back. Plus, you know that they are responsible honor roll students, too. Their parents *trust* their kids. . . . Don't you trust me?"

Unlike a conversation between a sixteen-year-old and her parent, I expect your public speaking presentation will have substantial points supported with credible sources. Integrating an emotional (pathos), ethical (ethos), and a logical (logos) argument into your persuasive speech may prove to be effective.

Take a look at the graphic organizers located in the appendix. They can be helpful in organizing your persuasive speech to make it clear in your mind how to lead your audience. The ***cause and effect, pros and cons,*** and the ***compare and contrast*** graphic organizers are great tools to use when preparing persuasive speeches—informative speeches, too. Good luck!

Key Terms:

Ethos
Hypersensitivity
Hyperreality
Hyperpraxis
Logos

Pathos
Symbol Manipulation
Symbol-sets
Symbol-substitution

Key Concepts:

Aristotle's Persuasive Appeals
Monroe's Motivated Sequence

Application Activity: *Does This Persuade You?* Intensify/Downplay Rate Sheet

Directions:

Watch the YouTube video infomercial. Note the statements, dialogue, signs, symbols, music, non-verbal cues, etc. and determine if it is an association, composition, confusion, diversion, omission, or repetition technique used to persuade.

YouTube Video: https://www.youtube.com/watch?v=RtpKjgwi4Sc&feature=kp

Exaggerate the Personal

_____
_____
_____
_____
_____
_____
_____
_____
_____
_____
_____
_____
_____

Underplay Others

_____
_____
_____
_____
_____
_____
_____
_____
_____
_____
_____
_____
_____

Underplay the Personal

_____
_____
_____
_____
_____
_____
_____
_____
_____
_____
_____
_____

Exaggerate Others

_____
_____
_____
_____
_____
_____
_____
_____
_____
_____
_____
_____

Note:
   a. Associations—linking ideas together
   b. Confusions—making small things unnecessarily big issues (mountains out of molehills)
   c. Compositions—graphic layouts and designs
   d. Diversions—shifting attention to bogus concerns
   e. Omissions—half-truths, slanted or biased evidence
   f. Repetitions—reoccurring themes or examples, slogans, jingles

MINI QUIZ

1. True or False: Hyperreality refers to well established concrete phenomenon.
2. Multiple Choice: This is a means of altering personal perception.
   A. Hyperpraxis
   B. Hypersensitivity
   C. Hyperreality
   D. Pathos
3. Fill in the Blank: Use of the term "collateral damage" for "civilian casualties" in war is

   an example of _____.
4. Essay: Think of a controversial topic that you have a strong opinion for. Discuss how you would use ethos, pathos, and logos to construct your argument for an audience you know may not agree with you.

CHAPTER 17

Argumentation

by Regina Williams Davis

Most individuals will find themselves in discussions where there is disagreement and will reach into their arsenal of information within their mind trying to prove their point. Those of us who are competitive, love to win arguments. But rarely are we taught specifically what argumentation actually is. **Argumentation** is a dialogic activity of developing and advancing opinions and of responding to the contrary point of view. It is a communicative exchange of thoughts and ideas with other people. Argumentation is often about personal opinions regarding money, politics, religion, education, art, and of course, relationships. Arguments are used to persuade someone to agree with you, to justify your position on an issue, and to inquire into a topic for increasing public or personal knowledge of the topic. Someone may state a claim connected with supportive reasons to promote a discourse. Those that are skillful at argumentation make great advocates for social causes.

It may be important to note that there is a difference in the lay term of "having an argument" such as a disagreement and "making an argument," which technically suggests a presentation of reasons that support a conclusion, a proposition, or a claim. An argument has a clear and concise **statement, reasons, conclusions,** and **inferences**. Once you have a series of arguments to support your claim and the same general conclusions, you, essentially, can build a case.

Please consider the examples below. Consider which statements in the paragraphs below represent the conclusion(s) and reason(s).

Example 1:
Making sexual jokes in conversations with women is a form of sexual harassment. (*conclusion*) This is because such jokes are almost always demeaning to women. (*reason*) Any activity that demeans women is sexual harassment. (*reason*)

Example 2:
Competency tests should be required for all public school teachers (*conclusion*), because these tests would establish a standard of performance for all teachers (*reason*) and also identify the least capable teachers. (*reason*)

If you were not sure if a statement is a reason or a conclusion, view the list below. It highlights potential cues, clues, and indicators of what part of the constructed argument each statement will represent:

1. *"In addition"* and *"moreover"* can signal the introduction of a new line of argument.
2. *"Although"* and *"nevertheless"* often signal that the speaker is aware of a counter-argument.
3. *"Because," "since,"* and *"the following evidence shows"* signal that a reason will follow.
4. *"And"* frequently indicates a parallel relationship between two statements.
5. *"First," "second,"* and *"finally"* are quantitative cues that designate a series of reasons for a conclusion.
6. *"Therefore," "thus," "so,"* and *"hence"* indicate that a conclusion will follow.

Anytime you are developing or creating an argument, you will always need to be thinking about how you will substantiate your assertions. You will require a collection of **evidence** or **"connectives."** These are both types of *reasons* you may use to advance your proposition. The distinctions between the two are outlined below:

Evidence vs. Connectives
1. Evidence – is a reason . . .
   a. Rooted in observation (scientific studies, eyewitnesses, etc.)
   b. Derived from expert testimony
   c. Are generally demonstrated as "true or false"
2. Connectives – are reasons . . .
   a. That consist of beliefs, values, assumptions, or generalizations that link evidence to a conclusion.
   b. They are assumed, presupposed, or taken for granted
   c. Examples:
      i. Marriage is defined as being between a man or a woman.
      ii. War is never justified.
      iii. Working hard is the only way to be successful.
      iv. Government should not legislate moral behavior.
      v. Gun control is necessary and there should be more of it.
   d. Connectives are reasons that reflect personal commitments such as beliefs and values or generalizations that are widely accepted.
   e. Connectives help to make inferences. If you recall from Chapter 5, a **fact** is a statement that can be demonstrated as true or false, regardless of our own personal beliefs. An **inference** involves personal preferences. Connectives create inferences and opinions.
      i. Example:
         1. Evidence: The Bureau of Transportation statistics indicate that every year more than sixteen thousand Americans are killed in car accidents caused by drunk drivers.

2. Connective: When a clear threat to public safety is present, strong laws are needed for protection from that threat.
3. Conclusion: Clearly we need strong laws to protect us from the drunk driver.

© Everett Collection, 2012. Used under license from Shutterstock, Inc.

Formal Debating

There are three categories of conclusions to arguments. I know that it may seem strange to discuss a conclusion, but your opining statement is, in essence, the conclusion you want your opponent to draw after they have heard your evidence. The three categories are propositions of *fact, value,* and *policy.* Propositions of facts report, describe, predict, or make fundamental assertions. Propositions of facts are often handled during court proceedings. Did the defendant murder the victim or not? The jury is the judge of the debated facts. Propositions of value promote judgments about morality, beauty, merit, or wisdom. Propositions of policy urge an action to be taken or ceased. Formal debate organizations are organized in this manner. The Lincoln-Debate format is used commonly in high school and college competitions. These debates generally argue propositions of value. The Cross Examination Debate Association or CEDA promotes propositions of policy issues with a focus on government action. These formal debate organizations are very controlled with specific rules and time constraints that must be obeyed.

© James Steidl, 2012. Used under license from Shutterstock, Inc.

Formal **debates** have two sets of speeches: constructive and rebuttal speeches. The first set of speeches is the **constructive** speeches, where the arguments in the debate are initially introduced and constructed. **Rebuttal** speeches are a response to the constructed speech and a continuation or extension of your argument. A new argument cannot be introduced in a rebuttal speech and would be deemed invalid. Good debaters learn to select their best arguments in a constructive speech because those are the only arguments they can address and defend in a rebuttal.

When a debate begins, the first speaker initiates what is called a **"first affirmative constructive."** You will hear the speaker greet and acknowledge their audience and their judges and will say, for example, "Resolved: The United States federal government should substantially increase its exploration and/or development of space beyond Earth's atmosphere." The debaters are divided into the **affirmative** and the **negative** teams. They will know their resolution, but they will not know if they are to debate the affirmative or the negative prior to their debate performance. This makes it interesting to watch the team members collaborate and quickly prepare to adjust to their proposition of policy. At the end of each constructive speech, the debater is directly questioned for three minutes by the opposing side. This is the **cross-examination**. Every person in a debate is involved in two cross-examination periods: one as the questioner and one as the respondent. Cross-examination is used to set up arguments and to clarify issues.

I teach policy debate and use the stock issue theory. The first affirmative constructive speech is typically organized or addresses five traditional *stock* issues. The affirmative debater's success could rest on how well these issues are appropriately addressed. The stock issues are significance, harms, inherency, topicality, and solvency. Significance and harms are both addressed by stating the importance of the problem, what the results will be if the plan the affirmative team suggests is not implemented, and/or demonstrate why we need to change the current policy. Inherency highlights the lack of an action plan in the current system, but provides evidence that the new idea (plan) set forth from the affirmative team is doable and has not been enacted already. Topicality is the most important stock issue. It spells out the process that the affirmative team's plan fits within the boundaries of the resolution. Solvency is the second most important stock issue in that there must be a plan in place. Solvency clearly outlines the way the affirmative team's plan solves issues for the significant harms.

Using the stock issue theory, your first affirmative constructive will be a prepared scripted speech that will acknowledge the audience and thank them for their time and attention. Then, the resolution will be clearly stated as well as your *affirmative* agreement with the resolution. Your next section (using three to four paragraphs) will address: (a) the significance and harms of the resolution; (b) the inherency; and then (c) your plan to (re)solve the significance and harms concern—solvency. Topicality is not a specific section in the first affirmative constructive because it must be inferred through the evidence presented throughout this speech. This is really a matter of staying focused on the resolution. If the affirmative team loses focus, the negative team has the responsibility to point out the failure of the affirmative to provide a reasonable plan within the boundaries of the topic or resolution, which would be a grave error of the affirmative team.

Both constructive affirmative and negative constructed arguments are expected to use either deductive or inductive reasoning. Read the outlines on the next page:

Deductive and Inductive Arguments

1. **Deductive arguments** are arguments that lead to necessary conclusions when their reasons are *true*!
   a. The "reasons" in a deductive argument are traditionally called premises.
   b. The typical structure of a deductive argument is to have a:
      i. Major premise (general principle)
      ii. Minor premise (more specific principle)
      iii. Necessary conclusion
      iv. Example:
         1. Men and women should receive equal pay for equal work.
         2. Jason and Sharita do equal work as editors for the paper.
         3. Therefore, Jason and Sharita should receive equal pay.

2. **Inductive arguments** are arguments whose reasons lead to probable conclusions (likely, but not necessarily, the conclusion).
   a. The structure moves from specific observations to a general conclusion.
   b. Example:
      i. In a salary audit of 50 major US businesses, male executives were paid (on average) 17 percent more than their female counterparts in comparable positions. (specific observation)
      ii. It appears that many US companies are still paying men more than women for similar work. (general likely conclusion)
   c. Inductive arguments typically involve an inductive idea—a process in which the conclusion of an argument moves beyond its stated evidence.

Logical Fallacies

I like to introduce my students to a series of logical fallacies as we delve into the anatomy of an argument. A **fallacy** is an error in reasoning or an argument that is invalid because it is unreliable (not consistent and unstable). Learning to recognize fallacious arguments will force the person whom you are debating to justify the reasonableness of their assertion. Learning to avoid making fallacious arguments or illogical statements will strengthen your ability to construct sound propositions. If you choose to point out that someone you are debating committed a fallacy, it is most appropriate to state the fallacy, explain why it is a fallacy and why it matters in this particular debate, and give an example of your explanation. Below is a list of some of the more common fallacies people tend to make:

a. *Argument to tradition*. If your opponent makes the popular statement "It's always been that way!" know that tradition does not justify continuing a policy.

b. *Argument directed at the person*. A respectable opponent should not attack the character or motive of the person they are debating. The attack should only be on the specific idea.

c. ***Argument or appeal to numbers***. This is an attempt to prove something by showing how many other people think it's true. No matter how many people believe something, that doesn't make it true or right!

d. ***Argument or appeal to authority***. This is when someone tries to demonstrate the truth of a proposition by citing some person who agrees, even though they have no expertise in the area. It is a fallacy to rely on an unqualified source.

e. ***Argument or appeal to pity***. "Think of all the poor starving Ethiopian children!" No amount of special pleading can make the impossible possible or make the false true. It is legitimate to point out the severity of the problem as part of the justification for adopting a proposed solution. The fallacy comes in when other aspects of the proposed solution are ignored and the pleading is the appeal.

f. ***Argument to the point of disgust*** (i.e., by repetition). This is trying to prove something by saying it again and again. No matter how many times you repeat something, it does not become any more true or false.

Read the policy debate format I use in my course located in the appendices. I use the format from CEDA (see http://cedadebate.org/) as a model, but adjusted the times and rounds to fit into the time frames reasonable for my students in class. My students participate in a simulation that resembles a formal debate and they experience preparing and delivering the constructive (scripted) and rebuttal speeches (extemporaneous), as well as the cross examinations (impromptu). The strategy for the negative team is outlined in the appendices. Remember that preparing for the debate means that you are prepared to be on either side of the issue and will still express your case strong enough to WIN!

Key Terms:

Affirmative Team	Deductive Arguments
Argumentation	Evidence
Argument of Tradition	Fallacy
Argument or Appeal to Authors	Fact
Argument or Appeal to Numbers	First Affirmative Constructive
Argument or Appeal to Pity	Inductive Arguments
Argument Directed at the Person	Inferences Negative Team
Argument to the Point of Disgust	Policy
Conclusion	Reasons
Connectives	Rebuttal Speeches
Constructive Speeches	Statement
Cross Examination	Value
Debate	

Application Activity: "We're Right—You're Wrong!" Learning How to Conduct a Debate

Time: At least 2 class periods

Objective:

- Students will experience researching, preparing, and delivering an impromptu presentation necessary to participate in a formal policy debate.

Requirements:

1. Timekeeper
2. Three judges
3. The Resolution (provided by the instructor)
4. Two (or more) Debate Teams, consisting of 3–4 students per team. (Note: Neither team knows if they will present the affirmative argument or the negative argument until approximately 10–15 minutes prior to the beginning of the debate).
5. Awareness of round-robin tournament elimination rules.

Directions:

1. Divide into teams
2. In advance:
   a. Research the Resolution provided by your instructor
   b. Prepare to argue both the affirmative or the negative side of the Resolution
   c. Prepare a written First Affirmative Constructive
   d. Practice privately with your team prior to the actual debate
   e. Study the policy debate format located in the appendix of your book
3. Debate Day:
   a. Your instructor will randomly select the affirmative team
   b. The judges are introduced and reminded of their responsibilities
   c. The Policy Debate Rules are read and signals the beginning of the debate
   d. Use round-robin tournament elimination rules

MINI QUIZ

1. True or False: "Therefore" is an example of a word that will be used to indicate a conclusion.
2. Fill in the Blank: Another name for an illogical statement presented in a debate is called

   a(n) _____.
3. Multiple Choice: An argument consists of
   A. Statement
   B. Reasons
   C. Conclusion
   D. Inferences
   E. All of the above
4. Essay: Now that you have a more specific and clear understanding of how an argument is constructed, search online for a resolution that interests you and prepare a "first affirmative constructive."

CHAPTER 18

Business and Professional Communication

by Regina Williams Davis

In some ways, it may seem strange to separate business and professional communication from other interpersonal communication and persuasion because there is a great deal of information that will overlap. However, I tend to view business and professional communication almost as an art. I am a manager in a state-supported organization and I run two business ventures. As a manager, I am a team leader. As a business owner, I am an entrepreneur. Consciously committed, concise, and sincere communication is a must. Understanding and recognizing human needs of the people you work for and work with is paramount. On any given workday, someone in your business world will have a personal issue or concern, and you, as the ethical and successful professional, must understand that human needs will come first in terms of Maslow's hierarchy (see Chapter 9, page 132). In this chapter, we will discuss interpersonal communication in business by learning:

a. How to produce concise powerful "good news" and "bad news" messages (spoken or written),
b. How to provide effective feedback,
c. Networking tips,
d. Concepts in negotiation,
e. Conflict management strategies,
f. About mentoring relationships,
g. About high performance teams, and
h. How to have effective meetings.

Effective "Good News" and "Bad News" Messages

Depending on how you want your audience to react to your message is how you should choose to organize it. In business communication, almost every word that is spoken or written, along with every action you make, must be well thought through in advance. In Sir Isaac Newton's third law of motion, he proves that with every action there is an equal and opposite reaction. I believe that this universal law applies to the actions we make as human beings. For that reason, before sending your message, reflect on the ethical philosophy of teleology is discussed (see Chapter 8). **Teleology** suggests that your ethical behavior is based on the anticipated outcomes. To practice a Teleological ethic, you must be proactive in your actions. A successful business professional is proactive in all of his/her communication. This would include determining which vehicle or medium you would choose to deliver your message. The successful business professional plans his/her messages extremely carefully. You must craft messages that your audience will likely find to be nice, kind, and/or considerate or craft messages that will have your audience react in a neutral manner. The objective is not to provoke your audience in a negative manner.

To craft a *good news* message or a *neutral* message (for people of an American culture), it should be organized using the **deductive reasoning model**. The major idea of your message should be stated first. The supporting information and details will follow in a logical structure. Then end with a considerate and polite tone that suggests a potential future opportunity to connect. These three parts are essential. They leave your audience feeling hopeful. Good news messages are messages that express appreciation, thanks, or an expression of encouragement or approval (see Figure 18.1).

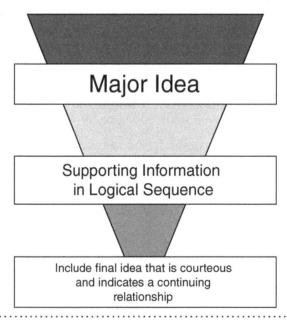

FIGURE 18.1 Deductive Reasoning Model

When having to craft a message where the content may potentially contain "*bad news*" for your audience, I would suggest using the following steps:

1. Make certain you are the person to deliver this message, if indeed this message is truly warranted.
2. Determine if this message should be delivered verbally, in writing, or both.
3. Your opening remark should be a courteous and sincere "Thank you." for either their time, effort, attention, inquiry, or something. Always find something positive to state in the beginning!
4. The next statement should sufficiently and clearly express to your audience what you are responding to in order to avoid confusion. For example, "I am responding to your inquiry regarding your recent job interview . . ."
5. Your first statement should not possess the *bad news*, but it should not be leading your audience to expect *good* news either.
6. Lead into the main reason for this communication—the *bad news*. Make every effort to de-emphasize the *bad news* statement with meaningful discussion.
7. Follow up the *bad news* with a comfort and hopeful statement that will create a more positive mood.
8. End with a positive statement that suggests a potential relationship in the future.

These steps are effective in both spoken and written messages. Just remember that anything that is written has the potential of becoming a matter of public record.

Effective Feedback

The ability to give and request feedback is essential in the business and professional world. Constructive use of this information helps individuals, organizations, and companies to be better. If we find the feedback useful, we can implement strategies for continuous improvements in areas where we are weak. There are many ways to acquire feedback, from surveys to focus groups. In this section, we will focus on the components of effective feedback.

Effective professional feedback in business communication has at least ten components. Effective feedback should be timely, specific, frequent, not personal, purposeful, documentable, balanced, descriptive, interactive, and expressed in a suitable environment. Timely feedback is most valuable immediately after an incident or activity. If someone produces a well-received program, let them know the value of appreciation promptly. Likewise, if there was an incident or complaint, it should be dealt with quickly. The feedback must be specific to a particular behavior. A general statement will not help anyone to identify how they can improve. Frequent feedback is helpful with continuous improvement. Personally, I like to know if my performance is improving when I am tweaking and adjusting to enhance specific processes.

It is definitely inappropriate to allow personal feelings and emotions to get in the way of professional communication. Again, focus on the behavior or activity. Purposeful feedback can contribute to the goals of the organization, the team, or for the individual's professional development. Documented feedback will assist tremendously in tracking improvements over a period of time. Balanced feedback is important for your audience to accept the comments with less emotion. Use the sandwich approach:

1. State or compliment the individual on something they do well.
2. Explain what they need to do to improve. And,
3. End with a statement that is positive and hopeful.

Please make your feedback descriptive instead of passing a judgment. Your audience needs enough data to know what, where, when, why, and how to improve. A simple, "I didn't like it . . ." does not provide constructive information. Create an opportunity for dialogue when discussing the feedback. This shows that you value the opinions of your audience and that you are open to learn from them as well. Be sure to conduct your feedback session in a location that will be suitable for a private discussion. It is important for your audience to feel welcomed and comfortable in your presence.

Effective feedback can be a powerful tool for organizational and professional enhancement!

Performance Feedback Script Activity:
1. Divide into small groups of four.
2. Select a timekeeper, a recorder, and a presenter.
3. Prepare a script for conducting a face-to-face feedback session with one of your employees or group members. (Ex. Addressing an employee who has been chronically late to work.)
4. Plan to act out your script in front of the class.
5. After every team has presented, discuss as a class the hardest part of developing the feedback script.

A Note on Networking

Networking is an essential skill for developing business and professional relationships that may become supportive in your future. It is a way for you to find resources and information as much as it is a way for others to find you.

Everyone will have a method that will work for them, but there is one method that I believe will be helpful. There will be many opportunities throughout your career where you will need to communicate quickly and concisely what you have to offer. You will need to share your skill set, experience, and other special information. However, most people do not have time to hear your entire life story. Therefore, it will benefit you to create a thirty-second elevator resumé brief that will give significant and pertinent information about you.

Identify three to four of your key strengths and incorporate these strengths into a summary statement. Order your statements to be first-engaging, second-peak interest for more information, and third-close with something memorable. Your objective is to leave your audience wanting to know more about you. Write your elevator resumé brief down and practice saying it until you have mastered it in a thirty-second time frame. You can do it!

Concepts in Negotiation

When it comes to **negotiating**, there are three primary areas of concern: Interest, Rights, and Power. Interests are our individual needs, desires, concerns, and fears. It includes all the things that we care about. Rights are the independent standard of perceived legitimacy of fairness such as laws, contracts, or social standards of concerns, like seniority. The power concern regarding negotiations is using the ability to coerce someone to do something that they normally would not do. Negotiation involves two or more parties who have something the other party wants. I believe that every potential transaction between two or more individuals is a negotiation. When sacrifices are made to reach a shared agreement, it is an exercise in bargaining. Bargaining is often an informal means of negotiating.

When preparing for negotiating, your approach should be simple, specific, and flexible. Taking the time to write down your thoughts prior to an upcoming negotiation is helpful. Part of your preparation should include being clear on your *purpose*—the objective of your negotiation; your *plan*, which will include where you will meet and will food or drinks be appropriate; your *pace*, which suggests that you consider how long you will allow the negotiation will go on; and the *personalities*, which is taking the time to understand the diversity of individuals involved in your negotiation and their needs.

I often recommend to my students that they consider conducting a SWOT analysis.

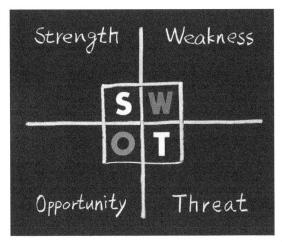

© Anson0618, 2012. Used under license from Shutterstock, Inc.

A **SWOT analysis** is a great tool to use to prepare for a negotiation meeting. It involves taking the time to assess your opponents' strengths, weaknesses, opportunities, and threats. I used this tool just recently when negotiating a five-year lease for a commercial property for one of the businesses that I manage. It was helpful for me to know that the owners of the property did not have renters occupying it for over two years. This helped me to understand that they might be eager to close the deal and to negotiate an acceptable price.

There are three bargaining strategies that are commonly used: Distributive Bargaining, Integrative Bargaining, and the Mixed Motive Strategy. **Distributive bargaining** will always end with a "win-lose" or "lose-lose" result. The goal of distributive bargaining is a scarcity mentality. The objective is to get the biggest piece of the pie. **Integrative bargaining** will result in a "win-win" for all parties involved. The goal of both parties will be to collaborate and generate multiple options or solutions that will expand the pie. The **mixed motive strategy** is the desire to create value with the "other" party and then claim your share. Tactics from both integrative and distributive bargaining methods are used.

It is important that the following behaviors are incorporated in all negotiations:

a. Show respect at all times.
b. Be guardedly informative about your interests.
c. Share more information as you develop trust.
d. Remain truthful.
e. Look for common ground and agree on basic principles.
f. Develop as many options as possible.
g. Pursue the "win-win."
h. Protect your interests.
i. Seek to expand the "pie" before dividing it.
j. Agree on the rules for dividing the "pie."

Know Your BATNA

Your "Best Alternative to a Negotiated Agreement" is referred to as your **BATNA**. According to Roger Fisher and William Ury (Spangler, 2003), any negotiation can be improved when you are aware of your best alternative. To identify your BATNA, you need to determine what will be your best option if the negotiation you are truly working toward does not work out. This will keep you from getting into a contract or agreement that you *really* did not want. Your BATNA gives you negotiating room and flexibility.

Negotiation Power Sources

There are so many ways to have perceived power when involved in a negotiation. It is good to be aware of these perceived power sources in order to have an understanding of how you may be perceived as a power source. These power sources include:

1. Positional power of authority – "Do what I say because I am the boss!"
2. Rewards – "If you do what he says, he will reward you handsomely, but if you don't . . ."
3. Sanctions – "If you continue to have these complaints, you will not be given this opportunity again."

4. Force – "I will make sure your child will not have a part in the next play!"
5. Information – "I know who to contact to get what you need."
6. Expertise – "She can create and edit commercials in all formats."
7. Charisma – "When he speaks, people listen and want to support his goals!"
8. Relationship – "I can work with her because I know her work ethic. She won't let me down."
9. BATNA – "The worst case scenario for me is to go back to my old unit . . . and that may be just fine with me!"

Conflict Management

Believe it or not, many companies deem that conflict is a benefit to their organization as long as it does not seriously affect cooperation and become an obstacle to the mission. Hence, conflict management is the process of planning to avoid quarrels and major disputes and resolve destructive disagreements quickly. If the desire of the manager is to create friendly competition or to promote unique and different ideas, this may turn into conflict and will need to be handled. Other causes of conflict are scarcity of resources, diversity in values, disagreements in priorities, and poor communication.

Giving individuals an opportunity to express themselves or vent in a safe place can help reduce conflict. However, when conflict becomes major in a workplace, sometimes collective bargaining is needed. Managing open conflict can require negotiating a compromise, mediation, or arbitration. **Collective bargaining** is a process where representatives from each group come together with a mandate to work out a solution. Integrative bargaining is the best strategy to use. **Mediation** is when an independent unbiased individual is asked to facilitate a settlement of the conflict. **Arbitration** is the appointment of an independent person to act as an adjudicator or judge in a dispute and they will decide on the terms of a settlement.

To reduce the potential for conflicts to rise to the point of mediation and arbitration, it is helpful for everyone in the organization or on your team to be aware of their conflict management strategy. These strategies include: competition, collaboration, compromise, avoidance, and accommodation.

Mentoring Relationships

It is valuable to seek a mentoring relationship to assist you with your goals for a successful career. We may have informal mentors and not even realize it. However, there are formal mentoring relationships in the professional world. If you want to have a mentor, there are a few things you may want to consider. Someone may see and learn something about you and choose you to be their protégé, or you may meet someone that you admire and would like to learn from them. In essence, you may find a mentor or a mentor may find you.

Mentoring relationships may have low to very high levels of self-disclosure and a variety of demands on time. However, all mentoring relationships must have high levels of trust. A mentor that will assist you in career development usually will share "tricks of the trade," will be honest with you about skills you need to improve, and will protect you from potentially damaging experiences in your professional life. Mentoring relationships should always lead to positive results. The key is to employ all of your communication skills for listening, speaking, receiving constructive feedback, and implementing the ideas your mentor suggests.

Some obstacles that affect being a good mentor are the lack of time, fear of a codependent relationship, and staying abreast of cultural changes. Therefore, if you are seeking a mentor, it will be helpful to be cognizant of these fears and attempt to address these concerns in the initial stage of your mentee/mentor relationship. Good luck!

How to Have a High Performance Team

Teams or groups can easily become dysfunctional. However, there are some techniques for developing high performance teams. Always seek individuals who have a commitment to producing quality work. First, orient teams by requesting each member to be a part of developing a mission statement so that we have a common goal. Next, discuss what the roles will be initially, although they may change as we progress. Finally, discuss how the team will operate and communicate via email, texting, etc. The most productive teams have three, but no more than four members. Additionally, I will disclose some of my weaknesses so that everyone feels comfortable and understands that commitment is more important than perfection.

It may be helpful to understand the different phases that most teams typically experience. These phases include: forming, storming, norming, performing, and concluding. When teams are forming, they are discussing ground rules and how they plan to manage and divide up the assignment or task(s). Teams are in the storming phase when mild conflict begins to arise. You will notice a variety of attitudes and questions about activities that were already agreed upon. If you are aware that this is typical, then you can prepare to step back from taking the comments personally and encourage positive communication and revisit some of the group decisions. In the norming phase, members begin to feel like they are on the right track and are pressing toward getting the mission accomplished. Everyone likes the performing phase, which is the opportunity to see the results of the team's hard work and their sacrifices in time. The last phase, concluding, is often bittersweet. There is a sense of satisfaction because the task has been completed, but sadness that the team may be disbanded. It may be good to have a parting party that will include tying up loose ends and evaluating what went well to help individuals on future teams.

Show your appreciation of your team members through verbal "thank-you's," accolades, treating them to a meal, and expressing concerns about things that are important to them ("How's your daughter doing today? I remembered you said she wasn't feeling well.") will demonstrate a caring concern for your team members. Showing old-fashioned thoughtfulness and consideration will take your team to the high-performance level of teaming!

Ways to Have an Effective Meeting

My colleagues and I initially thought that we might not need to have a section on effective meetings, but then we attended a meeting that was such a waste of our time. This made us decide to include some core principles for having a productive meeting.

As you are planning the meeting agenda, it is helpful to keep in mind your meeting attendees or those who should attend. It is necessary to invite the individuals who need to be aware of the topic(s) of discussion, who are affected by the topic(s) in some way, and/or who may have voting power on the topic(s). Know what your meeting goals are. The meeting agenda should list the tasks in order of priority and place an estimated time next to each one. This is to help control the length of your meeting as well as to send your agenda to the meeting attendees in advance. Try to select a time and place that will be comfortable and convenient for most of the individuals you are expecting. Start your meeting as close to the established time as possible. Facilitate your meeting by keeping people on topic. You may allow some digression for discussion or background purposes, but do so minimally. Close your meeting by summarizing the key issues discussed or resolved and suggest an action plan for those items that were not completed. After your meeting, it is good to get feedback from attendees. This will help you to improve the effectiveness of your next meeting.

Key Terms:

Arbitration	Negotiating
Collective Bargaining	Negotiation Power Sources
Conflict Management	Networking
Distributive Bargaining	Mediation
Effective Professional Feedback	Mentoring
High Performance Teams	Mixed Motive Strategy
Interrogative Bargaining	Teleology

Key Concepts:

Deductive Reasoning Model

SWOT Analysis

BATNA

Application Activity:

Write a "Good News" Letter and a "Bad News" letter. Share with a partner to find out how effective was your approach.

MINI QUIZ

1. True or False: The Deductive Reasoning Model is used to deliver unpleasant news.
2. Fill in the Blank: Interest, rights, and power are the primary areas of concern in _____.
3. Multiple Choice: This bargaining strategy will result in a "win-win" for all partners and is termed:
   A. Distributive
   B. Interrogative
   C. Mixed Motives
   D. None of the above
4. Essay: Describe how bargaining may be different in the business and professional setting as opposed to other interpersonal interactions.

CHAPTER 19

Audience Analysis: "Don't Talk to Strangers"

by Myra M. Shird

To know your audience is to relate to them based on their background and demographics. How can you know your audience when you've never met them? They're strangers, and mama always said, "Don't talk to strangers." One of the best ways to get to know your audience is to talk with the person who invited you to give the speech. This individual can provide you with background information such as how much the audience will know about the speech topic. Also, finding out such demographics as age, gender, and race of those in the audience will help you tailor your speech to your audience. Conducting an audience analysis will mean that on speech day, you succeed.

As a first requisite for communicating effectively, you must be aware of and sensitive to the major components of the speech process. These are 1. the self, 2. the "other," 3. the communication context.

Understanding How the Self Functions in the Public Speaking Event

"Know thyself," recommends the ancient adage. It's sound advice. You should try to formulate a clear concept of yourself *as a speaker*. Strive to see yourself *as others see you* in the act of speaking, attempting self-assessment as if you were an impartial, outside observer. As a first step, systematically make a careful, objective analysis of your feelings and behaviors in a number of speech communication *situations*.

Understanding the "Other" in the Public Speaking Event

When you are the speaker, the "Others" in the speech communication context will comprise your listeners—your audience. You should, therefore, learn as much about them as possible. That is, if you desire to interact with them effectively. The analysis of audiences begins and is inextricably interwoven with the history of rhetorical theory. In his dialogue, *Phaedrus*, Plato asserts that the good speaker must know the nature of his audience—must know their "souls." Aristotle, who also devoted much attention to audience analysis, discusses in the *Rhetoric* what an audience is likely to consider good. He touches upon several human emotions—anger, fear, love, shame, and pity—and examines the effects produced by the various emotions on listeners and the factors which create those effects. His discussion of the generation gap, hardly a new phenomenon, is a useful model of audience analysis and one pertinent for almost any era. Examine it and decide in what respects (if any) you agree, and to what extent.

What Is Their Motivation Here?

The analysis of audience behavior is also a central concern in contemporary research in communication. In fact, it has probably received more attention than any other single aspect of the oral interaction process. To know and to study the "subject matter" of an intended message is one thing; to know and analyze the nature, inclinations, and biases of the "others"—the audience members—is quite a different task—and a much more elusive one. And, of course, the larger the number of listeners, the more complex the assessment becomes. Here again, however, you can make certain preparations of both a general and a specific nature.

When preparing to speak with any audience (whether it be one good friend or a thousand strangers), you should try to assess the dominant values and motives which will be operative in the audience at the time of the speaking event. Because you will have to make your assessment well before the time you actually meet your audience face to face, your work will not be easy. To an extent, you will have to rely upon generalizations and speculations. But regardless of how you formulate your audience appraisal, the procedure can assist you in two important ways. First, it will reveal to you the nature of the audience you will face; you will become more aware of the types of personalities represented among your listeners. Second, by discovering the present thought position (and nature) of your audience, you can knowledgeably determine the directions and emphases your speaking must take in order to move the thinking of that audience to the desired position on the subject.

One means of accomplishing this goal is to ascertain the nature of the groups to which the listener(s) belong. Are they, for instance, predominately members of a single political party, or a church organization, or a certain social group? Do they come from a particular geographical region? Almost always, the individual identifies with one or more groups or collectives. By identifying with a certain group a person places himself in a category: he belongs to X group, she is one of the X. When you identify yourself with a group, you associate yourself with and support the attitudes, values, and motivations of that group. If you can accept the group memberships of your prospective listeners, you can use their associational attitudes, values, and motivations to bridge the communicational gap, to facilitate closer interactions.

In one research study, for example, a questionnaire containing some items opposing norms of the Roman Catholic faith was administered to two groups of Catholic students. Before filling out the questionnaire, group one was informed that they were all Catholics. Group two was not so informed. You can anticipate the results. Subjects in group one answered the questionnaire's critical items in clever accord with the positions prescribed for Catholics than did group two. The awareness of group membership clearly influenced group one to follow more closely the norms of their religious commonality.

A speaker will often wear his Legion cap when addressing the American Legion Convocation, thereby calling attention to the customs of the group and letting his audience know that he, too, is a member of their organization—one of them. Even if a speaker is not a member of the organization or group to whom she is addressing, she often tries to create the appearance of oneness with them by wearing a symbol of their organization or trade. A political campaigner, for example, might wear a hard hat when speaking to a group of construction workers. Almost any group can be expected to respond more favorably to one of its own or to one who shows evidence of a willingness to be "one" with them—especially if the speaker visibly emphasizes their common bond.

In analyzing an audience, you should seek out all of the information you can about the others who are or will be in the communication setting. Try to discover their views on the topic at hand, their beliefs and evaluations, their values and motives, the groups and viewpoints with which they associate themselves, and other characteristics or variables such as self-esteem, extremity of view, ego involvement, hostility, aggression, sex, etc.

This, admittedly, is no small task. It requires patience, perseverance, and a degree of ingenuity; but any speaker who hopes to interact effectively must do it. Never address an audience you can conceive of only in vague and general terms. Only address an audience that you are aware of and that you know. This applies to every communication. Each audience is a different audience. And if you fully realize this, you will readily understand why you may, on occasion, speak to your father very differently from the way you may speak to your mother, or why you would not use the same speech for a political gathering that you would use when addressing fellow graduates at a commencement, although many of the same people might be in both audiences.

The Feedback Principle

The thermostat is a common example of a mechanical feedback device. It controls the temperature in a room by receiving stimuli that indicate temperature levels, then sending this information to the furnace to produce changes in the physical environment. When the temperature falls to a certain level, the furnace is activated; when temperature rises to a certain level, the furnace is deactivated. Mechanisms regulating feedback occur and can be observed throughout nature. The human organism itself, for instance, contains numerous feedback mechanisms, which serve homeostatic purposes. These mechanisms keep body temperature, blood-sugar level, and many other physiological factors within desired ranges.

To pursue our first analogy a bit further, you might ask, "Does the temperature influence the thermostat, or does the thermostat influence the temperature? Which is cause and which is effect? The correct and crucial answer is that each is cause and each is effect; each is influencing, and at the same time, being influenced. The key factors in our analogy are interdependence and interaction of the elements or agents. The people in the speech communication context operate in an analogous situation: both influence and are influenced; both must agree to this joint participation.

From the vantage point of the speaker we need to answer the question: What can be done to gain and maintain the participation of the listening audience? In planning for a speech act, you must think in terms of your listeners and must plan with them in mind. In this preplanning, you will find that the principle of feedback functions in at least two very useful ways: (1) it enables you to allow for "feedforward," and (2) it enables you to adjust more readily and effectively to feedback from your listeners during the actual communication of your message. Actually, prior planning is feedforward, a counterpart of feedback.

Adjusting to Feedback from Your Audience

If, in your initial step in planning for a speech situation and event, you have carefully anticipated the nature of your prospective audience, have assessed their preferences and priorities, have taken into close account the variables of feedforward, and feel confident to carry the resultant adaptation into the speech context itself, you are ready to take a second important step toward effective interaction—adjusting to audience feedback.

This step involves an on-the-spot, face-to-face problem which you can detect and solve only with your actual audience before you. You must correctly interpret your audience members' responses as you are speaking, and you must adapt to that response very quickly. The requisite skill is adaptive readiness.

One of the key differences between planning for feedforward and adjusting to feedback is that in the former, you are, in effect, predicting probabilities, but in the latter you are facing immediate reactions. In the former, you can attempt specific preparation; in the latter you have to rely largely upon general preparation and flexibility. In adjusting to feedback, you must "think on your feet," and react immediately. In planning for feedforward, you are making allowances for what you believe might happen in a possible situation; in adjusting to feedback, you are making adjustments for what is happening in and to your audience. You must read reactions accurately, devise and assess possible new and unanticipated courses of action—"instantaneous feedforward"—and select the one that seems best to you at that particular instant.

If the facial expressions of your listener(s) reveal puzzlement, you may adjust by reiterating your point and amplifying it with clarifying materials. If your listener(s) appear bored, you may react by interjecting some humorous or novel material. If your audience is antagonistic or noisy negative, quite probably you will want to react promptly by voicing a pertinent value generally held by the preponderance of the audience members.

As an example of successful adaptation to audience feedback, consider an impromptu statement by Henry Ward Beecher. When an audience in Liverpool, suffering from the embargo during the American Civil War, reacted negatively by heckling a point in his speech, Beecher is reported to have said, "All I ask is simply fair play." Fair play apparently was a value embraced by most of the members of his audience. They allowed the speaker to proceed without further interruptions. Malcolm X, when speaking in favor of Black nationalism to a college audience, sensed a negative audience reaction to his rate and intensity of delivery. He attempted to adjust to this interpreted feedback by saying, "I'm sorry to be talking so fast, but I haven't much time, and I do have a lot to say." If you hope to be effective as a speaker, you must be sensitive to such audience cues, able to interpret them accurately, and able to react to them in ways that facilitate positive interaction.

Audience Rapport

Good rapport, the empathy that one human being has for another, and the relationship it seeks to identify should be one of your guiding goals as you plan and incorporate feedforward. You have no doubt heard the expression "having good vibes" to describe a feeling of natural understanding and sympathy. In the physical world, scientists use the term "sympathetic vibrations" to describe this principle. To demonstrate the principle, two tuning forks of equal frequency are placed in close proximity. When one fork is struck, the second tuning fork will be set into sympathetic vibration by a very small amount of sound-wave energy created by the vibrations of the first fork. If the second tuning fork has a vibration frequency different from the first fork, this phenomena will not occur. Sympathetic vibrations can also be produced with piano strings having the same frequency. The necessary condition for sympathetic vibrating is that the two bodies have identical resonant frequencies.

Similarity, if two or more individuals having similar psychological "resonant frequencies" are brought into association in a speech communication context, they seem to have a natural tendency to respond favorably to one another. They apparently have many characteristics in common—backgrounds, beliefs, values, attitudes, experiences, etc.—which seem to cause persons to respond to an event or events similarly. This is not a matter of mere conjecture. In persuasion, of the general findings of behavioral scientists is that a person is most significantly influenced by his close friends and associates, and by family. Voting behavior of young citizens, for example, appears to be determined to a greater extent by the predisposition of their parents than by the effects of a political candidate's charisma and speeches in particular election campaign. Of course, this parent-induced "sympathetic" behavior is not an instantaneous or automatic response.

Reacting to Absence of Feedback

Adjustment to feedback has, of course, certain advantages; but it also has its pitfalls; and as we will see, the total absence of feedback can produce serious obstacles to human interaction. The able communicator will therefore want to be alert to all of these possibilities.

At its worst, the inability to respond to others in real-life situations is a form of mental illness, and under so-called "normal" day-to-day conditions, failure to provide and receive feedback can do inestimable harm. One of the major problems in large organizations is that of "role ambiguity," in which a person feels that she doesn't quite know where she stands, what is expected of her or just how she fits in. She may be uncertain about the "task" elements of her job—the specific ethics—or she may feel insecure about the "socio-emotional" elements of the work—her interpersonal relationships. A frequent cause of this role ambiguity is the lack of communication or feedback from superiors. No matter how unsatisfactory the role itself may be, ambiguity about it is even worse. The deleterious effects of zero feedback doubtless extends to all speech communication settings. Outright heckling, for instance, is in many ways easier for the speaker to take than no reaction or indifference. As a speaker, you must do all you can to sense reaction in your hearers, and your hearers should do all they can reasonably do to provide "readable" reaction. You must learn to look at your audience to see people in it, and to see reaction. You must come to read reactions as "interest," "approval," "antagonism," "skepticism," "boredom," "polite blank stares," and so on.

Overreacting to Feedback

At the same time, both as speakers and listeners, you must be on guard against over reading or over responding to these or any other cues. Inherently, all feedback mechanisms, whether mechanical or human, have in them a tendency to overreact to stimuli. A radar-aimed antiaircraft gun programmed to zero in on a swiftly swerving, expertly maneuvered fighter jet tends to develop a momentum which carries it beyond a correct alignment with the target: it tends to overcorrect itself. The elusive target causes the gun to swing back and forth so rapidly that it has difficulty setting down on a straight line to the plane. Another example of this tendency to overcorrect is the boxer's response to the feinting jab employed by a skilled fighter to draw his opponent off guard and off balance.

Similarly, in the speech communication situation, a speaker may over react and over adjust for feedback and thereby lose sight of her basic purpose. Stated conversely, an audience—or even a small segment of it can provide such a strong or vociferous response as to cause the speaker, in turn, to over correct, distort, or lose sight of his intended message.

Over reaction to audience feedback is by no means exclusively a problem for beginning speakers. Experienced orators and seasoned political campaigners are highly susceptible on occasion. Indeed, there are some speakers, as you no doubt have observed, who are so eager to sense from which directions "the winds of change are blowing"—and to react instantaneously to those currents—that their values and goals seem to come more from their listeners than from themselves. Although they may be public figures and "leaders," they are, in fact, "followers," the epitome of the other-directed person.

Language Adaptation

As a public speaking communicator, you should be aware also that two persons having many experiences in common tend to develop similar categories and strategies for reasoning. You should be alert to the fact that, as you plan the phrasing of your ideas, propositions, and arguments, persons having these similar backgrounds are likely to have similar connotations for language symbols. Individuals with a good rapport or who have worked closely together in a school, business, or profession sometimes speak in a mutually-known jargon which strengthens their communicative bond. Various groups have their own verbal "shorthand"—they can count on the other's ability to fill in a cryptic message with appropriate detail. In Tolstoy's novel *Anna Karenina*, for instance, two lovers communicate by using the initial letter to each word, such as I - L - Y. If, in planning for feedforward you are cognizant of the range of language adaptability, your audience interaction will be much more effective.

Unfortunately, many participants in public speech scenarios do not have the close natural rapport and mutuality that we are describing in this section. Yet your goal as speaker is to try to discover the extent to which these bonds do exist among your listeners, and to strive for the feedforward which can facilitate and broaden their understanding of what you are trying to communicate to them.

To some degree, the functioning of this linguistic commonality is under your direct control as the speaker. Within reasonable bounds, you should adapt and attempt to "speak the language" of your listener. Behavioral research reveals ways that you, as a speaker, may do this. For example, speaking to the Methodist Women's club on water pollution, you may, relate your proposition to family life and social values. However, if later in the day you speak to the local Junior Chamber of Commerce, you may relate the same proposition to economic concerns. You will be less effective if you attempt to give the identical speech in two different settings. It is not enough to adjust the introductory material of your speech but the entire message must be fitted to the beliefs and evaluation and values of the audience.

In feedforward, your role as a speaker-to-be is to anticipate audience reactions and prepare for them. The greater your knowledge of the audience, the more accurately you will be able to predict their responses. In some special cases, as with a television address, attention to feedforward becomes of utmost importance because your audience is "faceless," and only delayed feedback will be possible. But for most forms of oral communication, including informal conversation, your anticipation of listener judgments and responses can help you achieve the desired interaction.

Stasis

Our study of feedforward would be incomplete without a consideration of what classical rhetoricians called stasis or the "status of the case." Assuming that you have accurately ascertained the beliefs, attitudes, values, and general backgrounds of your listeners, you now need to know what is their thinking about the ideas or prepositions you intend to advance. At what point in your speech do you "hook on" to their collective train of thought? If you assume, for instance, that your listeners have more background knowledge of your topic than they in fact possess, you will "lose" them at the outset; if you assume that they have less than they really have, they may quickly lose interest and become bored.

By asking specific questions the status of a case can be determined. Does the case focus on a question of fact, of definition, or of quality? For example, A is accused of murdering B. The first question (of fact) asks: Did A kill B? The second question (of definition) asks: Did the killing of B fit our legal definition of murder? The third question (of quality) asks: Was the act good or bad? Was it justified? The status of the argument could fall on either side of the issue. The issue might be: Did A kill B? If it is proved that A did intend to kill B, then the issue could become: Was it an act of murder? If murder is proved—or perhaps, admitted by A—the issue could become: Was the murder justifiable (self-defense, for instance), or was it premeditated and in cold blood? No effective communication will occur if you present an issue and your listener doesn't know enough about what you are talking about to understand your meaning; nor will any real communication take place if you are belaboring an issue already accepted by the listener.

When you are speaking on social issues, you may find it necessary to demonstrate the existence of a problem and, at other times, necessary to present a specific solution to the problem. If the listener already accepts the existence of the problem, you should talk about solutions and not waste time trying to persuade the listener of something he already accepts. On the other hand, there is little value in arguing for a specific solution and a new course of action if the listener doesn't feel that a problem even exists. If you hope to have the listeners respond maximally to your message, then you must be perceptive of the stasis of the listener(s). The degree to which you are capable of preplanning this adaptation will determine the degree of your effectiveness.

Understanding the Context of the Impending Communication

To know your audience is not enough. You must also know the communication context of the specific speaking situation or setting. The elements of the context will be multidimensional, multidirectional, and simultaneously operant within speaking situation because of the following factors:

1. The specific context constrains and directs your choices of materials and approaches.
2. The specific context helps you as the speaker to determine what is expected of you.
3. The specific context helps you to define what is desired of the speaker.
4. The specific context bears importantly upon what is required of the speaker.
5. And, over all, the context strongly influences the outcomes of the communication act.

Context has both physical and psychological dimensions that are significantly influenced by certain social, temporal, and cultural factors. They are the contemporaneous, causative, and circumstantial influences which bear upon an impeding communication event.

Contemporaneous Influences

Time and timing are significant elements of the context therefore, public speakers must be attuned to the tenor and timbre of the times. What are the common topics and issues of the day? What are the prevailing beliefs and practices? The length of speeches, like the length of women's skirts, vary from era to era. Standards for the "ideal" length of a speech change more slowly; however, some ages do go for maxi speeches while others seem to prefer the mini speech. The typical language (an unmistakable dating factor) of one age will appear ornate and artificial in another. You're the speaker—have some sensitivity to the contemporaneity of the context.

Causative Influences

The public speaker should also be aware of the **impetuses or forces which have continued to produce the specific speech situation**. What in this context has brought these particular people together at this particular time? Is the situation one of negotiation, where an antagonist and you—as protagonist—will attempt to arrive at a compromise that will bring to an end some impasse between you? Or does the situational milieu require you to enact the role of arbitrator in which you will attempt to create agitation among others in order to end an impasse between them? The problems may be similar, but there are different contextual requirements if your role is that of negotiator rather than arbitrator.

Perhaps, the situation is one of debate, where you are contending one person against another person in order to project your view to still other people. If so, design and marshal your arguments so that they will sway those listening to the debate. It is pointless to try to influence your opponent in a structured context of this kind.

Circumstantial Influences

As a speaker, you must know within the specific context not only to whom you are speaking, but also—and this is equally crucial—you must know what your audience expects of you. Are you being called to the specific situation to "present information" in a fairly unbiased manner? In that situation, outright advocacy may be objectionable, out of place, and ineffective. Or the situation might be calling for a polemic before a partisan crowd where you are expected to "pour it on." Is your presence a matter of genuine audience desire, or is it more of a perfunctory appearance? In the latter case you may choose to present "a few fitting and appropriate remarks" rather than a lengthy discourse. Is it a serious interview or social conversation? Audience expectations should, of course, help to shape every communication context.

Clearly, the circumstantial aspects of the occasion dictate significant differences in the content, thought direction, and delivery of a given message. A speaker addressing a routine Rotary Club luncheon on a given topic would not present the identical speech to the same group if they had convened for an evening meeting in a church social hall. As the speaker, you want to know in each instance what else, if anything, is planned for the program: who and what will precede your speech, and who and what will follow it; whether the general atmosphere of the occasion is to be serious or light; whether you will be seated at the head of a long dining table, or whether you will be speaking to the group from an elevation of some kind. If at all possible, you should make it a practice to inspect the physical facilities and arrangement some time before you are to speak. Always inquire about the occasion and ascertain the intended order of events—find out what "usually" happens at such a meeting.

Key Terms

Motivation

Audience Analysis

Rapport

Language Adaptation

Stasis

Feedback

Application Activity: *Persuasive Speech*

Time: 7–10 Minutes

Objective:

■ The purpose of the Persuasive Speech is to give your audience information, facts, and data in an organized and strategic manner that will force them to consider your point of view. Be sure to know your audience well enough to present your material in ways that may be engaging and meaningful to them. In this presentation, you are to promote your personal opinions, advance your thesis, or generate a call for action. Show your passion!

Directions:

PART ONE:

Prepare a video of your speech. Be sure to develop a clear thesis statement or "central message":

I. **Introduction**
   a. Attention-getter
   b. Credibility statement
   c. Preview of the main points contained in the body
   d. Thesis Statement
   e. Transition statement to the "Body"

II. **Body**
   a. Two or three main points; elaborate them using examples, explanations, or narrations
   b. Transition sentences or phrases between each point and a main transition statement to the "Conclusion"

III. **Conclusion**
   a. Signal that you're ending your speech
   b. Promote your "Call for action!"
   c. Memorable statement

PART TWO:

Show your ACCLAIM video to at least two of your classmates and request they complete a peer review. Your reviewers are to let you know if they were persuaded to consider your point of view.

PART THREE:

After reviewing your video and the feedback from your peers, prepare a typed, 1-page reflection paper, describing how you might improve your persuasive presentation, given the opportunity. Be specific.

Peer Evaluation—*The Persuasive Speech*

Directions: With four (4) being the highest and best score, please select the number to rate each component of the Persuasive Speech.

INTRODUCTION
Attention-Getter (Opening story, rhetorical question, quotations, etc.)

0	1	2	3	4

Credibility

0	1	2	3	4

Preview

0	1	2	3	4

Thesis Statement or Central Message

0	1	2	3	4

Transition Sentence

0	1	2	3	4

BODY
2–3 Appropriately Organized Points

0	1	2	3	4

Sufficiently developed with support for each point

0	1	2	3	4

Transition sentence

0	1	2	3	4

CONCLUSION
Signal of Wrapping-up/Transition Phrase

0	1	2	3	4

Summarize

0	1	2	3	4

Call-to-Action

0	1	2	3	4

Memorable Statement (Final, strong, connected . . .)

0	1	2	3	4

CHAPTER 20

Careers in Communication Studies and Communication Sciences and Disorders

......

Careers in Communication Studies

......

by Stephanie Sedberry Carrino and Regina Williams Davis

Communication Studies is a broad academic discipline, and students who graduate with a degree in Speech/Communication Studies are prepared for a wide variety of positions in high demand.

Though the study of communication often overlaps other fields of study, there is a core of content that defines the study of human communication. *Communication Studies* students examine forms of communication—spoken, written, and non-verbal—and the way people communicate in relationships, public discourse, and within organizations. Students study how people co-create meaning and how messages are interpreted in social, political, cultural, economic, and social contexts. The way the processes of communication relates to cultural differences, technology, and other social variables makes this major highly relevant in today's competitive job market.

Students majoring in *Communication Studies* learn to:

1. Analyze messages in a variety of contexts
2. Speak effectively
3. Think critically/Analyze problems
4. Listen effectively
5. Gather and analyze information
6. Create and analyze persuasive messages
7. Write clearly and effectively

These skills allow graduates to work across multiple industries, including:

Corporations

Healthcare Organizations

Non-Profit Organizations

Government Agencies

Educational Institutions

Media Outlets—Magazines/newspapers/television/film

Politics

Social and Human Services

Many students choose to attend graduate school after completing an undergraduate degree in *Communication Studies* and they are well prepared for entry into Law School and various Master's Degree Programs. However, many students are interested in joining the workforce and there are almost limitless options for careers with this degree program.

Job titles vary by industry, but the following list of job titles provides a starting point for students seeking employment with their communication studies degree:

Account Manager/Executive	Program Coordinator/Director
Activities Director	Public Administrator
Advertising Specialist	Public Information Officer
Admissions Counselor/Representative	Public Opinion Researcher
Announcer	Legislative Assistant
Claims Adjustor/Examiner	Lobbyist Fundraiser/Development Officer
Communication Consultant	Manager
Communications Assistant/Analyst	Market Research Analyst
Community Affairs Liaison	Marketing Representative/Assistant/Specialist/
Corporate Communications Specialist	Director
Corporate Trainer	Mediator
Customer Relations	Personnel Specialist
Employment Specialist	Public Relations Specialist/Coordinator
Event Planner/Convention Organizer	Publicist/Publicity Manager/Media Planner

Field Marketing Representative	Recreations Manager
Grants Writer	Recruiter
Health Educator	Risk and Crises Communication
Hospitality Manager	Sales Representative
Human Resources/Relations Specialist	Speech Writer
Human Rights Officer/Ethics Officer	Technical Writer
Information Specialist	Training and Development Specialist/Supervisor

Graduates who have a communications studies degree also work in the field of theater and performing arts. Many of our students take positions with the federal service, local and state government, including public information officers, legislative assistants, research specialists, program coordinators, and elected officials. Other communications related positions include:

Technical copywriter for high tech firms

Health communications analyst

International public service postings

Publications editor for nonprofit groups or government agencies

Legal reporter

Nonprofit executives

According to Aylesworth (2009), the U.S. Department of Education reports that the percentage of graduate degrees in communication studies has increased by more than 20% within the last ten years. Earning a master's will lead to higher salaries. I believe that the growth is because these graduates are hired for such a large variety of jobs and careers. Students who have graduated with a degree in communication have been hired by 3M and Sony. Others have been hired as communication directors for professional sports teams, such as the Carolina Panthers and the Minnesota Vikings. Many have gone to divinity school or law school. Clearly, mastering communication skills in persuasion and argumentation has been the key to the success of these students.

Careers in Speech-Language
Pathology and Audiology
"The Caring Professions: Helping
People Speak and Hear"

by Deana Lacy McQuitty

What is a Speech-Language Pathologist?

Speech-language pathologists are specialists in communication who evaluate and treat problems with speech, language, and swallowing in patients that represent the lifespan (pediatrics–geriatrics). Such problems include difficulties with articulation (pronunciation of the speech sounds) as in the example with my nephew, fluency (such as stuttering), vocal nodules caused by improper voice use, as well as problems with organizing heard or spoken language that result from brain disorders or strokes. These professionals also work with patients who have conditions such as cleft palate, exceptionalities, and hearing loss. Speech-language pathologists work closely with **Audiologists**, to treat children and adults whose hearing problems affect their communication skills.

What is an Audiologist?

Audiologists are health-care professionals whose primary purpose is the evaluation, diagnosis, treatment, and management of hearing loss and balance disorders across the life span (American Academy of Audiology, n.d.). The clinical doctoral degree (AuD) is the entry level into the field and, in most states, audiologists must be licensed to practice. Audiologists can work in a variety of settings such as public schools, universities, ENT offices, private practice, medical centers, and hospitals. For more information about audiology and audiologists visit the American Academy of Audiology webpage at www.audiology.org.

What are ASHA and the CCCs all about?

The **American Speech-Language and Hearing Association (ASHA)** is the governing and credentialing body for communication sciences and disorders professionals around the world. ASHA outlines the scope of practice and best practices for providing services to the public. Furthermore, ASHA is responsible for outlining the standards needed to earn the clinical credentials within the field, the **Certificate of Clinical Competence** (CCC). The CCC can be earned in speech-language pathology, audiology, or both professions. This credentialing signifies that you have met all the necessary requirements to practice speech-language pathology and/or audiology. In order to be licensed by each prospective state, you must contact the Board of Examiners office for the state you reside in before you can be a practicing speech-language pathologist and/or audiologist.

Careers/Service Delivery Settings

One of the benefits of this profession is the wide variety of employment opportunities and job marketability. As stated earlier, speech-language pathologists serve clients across the lifespan from the premature infant in the neonatal intensive care unit because he/she has not learned the suck/swallow pattern to the 80-year-old who recently suffered a stroke. Service delivery settings include schools, medical centers, skilled nursing facilities, private practice, prisons, universities, telepractice, professional/cooperate setting, home health, and center-based settings. Within these settings, speech-language pathologists serve a number of conditions such as language-based disorders, articulation, fluency (stuttering), hearing impairment, stroke victims that are exhibiting deficits with speaking clearly, cognitive issues for individuals who have suffered from a traumatic brain injury, and accent modification, to mention a few.

The Signs of the Times in Speech-Language Pathology

One of the growing trends in the profession of speech-language pathology in particular has been the concept of telepractice technology in the field. This phenomenon opens another clinical service delivery model. Briefly, telepractice is a mechanism in which speech-language services are rendered at a distance for clientele that may not be able to travel to a clinical site for therapy. The set-up is similar to Skyping where each participant has webcam capability and views each other from a distance. Such need for telepractice addresses speech-language pathology shortages in rural parts of the world. The speech-language pathologist providing these services must also consider the technology savvy of their clients regarding the use of equipment.

In addition to the use of telepractice within the field, there is a growing number of clinicians that have begun to incorporate technology within clinical practice for treating a variety of communication disorders. Technologies, such as the IPAD third generation, have been used in clinical practice to address such disorders as autism, aphasia, articulation, and other speech and language-based disorders. Companies such at Smarty Ears © and Geek SLP © are two well-known agencies providing applications for smart devices being utilized within the profession of speech-language pathology and audiology.

Professional Etiquette for Speech-Language Pathologists and Audiologists

It is important that we have effective oral and written communication skills within this profession. A large percentage of our career is spent interacting with other people. Therefore, we must always remember to present information, both orally and in writing in a manner that is understood by all individuals. Sensitivity to and the acknowledgement of a listener's or reader's nonverbal communication language style, emotional needs, in both culturally and linguistically diverse populations must be shown. Paul (2009) outlined principles of effective clinical communication in both oral and written communication. He stated that clinicians: "must clearly introduce the topic about which they are writing and speaking, organize all information in a logical, cohesive manner by subtopic, avoid technical language whenever possible, explain technical terms, use people-first language (e.g., a man who suffered a stroke) rather than referring to people as disabilities (e.g., "a stroke victim"), attend to the comfort of the listener, establish trust by being an active listener, allow the person with whom you are communicating to be an active participant, be sensitive to cultural differences, and watch for both verbal and nonverbal cues from your listener" (184–185).

Explore Further:

1. Visit your local school district, hospital, and other clinical setting where a speech-language pathologist may be employed. Observe the workday and job shadow to increase your awareness of what their roles and responsibilities are. Who knows, you may find yourself in this career field helping others through the power of communication.
2. Visit a university or explore their website about a Master's program in speech-language pathology or the doctor of audiology (AUD). Identify their curriculum and entrance requirements.
3. Visit www.asha.org to learn more interesting facts about this fascinating profession.

Key Terms:

ASHA	Communication Studies
Audiologist	Speech-Language Pathologist
Certificate of Clinical Competence	Telepractice

Vignettes are portrayals of a brief evocative description, account, or episode that will illustrate an important lesson.

VIGNETTE D: AUDIENCE ANALYSIS

One of the biggest mistakes a communicator can make is to ignore the characteristics of their audience. Have you been offended from a comment made by a speaker or a manager? Often when it happens we will shut anything else they say out! Not knowing your audience before you deliver a message is a classic mistake! This becomes extremely important when you are delivering "bad news" messages. Your audience may be any group of people or individual to whom you must communicate a specific message. Think of a time when you thought you were sharing "good new" information, but received an unexpected negative reaction from the people who were listening to you. Think of a time when you reacted to a speaker in a similar manner. How might you analyze your audience in advance of delivering a message? Create a vignette that will demonstrate this lesson.

MINI QUIZ

1. True or False: Speech-Language Pathologist represents a career in high demand.
2. Multiple Choice: Which of the following specialists work with individuals with hearing problems?
   A. Speech-Language Pathologist
   B. Audiologist
   C. Both A and B
   D. None of the above
3. Fill in the Blank: This service delivery model allows a speech and hearing specialist to work with clients who are physically in different geographical locations during therapy

   _____.

4. Essay: Briefly discuss the role of the speech-language pathologist and the audiologist in the overall field of communication. Discuss how their roles are vital in assisting people to be more effective communicators.

APPENDIX

COMPARE AND CONTRAST

Instructions: Use this form to help you brainstorm relative points for your presentation. Identify similarities and differences between information that you may present during your presentation. Be sure to include your original thesis statement to help generate ideas. You may find that your thesis statement changes as ideas are generated. Use the generated similarities and differences to support the key points in your presentation as well.

Topic: _____

Problem or Issue: _____

Thesis Statement: _____

Adapted Thesis Statement: _____

Compare and Contrast

Item 1:		Item 2:
Differences	Similarities	Differences

Snipes (2012)

CAUSE & EFFECT

Instructions: Use this form to help you brainstorm relative points for your presentation. Identify the problem or issue you will be addressing in your presentation. What are the possible causes and effects that may impact the topic? Be sure to include your original thesis statement to help generate ideas. You may find that your thesis statement changes as ideas are generated. Use the generated "cause and effect" list to support the key points in your presentation as well.

Topic: _____

Problem or Issue: _____

Thesis Statement: _____

Adapted Thesis Statement: _____

Cause	Effect

Snipes (2012)

PROS & CONS CHART

Instructions: Use this form to help you brainstorm relative points for your presentation. Identify the positive aspects of the issue (pros) and the negative aspects of the issue (cons). List the "pros" and "cons" below. Utilize information generated from this list to help strengthen the key points in your presentation. Be sure to include your original thesis statement or purpose statement to help generate ideas. You may find that your thesis statement changes as ideas are generated.

Topic: _____

Thesis Statement/Purpose: _____

Adapted Thesis Statement: _____

Pros	Cons

Snipes (2012)

POLICY DEBATE FORMAT

First Affirmative Constructive (3–5 minutes) *can be completely written and practiced in advance! Delivery and emphasis on specific points will help!*

Introduction

- Opening – State your name and partner's name and that you are speaking for the affirmative; express pleasure for the opportunity to debate the topic; state the resolution.
- Define key terms.
- Present your thesis statement to show where you are going (e.g., *This is a serious problem and the present system will not solve the problem; our plan will solve the problem.*).

Body

- Describe the issue using a combination of logos, ethos, and pathos.
- Support the affirmative case with 4–6 contentions. Have at least three supporting pieces of evidence and reasoning (save at least one for rebuttal).
    - Establish the need for change (why this is a serious problem) and the significance and harms (qualitative/quantitative).
    - Establish the harm of the present system—people or other living beings are hurt physically, emotionally, financially, and socially.
    - Establish how the present system contributes to the problem (inherency).
- Briefly introduce your ***plan*** and how it solves the problem (solvency).

Conclusion

- Summarize your position. Say "Thank you."

First Negative Constructive (3–5 minutes)

Introduction

- Greet – State your name and partner's name and that you are speaking for the negative; express pleasure for the opportunity to debate the topic of _____.
- Either accept the affirmative's definitions or correct the definitions presented by the affirmative.

- Describe the issue from the point of view of the negative.
- Introduce your case with your thesis statement: *"We intend to prove that there is no need to . . . ."*

Body

- State negative philosophy by presenting 4–6 contentions. Have at least three pieces of evidence and reasoning to support them (save at least one to reestablish during rebuttal).
  - Refute the need for change; explain why the status quo is preferable (defend present system).
  - Deny that the present system contributes to the problem (inherency).
  - Explain why there is no reason for change; diminish significance (quantitative/qualitative).
  - Explain why change could be worse than the present system.
- Attack the need for a plan; possibly why it will cause more harm than good.
- *(Optional advanced strategy! You can accept that the status quo could be changed in a MINOR way; then introduce a counter plan that is significantly different from the affirmative's plan.)*
- Discriminate: Refute affirmative's points with evidence and reasoning.

Conclusion

- Summarize the negative case so far. Say "Thank you."

Second Affirmative Constructive (3–5 minutes)

Introduction

- Present overview of the debate so far and contrast affirmative and negative positions.
- Defend definitions of terms and topicality, if necessary.
- Present a thesis statement to show where you are going (e.g., _____ *is a problem that must be solved and our plan will do it.*).

Body

- Attack the negative philosophy defending the present system, especially harm and significance.
- Discriminate. Directly address each of the specific challenges issued by the negative.
- Reestablish why change is necessary.
- Explain your plan with details; describe the benefits of the plan and how the plan will solve the problem.

Conclusion

- End with an appeal to adopt the resolution. Say "Thank you."

Second Negative Constructive (3–5 minutes)

Introduction

- Review/reinforce negative philosophy.
- Present thesis (e.g., *We will prove that there isn't a problem, that the plan is bad, that the plan is unnecessary.*).

Body

- Present contentions and attack the plan as undesirable, unable to solve needs, or unnecessary.
  - Practicality, workability—specific elements of the plan.
  - Solvency—demonstrate that the plan is not capable of solving the problem.
  - Disadvantages—explain that more harm will result from the plan than the status quo.
  - Injustices—explain that the plan affects some individuals or groups more than others.
  - Deny the supposed benefits of the plan.
- If the affirmative neglected to present a plan, make a **HUGE** deal of its omission.
- Discriminate. Counter all affirmative challenges directly and specifically.
- Refute the affirmative case as a whole.

Conclusion

- Summarize problems of the plan; say: *That is why we cannot adopt the resolution. Thank you.*

First negative rebuttal speech (2–3 minutes)—Summarize and reiterate.

- Discriminate: Refute the arguments introduced by the second affirmative, point by point.
- Again attack affirmative's justification for change.
- Summarize the entire negative block.
- End with instructions: *We must not allow . . . .*

First affirmative rebuttal speech (2–3 minutes)—*Be the savior and regain control after eight negative minutes!*

- Refute negative's plan objections; point out fallacies in reasoning.
- Rebuild your case at major points of attack; offer new evidence to support your contentions.
- Discriminate. Respond to all the arguments from the second negative constructive arguments and first negative rebuttal; defend and re-support the arguments you can.

Second negative rebuttal speech (2–3 minutes)—*Last chance for the negative side to speak.*

- Rebuild your case at major points of attack; offer new evidence to support your contentions.
- Explain why your side should win: Review plan objections and disadvantages. Refute affirmative's responses; point out any issues dropped by the affirmative.
- Summarize the negative position in a dramatic way; call for rejection of the proposal.
- Thank the audience and judge(s).

Second affirmative rebuttal speech (2–3 minutes)—*Last speech!*

- Point out any arguments dropped by the negative; these are considered your points now.
- Respond to objections the negative made to your plan and point out those that were dropped by the second negative rebuttalist. Dropped arguments are conceded arguments!
- Remind the judges of your arguments and why they are more important than the negative's.
- Be dramatic in your big picture. Make your audience care! End with a strong appeal to adopt the resolution and to accept the proposal.
- Thank the audience and the judge(s).

NEGATIVE STRATEGY IN POLICY DEBATE

1. Negative debaters cannot script their first constructive speech.
2. The negative team is expected to respond specifically to the example of the resolution advocated in the affirmative case.
3. Negative team must be pre-prepared with strategies for the likely affirmative cases.
4. Five recommendations for building a negative strategy:
   a. Advocate something.
      i. Let the judge know what you are for, not just what you are against.
      ii. Prepare to counter-plan (not necessarily every time).
      iii. Latch on to something the present system is already doing.
   b. Minimize and then outweigh.
      i. Find a direct clash with the affirmative case.
      ii. Many negative teams make the mistake of focusing entirely on their own arguments while ignoring the claims made in the affirmative case.
      iii. Find issues in (Significance, Harms, Inherency, Topicality, Solvency).
      iv. Show the affirmative harm itself is exaggerated.
   c. Think backwards from disadvantages.
      i. The best negative teams win debates with powerful disadvantage arguments.
      ii. Select a disadvantage or two that can outweigh the affirmative case.
   d. Limit the number of strategies.
      i. An advantage of being the affirmative is that you are debating the same thing in half of your debate rounds.
      ii. Learn to bring that same advantage to the negative side as well.
   e. Take what the resolution gives you.
      i. The affirmative team is defending the resolution.
      ii. The negative team is defending the nonresolution.

5. Challenging topicality
    a. If challenging topicality, it should be presented in the first negative constructive speech.
    b. It loses credibility if you wait too far into the debate.
6. Remember
    a. Clarity
    b. Correspondence
    c. Simplicity

REFERENCES

Allen, B. J. 1995. "Diversity and Organizational Communication." *Journal of Applied Communication Research* 23:143–55. Berger, R. M. 1992. "Passing and Social Support Among Gay Men." *Journal of Homosexuality* 23:85–97.

Ambady, N., and Rosenthal, R. 1992. "Thin Slices of Expressive Behavior as Predictors of Interpersonal Consequences: A Meta-Analysis." *Psychological Bulletin* 111: 256–274.

Ambady, N., and Rosenthal, R. 1995. "On Judging and Being Judged Accurately in Zero-Acquaintance Situations." *Journal of Personality and Social Psychology.* 69:518–529.

Amster, B. J. 1999. *Speech and Language Development of Young Children in the Welfare System.* In Silver, J. A., B. J. Amster, and T. Haekcer. *Young Children in Foster Care: A Guide for Professionals* 117–38. Baltimore: Paul H. Brookes, Publisher.

Anderson, R. 2002. "Questions of Communication," 3rd ed. Boston, MA: Bedford/St. Martin's 2002.

Anderson, N., and D. Battle. 1993. "Cultural Diversity in the Development of Language." In D. Battle, ed. *Communication Disorders in Multicultural Populations* 158–82. Boston: Andover Medical.

Anderson, N., and D. Battle. 2002. "Cultural Diversity in the Development of Language." In D. Battle, ed. *Communication Disorders in Multicultural Populations*, 2nd ed. 106–203.

Anderson-Yockel, J., and W. Haynes. 1994. "Joint Picture-Book Reading Strategies in Working-Class African American and White Mother-Toddler Dyads." *Journal of Speech, Language, and Hearing Research* 37(2):583–93.

Arnett, R. C. "The Status of Communication Ethics Scholarship in Speech Communication Journals from 1915 to 1985." In K. J. Grenberg. "Conversations on Communication Ethics." 1991:55–72. Norwood, NJ: Ablex.

Atchison, B. J. 2007. *Sensory Modulation Disorders Among Children with a History of Trauma: A Frame of Reference for Speech-Language Pathologists.* "Language, Speech, and Hearing Services in Schools" (38):109–16.

Aylesworth-Spink, Shelley. 2009. "Why Get a Communications Degree?" Vancouver, Canada. Accessed June 3, 2013 from http://suite101.com/article/why-get-a-communications-degree-a144902.

Ayoko, O. B., E. J. Hartel, and V. Callan. 2001. "Disentangling the Complexity of Productive and Destructive Conflict in Culturally Heterogeneous Workgroups: A Communication Accommodation Theory Approach." *Academy of Management Proceedings and Membership Directory,* CM, A1–A6.

Ball-Rokeach, S. J. 1985. "The Origins of Individual Media-System Dependency: A Sociological Framework." *Communications Research* 12 (4):485–510.

Bandura, A. 1997. *Self-Efficacy: The Exercise of Control.* New York: W. H. Freeman.

Baker, Matt. 2011. www.usefulcharts.com/psychology/piaget-stages of cognitive-development.html. Retrieved May 8, 2012.

Barber, B. 1992. Jihad vs. McWorld. *The Atlantic Monthly, 269*(3), 53–65.

Barnhart, Clarence L., and Robert K. Barnhart, eds. *World Book Dictionary,* Chicago: Childcraft International Inc., 1980.

Bartley, S., P. Blanton, and J. Gilliard. 2005. "Husbands and Wives in Dual-Earner Marriages: Decision-Making, Gender Role Attitudes, Division of Household Labor, and Equity." *Marriage & Family Review* 37 (4):69–94.

Battle, D. 1996. "Language Learning and Use by African American Children." *Topics in Language Disorders* 16 (4):22–37.

Boyd, D. M., and N. B. Ellison. 2007. "Social Network Sites: Definition, History, and Scholarship." *Journal of Computer-Mediated Communication* 13 (1):210–30. doi:10.1111 /j.1083-6101.2007.00393. Boswell, Susan. 2002. *Professions on Fast Track.* ASHA Leader, April 30.

Breiding, M. J., M. C. Black, and G. W. Ryan. 2008. *Chronic Disease and Health Risk Behaviors Associated with Intimate Partner Violence.* Annual Epidemiology 18:538–44.

Brown, Hallie Q. 1892. "A Great Slight to the Race." Editorial. *The Freeman* (Indianapolis, Indiana). www.womhist.binghamton.edu.

Brown, Hallie Quinn. 1880. Bits and Odds: *A Choice Selection of Recitation for School, Lyceum and Parlor Entertainments.* Xenia, Ohio: Chew Press. _____. 1920. "First Lessons in Public Speaking." Appendix C, "Sample Manuscript of Text" in McFarlin. _____. 1926. *Homespun Heroines and Other Women of Distinction.* Xenia, OH. _____. "Not Gifts But Opportunity." Appendix C, "Sample Manuscript of Text" in McFarlin. _____. 1925. Tales *My Father Told and Other Tales.*

Buber, M. "I and Thou." Translated by R. G. Smith. New York: Scribner, 1958.

Bybee, J. 2002. "Word Frequency and Context of Use in the Lexical Diffusion of Phonetically Conditioned Sound Change." *Language Variation and Change* 14:261–290.

Caplan, E. S., E. M. Perse, and J. E. Gennaria. 2007. "Computer-Mediated Technology and Social Interaction." In C. A. A. Lin, D. J., ed. *Communication Technology and Social Change: Theory and Implications* 43. Mahwah, N.J.: Lawrence Erlbaum Associates.

Carnevale, A. P., and S. C. Stone. 1995. *The American Mosaic: An In-Depth Report on the Future of Diversity at Work.* New York: McGraw-Hill, Inc.

Carrino, S. 2012. Intercultural communication. In R. W. Williams, D. L. McQuitty, & T. Snipes (Eds.), *ttyl…The fundamentals of speech communication in the digital age.* Dubuque, IA: Kendall Hunt.

Carrol, B. C., A. Raj, S. E. Noel, and H. Bauchner. 2011. *Dating Violence Among Adolescents Presenting to a Pediatric Emergency Department.* Archives of Pediatric Medicine 165 (12):1101–06.

Chapman, G. 2010. *The Five Love Languages: The Secrets To Love That Lasts.* New Edition. Chicago, IL.

Chemers, M. M., S. Oskamp, and M. A. Costanzo, eds. 1995. *Diversity in Organizations: New Perspectives for a Changing Workplace.* London: SAGE.

Cheney, G. 1995. "Democracy in the Workplace: Theory and Practice from the Perspective of Communication." *Journal of Applied Communication Research* 23:167–200.

Cheseboro, J. L., and J. C. McCroskey. 2002. *Communication for Teachers.* Boston, MA: Allyn & Bacon.

Chomsky, N. 2003, February 5. *Confronting the empire—Noam Chomsky speech.* Retrieved April 17, 2010, from Scoop New Stories: http:www.scoop.co.nz.stories

Coker, A. L., K. E. Davis, L. Arias, M. Sanderson, and H. M. Brandt. 2002. "Physical and Mental Health Effects of Intimate Partner Violence for Men and Women." *American Journal of Preventive Medicine*, 24 (4):260–68.

"Communication Facts: Special Populations: Traumatic Brain Injury." 2010. www.asha.org /research/reports/tbi

Coontz, S. 2005. *Marriage, a History: From Obedience to Intimacy.* Penguin Publishing, New York.

Cormode, G., and B. Krishnamurthy. 2008. Key Differences between Web 1.0 and Web 2.0. Retrieved December 21, 2011, from http://citeseerx.ist.psu.edu/viewdoc/download? doi=10.1.1.145.3391&rep=rep1&type=pdf

Cutrona, C. E., and J. A. Suhr. 1992. "Controllability of Stressful Events and Satisfaction with Spouse Support Behaviors." *Communication Research* 19:154–74.

Daniel, J. L., and G. Smitherman. 1976. "How I Got Over: Communication Dynamics in the Black Community." *Quarterly Journal of Speech* 62:26–39.

Dewey, J. 1949. "Knowing and the Known." Boston: Beacon.

Dick, Marissa. "Personal Communication" (lecture, 2009).

Dollaghan, C. A., T. F. Campbell, J. L. Paradise, H. M. Feildman, J. E. Janosky, and D. N. Pitcairn, et al. 1999. "Maternal Education and Measures of Early Speech and Language." *Journal of Speech, Language, and Hearing Research* 42 (6):1532-544.

Dominick, J. R. 2011. "The Dynamics of Mass Communication: Media in Transition," 11th ed., 72. New York: McGraw-Hill.

DPhil, J. S. 1994. "Gay Rights and Affirmative Action." *Journal of Homosexuality* 27 (3/4):179–222.

Drago, K. 2010. *Sociophonetic Variation in Speech Perception: Language and Linguistics Compass* 4/7:473–480.

Farran, D. C. 1982. "Mother-Child Interaction, Language Development and the School Performance of Poverty Children." In Feagans, L. and D. Farran, eds. *The Language of Children Reared in Poverty: Implications for Evaluation and Intervention* 183–256. New York: Academic Press.

Farran, D. C., and C. T. Ramsey. 1980. "Social Class Differences in Dyatic Involvement During Infancy." *Child Development* 51 (1):254–57.

Foucault, M. 1977. Discipline and punishment: *The birth of the prison*. New York, NY: Vintage.

Foucault, M. 1984. Power/knowledge: Selected interviews and other writings, 1972–1977. In P. Rabinow (Ed.), *The Foucault reader* (pp. 51–75). New York, NY: Pantheon Books.

Fraleigh, D. M. 1997. "Freedom of Speech." Boston, MA: Bedford/St. Martin's Press.

Friedman, M. 1974. "Touchstones of Reality: Existential Trust and the Community of Peace." New York: Dutton.

Friedman, T. 2007. *The world is flat*. New York, NY: Picador.

Fukuyama, F. 1992. *The end of history and the last of man*. New York, NY: Avon Books.

Giddings, Paula. 1984. *When and Where I Enter: The Impact of Black Women in Race and Sex in America*. New York: Bantam Books. Kates, Susan. 1997. "The Embodied Rhetoric of Hallie Quinn Brown. " *College English* 59:59.

Gilbert, D. T. and P. S. Malone. 1995. "The Correspondence Bias." *Psychological Bulletin* 117:21–28.

Gollwitzer, P. M. 1986. "Striving for Specific Identities: The Social Reality of Self-Symbolizing." In R. F. Baumeister, ed. *Public Self and Private Self* 141–59. New York: Springer-Verlag.

Gorham, J. 1988. "The Relationship Between Verbal Teaching Immediacy Behaviors and Student Learning." *Communication Education* 17:40–53.

Gouran, Dennis, W. E. Wiethoff, and J. A. Doelger. 1994. *Mastering Communication*, 2nd ed. Boston: Allyn and Bacon.

Gray, H. M. and V. Foshee. 1997. "Adolescent Dating Violence: Differences Between One-Sided and Mutually Violent Profiles." *Journal of Interpersonal Violence* 12 (1):126–41.

Green, D. M., and F. R. Walker. 2004. "Recommendations for Public Speaking Instructors for the Negotiation of Code-Switching Practice Among Black English-Speaking African American Students." *The Journal of Negro Education* 73:435–442.

Griggs, B. 2013. *7 social media resolutions for 2014*. Retrieve January 5, 2014, from the CNN website at http://www.cnn.com/2013/12/31/tech/social-media/social-media-resolutions/

Gunn, A. M. 1998. *Lesbian Passing in the Workplace: A Strategy for Negotiating an Absence of Power.* Masters' Thesis. Keaton-Jackson, Karen. "Re: Update." Message to the Author. (February 28, 2012) E-mail.

Halpern, C. T, S. G. Oslak, M. L. Young, S. L. Martin, and L. L. Kupper. 2001. "Partner Violence Among Adolescents in Opposite-Sex Romantic Relationships: Findings from the National Longitudinal Study of Adolescent Health." *American Journal of Public Health* 91 (10):1679–85.

Hamachek, D. 1992. *Encounters with the Self,* 3rd ed. Fort Worth: Harcourt Brace Jovanovich. Jones, E. E. 1979. "The Rocky Road from Acts to Dispositions." *American Psychologist* 34:107–17. 64 Unit 1 Foundations of Human Communication 02_Shird.qxd 7/31/07 11:47 AM Page 64.

Hammer, C. S. 2001. "Come and Sit Down and Let Mama Read: Book Reading Interactions Between African American Mothers and Their Infants." In Harris, J. L., A. G. Kamhi, and K. E. Pollock, eds. *Literacy in African American Communities* 21–43. Mahwah, NJ: Erlbaum.

Hammer, C. S. and A. L. Weiss. 2000. "African American Mother's Views of Their Infant's Language Development and Language-Learning Environment." *American Journal of Speech-Language Pathology* 9 (2):126–41.

Hammer, C. S. and A. L. Weiss. 1999. "Guiding Language Development: How African American Mothers and Their Infants Structure Play Interactions." *Journal of Speech, Language, and Hearing Research* 42 (5):1219–33.

Hampton, K., L. G. Sessions, L. Raine, and K. Purcell. 2011. "Social Networking Sites and Our Lives." (December 2011) http://www.pewinternet.org/Reports/2011/Technology-and -social-networks/Summary.aspx

Heath, S. B. 1983. *Sociocultural Contexts of Language Development: In Beyond Language.* Los Angeles: Evaluation, Dissemination, and Assessment Center.

Hecht, M. L., M. J. Collier, and S. A. Ribeau. 1993. *African American Communication: Ethnic Identity and Cultural Interpretation.* Newbury Park: Sage Publications.

Hecht, M. L., R. L. Jackson II, and S. A. Ribeau. 2003. *African American Communication: Exploring Identity and Culture.* Lawrence Erlbaum Associates, Publishers: London.

Held, D., A. G. McGrew, D. Goldblatt, and J. Perraton. 1999. *Global Transformations: Politics, Economics, and Culture.* Stanford, CA: Stanford University Press.

Hill, D. K. 2009. "Code Switching Pedagogies and African American Student Voices: Acceptance and Resistance." *Journal of Adolescent and Adult Literacy* 53:120–131.

Hill, S. A. 2006. "Marriage Among African American Women: A Gender Perspective." *Journal of Comparative Family Studies* 37 (3):421–40.

Houston, Whitney. 2012. Whitney. (March 4, 2012) https://www.facebook.com/#!/WhitneyHouston

Humphreys, J., and J. C. Campbell. 2004. *Family Violence and Nursing Practice.* Philadelphia, PA: Lippincott.

Jamjoom, M. 2013. Saudi Arabia issues warning to women drivers, protesters. Retrieved January 10, 2014, from the CNN website at http://www.cnn.com/2013/10/24/world/meast/saudi-arabia-women-drivers/

Johannesen, R. 1990. "Ethics in Human Communication," 3rd ed. Prospect Heights, IL: Waveland.

Kalafatoğlu, T. 2013. *The spread of culture under the umbrella of globalization.* In K. St. Amant & B. Olaniran (Eds.), *Globalization and the digital divide.* Amherst, NY: Cambria Press.

Kaplan, A. M. and M. Haenlein. 2010. "Users of the World, Unite! The Challenges and Opportunities of Social Media." *Business Horizons* 53 (1):59–68.

Keaton-Jackson, Karen. Southeastern Writing Center Association Conference. Marriott Hotel, Greensboro, NC. (February 28, 2009) Address.

Kennard, J. 2007. *Definition of Intimate Partner Violence.* http://menshealthabout.com/od/relationships/aBattered_Men_2.htm.

Kennedy, J. 2005. *Types of Verbal Abuse.* http://www.abigails.Org/Sin/types-of-verbal abuse.htm.

Kwako, L. E., N. Glass, J. Campbell, K. C. Melvin, T. Barr, and J. T. Gill. 2011. "Traumatic Brain Injury in Intimate Partner Violence: A Critical Review of Outcomes and Mechanisms." *Trauma, Violence, & Abuse* 12 (3):115–26.

Lechner, F. 2005. Globalization. In G. Ritzer (Ed.), *Encyclopedia of social theory.* Thousand Oaks, CA: Sage.

Lewin, T. 2010. "If Your Kids are Awake, They're Probably Online." *New York Times* A1. http://www.nytimes.com/2010/01/20/education/20wired.html

Leys, C. (2001). *Market-driven politics: Neoliberal democracy and the public interest.* London: Verso Books.

Luft, Joseph. 1969. *Of Human Interaction* 177. Palo Alto, CA: National Press.

Mansfield, H. 2012. *Social Media for Social Good.* New York: McGraw-Hill. Mobile Phone Use by Kids and Teens on Rise. 2010. (December 19, 2011) http://www.adweek.com/news/technology/mobile-phone-use-kids-and-teens-rise-102754

Mazer, J. P., and S. K. Hunt. 2008. " 'Cool' Communication in the Classroom: A Preliminary Examination of Student Perceptions of Instructor Use of Positive Slang." *Qualitative Research Reports in Communication* 9:20–28.

McFarlin, Annjenette Sophie. 1975. "Hallie Quinn Brown—Black Woman Elocutionist." Diss. Washington State University.

McLaughlin, S. 1998. Introduction to Language Development. San Diego: Singular Publishing Group.

Mehrabian, A. 1971. *Silent Messages.* 1st ed. Belmont, CA: Wadsworth.

Monroe, A. H. 1943. Monroe's Principles of Speech (military edition). Chicago: Scott, Foresman PN4121.M578.

Mottet, T. P., and Richmond, V. P. 1998. "An Inductive Analysis of Verbal Immediacy: Alternative Conceptualization of Relational Verbal Approach/Avoidance Strategies." *Communication Quarterly* 46:25–41.

Nsouli, S. 2008. *Ensuring a sustainable and inclusive globalization.* Speech delivered at Universal Postal Union Congress (pp. 1–4). Geneva: International Monetary Fund.

Nye, J. 2002, April 15) *Globalism vs. globalization.* Retrieved November 13, 2009, from http://www.theglobalist.com

Nye, J. 2009, April 12. *Which globalization will survive?* Retrieved September 27, 2009, from http://www.realclearworld.com/articles/2009/04/nye_globalization_will_survive.html

Ogbu, J. U. 1999. "Beyond Language: Ebonics, Proper English and Identity in a Black-American Speech Community." *American Educational Research Journal* 36:147–184.

Okin, S. 1989. *Justice, Gender, and the Family.* Basic Books, Inc. Rawlins, W. 2008. *The Compass of Friendship: Narratives, Identities, and Dialogues.* Thousand Oaks, CA: Sage.

Osofsky, J. D. 1995. "Effects of Exposure to Violence on Young Children." *American Psychologist* 50 (9):782–88.

Overwalle, F. V. 1997. "Dispositional Attributions Require the Joint Application of the Methods of Difference and Agreement." *Personality and Social Psychology Bulletin* 23:974–80. Seiler, W. J. and M. L. Beall. 2002. *Communication Making Connections,* 5th ed. Boston, MA: Allyn & Bacon.

Palley, T. 2006, April 13. *Could globalization fail?* Retrieved September 21, 2009, from http://yaleglobal.yale.edu

Paul, Rhea. 2009. "Introduction to Clinical Methods in Communication Disorders." Baltimore, MD: Brookes Publishing Co.

Perkovich, G. H. 2006. *Is globalization headed for the rocks? Carnegie Endowment for International Peace* (pp. 1–6). Washington, DC: Carnegie Endowment for International Peace.

Prague protests renew 'Battle of Seattle.' 2000, September 27. *The Seattle Times.* Retrieved November 30, 2009 from http://community.seattletimes.nwsource.com/http://community.seattletimes.nwsource.com/archive/?date=20000927&slug=4044799

Rahman, J. 2008. "Middle Class African Americans: Reactions and Attitudes Toward African American English." *American Speech* 83:1410–176.

Rawlins, W. 2008. *The Compass of Friendship: Narratives, Identities, and Dialogues.* Thousand Oaks, CA: Sage.

Renner, L. M. 2009. "Intimate Partner Violence Victimization and Parenting Stress: Assessing the Mediating Role of Depressive Symptoms." *Violence Against Women* 15 (11):1380–1401.

Restivo, Sal P. 1994. "Science, Society and Values: Toward a Sociology of Objectivity." Bethlehem, PA: Lehigh University Press.

Rice, M. L., F. L. Wexler, and Hershberger, S. 1998). "Tense Over Time: The Longitudinal Course of Tense Acquisition in Children with Specific Language Impairment." *Journal of Speech, Language, and Hearing Research* 41:1412–31.

Richardson, Elaine B. 2004. "Coming from the Heart: African American Students, Literacy Stories, and Rhetorical Education." *African American Rhetoric(s) Interdisciplinary Perspectives*. Richardson, Elaine B. and Ronald L. Jackson II, eds. Carbondale, IL: Southern Illinois UP. Print.

Richmond, V. P. 2002. "Teacher Nonverbal Immediacy." In ed. Cheseboro, J. L. and McCroskey, *Communication for Teachers.*

Ritzer, G. 2000. *The McDonaldization of society.* Thousand Oaks, CA: Pine Forge.

Ritzer, G. 2004. *The globalization of nothing.* Thousand Oaks, CA: Pine Forge.

Royster, Jacqueline Jones. 2000. *Traces of a Stream: Literacy and Social Change Among African American Women.* Pittsburgh; University of Pittsburgh Press.

Sanders, Rose. "An African American Manifesto on Education." *In Motion Magazine.* http://www.inmotionmagazine.com.

Scanzoni, J. 1982. "Sexual Bargaining: Power Politics in the American Marriage." Chicago: University of Chicago.

Schafer, J., R. Caetano, and C. L. Clark. 1998. "Rates of Intimate Partner Violence in the United States." *American Journal of Public Health* 88 (11):1702–04.

Schofield, J. W. 2001. "Improving Intergroup Relations." In Banks, J. A. and C. A. M. Banks, eds. *Handbook of Research on Multicultural Education* 635–46. San Francisco: Jossey-Bass.

Sewall, Mary Wright. 1894. *The World Congress of Representative Women: The World Congress Auxiliary.* Chicago and New York; Rand McNally and Company. http://womhist .binghamton.edu/ibw/congress.htm.

Shird, M. M. 2001. "Scars of Struggle, Marks of Strength: Models of Mentoring Black Men." Dissertation Institution: The University of North Carolina at Greensboro 0154 ISBN: 0-493-19168-2.

Silverthorne, J. 2009. "Understanding Users of Social Networks." *Working Knowledge: The Thinking that Leads.* (December 23, 2011) http://hbswk.hbs.edu/item/6156.html

Smith, A. 2011. "Why Americans Use Social Media." (December 27, 2011) http://www .pewinternet.org/Reports/2011/Why-Americans-Use-Social-Media/Main-report.aspx

Smitherman, Geneva. 1977. "From Africa to the New World and Into the Space Age." *Talkin and Testifyin: The Language for Black America* 1–15. Detroit: Wayne State UP. *Books.google .com.* Web. (March 1, 2012)

Smitherman, Geneva. 1977. *Talkin and Testifyin: The Language of Black America*. Boston; Houghton Mifflin Co.

Smitherman, Geneva. *Talkin that Talk: Language, Culture and Education in African America*. London: Routhledge. 1999. *Library.ncat.edu*. Bluford Library North Carolina A&T State University. 2012. Web. (February 28, 2012)

Snow, C. E., M. S. Burns, and P. Griffin, eds. 1998. *Preventing Reading Difficulties in Young Children*. Washington, DC: National Academy Press.

Sommers, Nancy. "Writing in the Margins: Why Students Find Some Comments Useful and Ignore Others." Conference on College Composition and Communication. Marriott Marquis Atlanta. (April 8, 2011) Lecture.

Sorenson S. B., D. M. Upchurch, H. Shen. 1996. "Violence and Injury in Marital Arguments: Risk Patterns and Gender Differences." *American Journal of Public Health* 86 (1):35–40.

Sorrells, K. A. 2008. *Linking social justice and intercultural communication in the global context*. Portland, OR: Intercultural Communication Institute.

Sorrells, K. A. 2013. *Intercultural communication: Globalization and social justice*. Thousand Oaks, CA: Sage.

Sorrells, K. A., & Nakagawa, G. 2008. Intercultural communication praxis and the struggle for social responsibility and social justice. In O. Swartz (Ed.), *Transformative communication studies: Culture, hierarchy, and the human condition* (pp. 23–61). Leicester, UK: Troubador.

Spangler, Brad. "Best Alternative to a Negotiated Agreement (BATNA)." *Beyond Intractability*. ed. Heidi Burgess. Conflict Research Consortium, University of Colorado, Boulder, Colorado, USA. Accessed June 3, 2013 from http://www.beyondintractability.org/bi-essay/batna.

Sterling, Dorothy, ed. 1984. *We Are Your Sisters: Black Women in the Nineteenth Century*. New York: W.W. Norton and Co.

Straus, M. A. 2004. "Prevalence of Violence Against Dating Partners by Male and Female University Students Worldwide." *VIOLENCE AGAINST WOMEN* 10 (7):790–811.

Stockman, I. 1996. "The Promise and Pitfalls of Language Sample Analysis as an Assessment Tool for Linguistic Minority Children." *Language, Speech, and Hearing Services in Schools* 27 (4):355–66.

St. Amant, K., & Olaniran, B. A. (Eds.). 2013. *Globalization and the digital divide*. Amherst, NY: Cambria.

Sullivan, P. M. and J. F. Knutson. 2000. "Maltreatment and Disabilities: A Population Based Epidemiological Study." *Child Abuse & Neglect* 24 (20):1257–73.

Swartz, O., Campbell, K., & Pestana, C. 2009. *Neo-pragmatism, communication, and the culture of creative democracy*. New York, NY: Peter Lang.

Sypher, B. 1984. "Seeing Ourselves As Others See Us." *Communication Research* 11:97–115.

Tjaden, P. and N. Thoennes. 2000. "Full Report of the Prevalence, Incidence, and Consequences of Violence Against Women: Findings from the National Violence Against Women Survey." Washington, D.C.: Department of Justice, 2000.

Traupmann, J. 1978. *Equity in Intimate Relationship: An Interview of Marriage.* Unpublished Ph.D. Dissertation, University of Wisconsin–Madison.

Traupmann, J., R. Petersen, M. Utne, and E. Hatfield. 1981. "Measuring Equity in Intimate Relationships." *Applied Psychological Measurement* 5:467–80.

Trenholm, S. and Jensen. A. (2004). Interpersonal Communication (5th ed.). New York: Oxford Univ. Press.

Tomblin, J. B., N. L. Records, P. R. Buckwalter, X. Zhang, E. Smith, and M. O'Brien. 1997. "Prevalence of Specific Language Impairment in Kindergarten Children." *Journal of Speech, Language, and Hearing Research* 40:1245–60.

Valkenburg, P. M., J. Peter, and A. P. Schouten. 2006. "Self Esteem and Social Media Among Adolescents." *CyberPsychology & Behavior* 9 (5):584–90. doi:10.1089/cpb.2006.9.584.154. Creskill, NJ: Hampton Press.

Verderber, R. F. and K. S. Verderber. 2002. *Communicate.* Belmont, CA: Wadsworth Press.

Vernon-Feagans, L. 1996. *Children's Talk in Communities and Classrooms.* Cambridge, MA: Blackwell.

Vernon-Feagans, L., A. Miccio, E. Manlove, and C. Hammer. 2001. "Early Language and Literacy Skills in Low-Income African American and Hispanic Children." In Neuman, S., and D. Dickinson, eds. *Handbook on Research in Early Literacy* 192–210. New York: Guilford.

Westby, C. E. 2007. "Child Maltreatment: A Global Issue." *Language, Speech, and Hearing Services in the Schools* 38:140–148.

Welc, J. B. 2010. "Understanding the Impact of Abuse on Speech-Language Development." [PowerPoint slides]. http://search.asha.org/default.aspx?q=child Abuse

What is an Audiologist (n.d.). Accessed May 2013 from http://www.audiology.org/resources /consumer/documents/fsaudiologist08.pdf

Why does Kenya lead the world in mobile money? 2013, May 27. *The Economist Newspaper Limited.* Retrieved January 3, 2014, from http://www.economist.com/blogs/economist -explains/2013/05/economist-explains-18

Wikipedia. 2012. "Anthony Weiner Sexting Scandal." http://en.wikipedia.org/wiki /Anthony_Weiner_sexting_scandal

Wilson, Gerald L. 1999. "Groups in Context: Leadership and Participation in Small Groups," 5th ed. 123–26. Boston: McGraw-Hill College.

Wood, J. (2006). *Communication in our lives* (4th ed.). Belmont, CA: Wadsworth.

Woods, J. T. 2009. "Communication in Personal Relationships. Communication in Our Lives." Boston, MA: Wadsworth/Cengage Learning.

Woods, Sherry E., and Karen Harbeck. 1991. "Living in Two Worlds: The Identity Management Strategies Used by Lesbian Physical Educators." In ed. Karen Harbeck *Coming Out of the Classroom Closet: Gay and Lesbian Students, Teachers, and Curricula*. New York: Haworth Press, Inc.

World Bank. 2009, September 22. *World Bank*. Retrieved December 6, 2009, from http://www.worldbank.org/financialcrisis/bankinitiatives.htm

Young, R. 2001. *Postcolonialism: An historical introduction*. Malden, MA: Blackwell.

Zook, K. 2006. *Black Women's Lives: Stories of Power and Pain*. New York: Nations Books.

INDEX

Note: Page references in *italics* refer to figures.